GENERATIONS OF
·PRAISE·
THE HISTORY OF WORSHIP

GENERATIONS OF
·PRAISE·
THE HISTORY OF WORSHIP

BRUCE E. SHIELDS & DAVID A. BUTZU

COLLEGE PRESS PUBLISHING COMPANY· JOPLIN, MISSOURI

Cover design by Mark A. Cole

Library of Congress Cataloging-in-Publication Data

Butzu, David A. (David Alan), 1967–
  Generations of praise : the history of worship / by David A. Butzu and
Bruce E. Shields.
      p. cm.
  Includes bibliographical references.
  ISBN 0-89900-941-7 (softback)
  1. Worship—History. I. Shields, Bruce. II. Title.
  BV5.B88 2006
  264.009—dc22

                                            2006021938

Table
of
Contents

Introduction

*P*erhaps a history of worship should be written by people who are not professional historians—at least once in a while. In this volume we intend to cover two aspects in relation to the history of worship: from ancient Israel to the present, and global space. We are naïve enough to think we can do this in a way which will be understandable and helpful to people who plan and lead worship, either as paid staff or as members of church worship committees. We are convinced that an understanding of how worship has developed over the centuries in various cultures will help us to develop services of worship suitable for congregations of the twenty-first century.

This is not to say we are unqualified to undertake the project. One of us has been teaching seminary courses on worship for over twenty years, and the other has been leading worship and studying its development, especially in the early church, as part of his doctoral studies.

We write from our vantage point within the Stone-Campbell Movement and especially its descendants among so-called independent Christian Churches and Churches of Christ. However, since we live in hope of increasing the unity of Christ's followers across denominational lines, we pray that the book will prove helpful both inside and outside our tradition.

CHAPTER ONE

Jewish Backgrounds to Christian Worship

While this is a book about Christian worship, we are going to begin in the Old Testament. It should not surprise the reader to hear that Christian worship has roots in the worship practices of ancient Israel and Judaism. After all, Jesus himself was a Jew, as were all his original disciples.[1] As apostle to the Gentiles, Paul carried with him his Jewish worship traditions, although we shall see at least some of his churches developed some practices that seemed foreign to Paul's kinfolk. We shall begin by looking at the development of worship in the Old Testament in more or less chronological order.

But first a word about sources and our understanding of them. In addition to the Bible we have available a number of other Jewish documents offering information about worship activities. The *Mishnah* is a collection of tractates dealing with various events in Jewish life and decisions of various rabbis on questions about the law and other Scripture texts. This collection was finally brought together in about A.D. 200, so it deals with first-century issues from that later historical viewpoint. It purports to be a collection of the oral *Torah* (what we translate as "law") given to Moses at the same time he received the written code that was handed down to teachers in each generation. The problem for us, of course, is deciding what descriptions of worship activities were practiced by the Jews in Judea and Galilee at the time of Jesus and the early church. Likewise, we are faced with the same challenge in the *Tosefta*, additions to the *Mishnah,* where we find much valuable information. This same difficulty pertains to the *Talmud,* an even later compilation of most of the *Mishnah* plus commentary on it (*Gamara*), and to the *Tefilla,* the Eighteen Benediction prayer, that we look at in detail below. Much scholarly work is being done on these sources at present to try to sort out the historical questions and so give us a clearer picture of Jewish worship at the time of the birth of the church. However, since information is sketchy and surrounded by historical questions, we proceed with caution to deal with the information we have about these Jewish backgrounds.

Worship in the Old Testament

Worship in Ancient Israel

In this section we shall look at a few special people in the Hebrew Bible to see how they worshiped and what we can learn from their examples. It is not our intention to deal with scholarly issues about the Old Testament texts, but it is relevant to note that scholars generally recognize the hand of a priestly editor in the final form of the Pentateuch, which indicates an overriding interest in worship in the early books of the Bible.

We find some hints about the meaning of sacrifices in Genesis 4:1-7 and 8:20-22. The former is the account of the offerings of Cain and Abel and the latter tells of Noah. In both cases we are told that the efficacy of a sacrifice depends on its acceptability to God. However, the details are so sparse here that we must turn to Abraham to begin to get the fuller picture of what God expects and does not expect in sacrificial worship.

Abram (as he was then called) according to Genesis 12:7, after receiving the promise of God that his offspring would receive the land, "built there an altar to the LORD, who had appeared to him." The very next verse describes his building another altar, this time east of Bethel, where he "invoked the name of the LORD." Then after his trip to Egypt, 13:4 tells us he returned to the altar east of Bethel and "called on the name of the LORD." Here we see an early indication of an interest in the sacred nature of some places in the history of Israel.

Genesis 14:18-24 gives us the strange story of Abram and Melchizedek, a figure even the New Testament book of Hebrews (7:1-17) points to as mysterious, taking the messianic-sounding words of Psalm 110 to portray Christ as fulfilling the typology of Melchizedek. We should not permit the mystery surrounding the person of Melchizedek to overshadow the information here about him as a "priest of God Most High" (v. 18) and about Abram's worship through this priest. Melchizedek brought out bread and wine and blessed Abram, who gave Melchizedek a tithe (one-tenth) of everything he had won in battle. Here for the first time we see participation in a meal, a blessing, and an offering other than animal sacrifice connected with the worship of God.

Then we come to the disturbing account called the binding of Isaac in Genesis 22:1-19. The whole history leading up to the birth of Isaac lies in the background. The narrator introduces the story by telling us, "God tested Abraham" (v. 1). Then we find the details of Abraham's receipt of God's command to sacrifice Isaac on a mountain in Moriah, his preparations for the journey, the trip itself, and the actual preparation of the ceremony of sacrifice. Abraham assures Isaac that "the Lord will provide," or perhaps "the Lord sees," a Hebrew statement often transliterated as *Jehovah Jireh*. At that point, of course, the angel intervenes, Abraham sees the ram caught in the thicket, and Isaac is spared by the sacrifice of the ram in his place. The angel then reiterates God's promise to bless Abraham and make him the father of many offspring by whom all nations will be blessed (Gen 12:1-3). In this disturbing story we hear that God is pleased with the willingness of Abraham to sacrifice— at God's command—what he holds dearest and that God blesses such loyalty. At the same time we should note that God never again asks for such a show of loyalty. In fact in Leviticus 18:21, 20:2-5 the Israelites are strictly forbidden to offer their offspring (to Molech). Thus even though human sacrifice was practiced by people around them, the story of the binding of Isaac was a constant reminder to Israelites that this was not the will of their God.

Abraham became the exemplar for both Jews and Christians of the life lived loyal to God. His loyalty is seen most clearly in his worship, in which he calls on the name of the Lord, shows respect for God's chosen leader, and displays willingness to give what is most precious to him when he is convinced that it is God's will. Such loyalty undergirds acts of worship of all kinds then and now.

The story of **Jacob** is a tangled web of deceit by which Jacob wins the blessing of his father Isaac and thus the inheritance of the elder son. He forces another blessing in a wrestling match with the mysterious opponent on the bank of the Jabok (Gen 32:22-32). Then Genesis 35:1-4 brings us back to Bethel, where Abram built an altar and where Jacob had his vision of the ladder to heaven (Gen 28:10-22). As a result of hearing the voice of God renew the Abrahamic covenant with him, Jacob vowed his loyalty and his tithe to God. Later Jacob prepared his household for worship at Bethel by getting rid of all their household idols. They then journeyed to Bethel, where Jacob erected a pillar-altar and anointed it with oil. At this time the covenant was again renewed and Jacob was given the name Israel. If Abraham is the exemplar of faithfulness in worship, Jacob shows us that acceptable worship is not always linked with acceptable living. The story of Jacob is not that of an exemplary person, but God led him to be a worshiper in spite of his questionable morals and ethics, thus making a clear connection between repentance and acceptable worship (see Gen 31:36-51 and 33:1-11).

Up to this point worship has been a practice for individuals and families, but as we come to the exodus story and the leader Moses, we begin to find worship as a national experience. The Lord is no longer just "the God of Abraham, Isaac, and Jacob." The Lord is now the one who has redeemed the people of Israel from their bondage in Egypt and is leading them to the land promised to those patriarchs and their numerous descendants. Therefore with Moses we find a turn toward corporate worship of a whole people.

Moses himself is presented to us as a special case. His relationship with God is so intimate and deep that he becomes Israel's example of a priest, a judge, and a warrior leader. In Exodus 25:1–30:38 we find Moses receiving from the Lord detailed instructions for gathering free-will offerings from the people to construct the tabernacle and its furnishings as a movable worship place and to ordain and purify a priesthood. Earlier, according to 20:24-26, God had given general instructions about altars before the tabernacle:

> [24]You need make for me only an altar of earth and sacrifice on it your burnt offerings and your offerings of well-being, your sheep and your oxen; in every place where I cause my name to be remembered I will come to you and bless you. [25]But if you make for me an altar of stone, do not build it of hewn stones; for if you use a chisel upon it you profane it. [26]You shall not go up by steps to my altar, so that your nakedness may not be exposed on it."

Now we find the developing procedures, space, and rituals for the regularizing of the worship of the Lord. This set the basic pattern for sacrificial worship in Israel until the destruction of Herod's temple in A.D. 70. Exodus 23:12-13 sets the seventh day as a special day for God's people and the seventh year as a time of rest of the land. Then Exodus 23:14-19a sets three annual festivals for Israel: the festival of unleavened bread at the time of the barley harvest in spring; the festival of harvest (usually called "weeks") in June when grain is harvested; and the festival of ingathering at the end of the fall harvest of grapes and olives.[2] This calendar is repeated in Exodus 34 and later expanded upon in Leviticus 23, Numbers 28–29, and Deuteronomy 16. Then in Exodus 25:1–28:43 Moses receives the detailed plans for the tabernacle and the robes for the priests, which is followed in chapter 29 with instructions for the service of ordination of Aaron and his sons to the priesthood. Exodus 30 gives instructions for daily incense offerings and the annual sacrifice of atonement, followed by detailed instructions on how these offerings are to be made.

Joshua set another pattern that we find repeated by the

prophets and other leaders during the time of the judges—the pattern of worship as covenant renewal. The beautiful address in Joshua 24 reminds the people what Yahweh did for them and calls them to put away other deities and commit themselves to the covenant with Yahweh.

The **former prophets**, like Deborah, Nathan, Elijah, Elisha, Micaiah, and, perhaps most important, Samuel, all called Israel from their worship of the Baals (an ecstatic, often sex-oriented ritual) and back to the covenant relationship with Yahweh.[3] As later happened under the leadership of Ezra, the communal renewal of this covenant was a ceremony in which the people reiterated their vows to God. This theme was later developed in the Psalms, where worshipers "paid their vows" (Ps 2:25) or "performed" them (Ps 56:12) as a covenant renewal. And, of course, the "new covenant" language connected with the last supper continues this significance in the early church (1 Cor 11:25, Matt 26:28, Mark 14:24, Luke 22:20).

The prophet **Samuel** is our next pivotal figure. He proved to be a more worthy and able leader than the priests, the sons of Eli. They were killed in the battle in which the ark of the covenant was captured. On hearing that the ark had been captured, Eli died. That left Samuel as the recognized spiritual leader when the ark of the covenant was returned by the Philistines who had captured it (1 Samuel 4–7). It was Samuel who later (8:4–12:25) appointed Saul to be the first king of Israel but who at the same time warned the people that this would bring calamity on them. He then led them in acts of repentance, assuring them he would continue to pray for them and that God would not forsake them. Even though not of a priestly family, Samuel gained the respect of the people for his relationship with God, and he led them to see that religious exercises without accompanying godly living were useless. He told King Saul directly (1 Sam 15:22):

> Has the LORD as great delight in burnt offerings and sacrifices,
>   as in obedience to the voice of the LORD?

Surely, to obey is better than sacrifice,
　　and to heed than the fat of rams.[4]

Samuel set the scene for **David**, who would usher in a new era in beautiful and heartfelt worship. David began the process of centralizing the worship of Yahweh in Jerusalem by bringing the ark of the covenant into the capital city. After giving the ark a secure home in Jerusalem, David prays an interesting and heartfelt prayer, recorded in 2 Samuel 7:18-29. In verse 27 he uses two different forms of the word that would become a favorite word for prayer: the Hebrew term *tefilla*. It appears here in both noun and verb forms. The Greek translation is *proseuche* (LXX). The Hebrew word appears here for the very first time in the Bible. The ark's arrival in Jerusalem is recorded again in 1 Chronicles 16 and 17, but here David is depicted as establishing the singing of praises to the Lord (16:7) and composing a psalm (16:8-34), a petition, and doxology to which the people said their "Amen!" and praised the Lord (16:35-36). David then organized priests to minister regularly before the ark (16:37-42). From that time David was known as the singer of Israel. Seventy-four of our biblical psalms are ascribed to him, so we can thank David for bringing music into the regular worship of Israel and, since the book of Psalms was a primary source of early Christian music, of the church, too.

So David not only centralized governmental power in Jerusalem, he also gradually brought the worship of Yahweh under the control of his priests in the capital. As one historian put it,

> The economic boom which Israel experienced through the monarchy made it possible to equip the cult in quite a different way, especially in the state sanctuaries, in terms not only of buildings, vessels and temple personnel but also of the dimension of the liturgical festival itself: attracted by the development of state splendour, great liturgical gatherings took place with people streaming in from all parts of the country to the annual feasts.[5]

While David may have suffered disappointment because God refused his request to build a temple in Jerusalem, the task was left to David's son, **Solomon**. The finishing of the temple completed the centralizing of religious authority in Jerusalem. The construction work is described in 2 Chronicles 1–4, probably during the years 959–952 B.C. Chapter five describes the entrance of the ark of the covenant into the temple and the praise of the priests, Levites, and all the people, whereupon the building was filled with a cloud, "for the glory of the LORD filled the house of God." (2 Chr 5:14). Solomon's response to this is recorded in chapter 6 in what amounts to a covenant-renewal ceremony. He reminded the people of what God had accomplished among them (vv. 1-2), he blessed the people (v. 3), he reminded them that God had brought them out of Egypt (vv. 4-11), and then he prayed a beautiful prayer of dedication (vv. 14-42), setting aside another sacred space that would orient the worship of Israel even when they were away from their land. Chapter seven describes fire coming from heaven and consuming the sacrifices and God's warning to Solomon to continue to walk before the Lord. This is also recorded in 1 Kings 5–9.

The major elements of worship in ancient Israel appear to be praise and prayer, connected after Moses (see especially Exodus 19–24) with holy living. The prayers are excruciatingly honest, often taking the form of lament. The sacrifices prescribed in Leviticus and elsewhere and described even in the narratives of David and Solomon seem secondary during this early period. However, as we shall see, the sacrificial system became central to Israel's worship with the establishment of Solomon's temple in Jerusalem and remained primary until the destruction of Jerusalem and its temple in about 587 B.C.

Worship in the First Temple

The construction of Solomon's temple completed the work of cultic centralization started by David. Until its destruction in 587 B.C., the temple remained the symbol of the reign of Yahweh and the rallying place of all Israelites. This gave the temple personnel— the priests and Levites—great influence over life on all levels of society.

The building and its furnishings are described in 1 Kings 6 and 7. Scholars differ on the meanings of the many technical terms and the extent of later changes in the text that reflect the second temple. However, the description portrays a magnificent structure. The temple proper was rectangular, about 90 feet long, 30 feet wide, and 40 feet high (1 Kings 6:2). The walls must have been about 10 feet thick. There was a porch (vestibule) the length of the front (east) side that was about 15 feet deep. The interior space was divided into two rooms, the larger called the holy place and the smaller called the Holy of Holies. This inner room was just half as long as the outer—a cube of about 30 feet.[6] In addition, there were buildings around the sides and rear of the temple proper, plus a walled courtyard that covered several acres of ground.[7]

The furnishings of the courtyard and temple must have made it a breathtaking sight. In front of the main entrance to the temple itself stood an altar of burnt offering that was 30 feet square and 15 feet high. This altar was later replaced several times with succeedingly larger structures. Between the altar and the temple, and slightly to the south was the so-called brazen sea, a bronze basin 15 feet across and 7 feet deep, holding probably 16,000 gallons of water for ritual purposes. The basin rested on the backs of 12 bronze oxen in groups of 3, facing the four directions of the compass. In addition, there were four smaller basins (lavers) on wheels. These were about 6 feet in diameter and held about 325 gallons. The porch itself was flanked by two pillars that, oddly enough, were given the names of Jachin and Boaz. Within the temple proper was a table of showbread, used first in the tabernacle, and two large lampstands, one on either side of the door to the holy of holies. Within this inner sanctum, facing the door were two statues of golden cherubim, guarding the ark of the covenant. The cherubim appear to have represented the throne of Yahweh, with the golden lid of the ark as Yahweh's footstool. Here was the presence of God for people taught that no material representation of God could be used, and here the high priest took the blood of the sacrifice of atonement each year on the Day of Atonement (see below).

The temple worship orders are described briefly in 2 Chronicles 8:12-13. Here we find Solomon offering "up burnt offerings to the Lord on the altar of the Lord that he had built in front of the vestibule, as the duty of each day required, offering according to the commandment of Moses for the Sabbaths, the new moons, and the three annual festivals—the festival of unleavened bread, the festival of weeks, and the festival of booths." This set pattern of weekly, monthly, and annual gatherings for worship follows the description of the dedication of the Jerusalem temple (1 Kings 8, 2 Chronicles 6). The weekly Sabbath (seventh day) became the most basic holy day in the Jewish experience. It was a day of rest, with stipulated limits on work and travel from sundown Friday to sundown Saturday. It was also the day each week when two daily sacrifices were made in the temple. On the first day of each lunar month special sacrifices were offered in the temple. As we noted above, the special worship festivals that developed in Israel were connected with annual cycles of planting and harvesting, now that the people were settled in the land. However, they were also connected to major events in the history of Israel. The seven day Festival of Unleavened Bread was celebrated in the early spring (March or April) at the time of the barley harvest. It ends with the celebration of Passover, reminding people of the exodus from Egypt. The Festival of Weeks came seven weeks after Passover, as a celebration of the wheat harvest. It was also called Pentecost, reflecting the fifty days from Passover. It served as a reminder of the giving of the law to Moses on Mount Sinai. The Festival of Booths or Tabernacles is in the fall (September or October), at the time of the grape and olive harvest. During this week the people lived outdoors in makeshift shelters to reenact the forty years their ancestors spent in the wilderness. Scholars differ as to when the Day of Atonement came into the Jewish calendar, but it became the high holy day for the temple, as the Passover was for the Jewish family. On that day (in the fall) the sin offering sacrifice was made, the scapegoat was released, and the high priest carried the blood of the sacrifice into the Holy of Holies to sprinkle it around the ark of the covenant, thus graphically ritualizing the forgiving of the sins of the people of God. The presently popular holidays among Jews, Purim (February or March) and Hanukkah (December), were developed later, the former memorializing the salvation of the Jews by the actions of Queen Esther and the latter the rededication of the temple after the Maccabean revolt wrested it from the control (and desecration) of the Hellenistic overlords.

However, there remained points of conflict, most of which centered on prophets (see Elijah in 1 Kings 18). The prophets refused to allow the set patterns of worship in the temple to crowd out of the consciousness of Israel its relationship with Yahweh. That relationship, they reminded the people, was based on God's gracious choice of them as his special people and God's claim on them as a holy people. Thus holy living, and not just ritual purity, was to be the outcome of Israel's worship.

The process of centralization was brought to its zenith by King Josiah, according to 2 Kings 22–23. Josiah's reform called people back to the patterns prescribed in the *Torah*, but it also destroyed outlying sites for worship, which left many of the people too far distant for worship to play much of a role in their lives. The sacrificial system set out in great detail in Leviticus was dutifully carried out by the priests and Levites, but for most inhabitants of Judea and Galilee worship in Jerusalem was an annual experience at best.

Relationships between priests and prophets continued to be rocky, as preachers like Jeremiah, known as the man of prayer, and Isaiah, who appears to have been closely connected to temple officials, called people back to true worship that showed itself in righteous living. The Psalms were written, collected, and used during this period as the worship book of the people, but again most of this use was confined to Jerusalem and its temple environs.

Worship in the Second Temple Period

During the Babylonian captivity, certain important develop-ments appeared. As the people were separated from their homeland and their now ruined temple, they found other ways to express their relationship with Yahweh. Whereas we find no mention of syna-gogues or Pharisees in the Hebrew Bible, they both appear in Jewish literature of the intertestamental period. We discover that prayer and *Torah* study supported Israel's faith during the captivity. People learned to gather in smaller groups to share their faith and to build up one another in that faith. A new kind of leadership developed to serve these smaller gatherings. People discovered that they could worship without the aid of an order of priests.

So when the people returned to Jerusalem in 538 B.C., they began rebuilding the temple, but they continued also in their wor-ship at the local level. The temple, the restoration of which was completed in 515 B.C., was not unaffected by these developments. When Ezra arrived around 458 B.C., he led a covenant renewal cer-emony and movement and reinstituted the priesthood and services prescribed in the Torah, which indicates that these services were not being performed according to regulations. However, we find now that temple services made much broader use of psalms and lay prayers. We can see this in the rabbinic description of the daily tem-ple whole-offering (sacrifice) recorded in the *Mishnah* tractate, *Tamid* 5. Here is recorded:

> The officer said to them, 'Recite ye a Benediction!' They recited a Benediction, and recited the Ten Commandments, and the *Shema* [Deuteronomy 6:4-9], and the *And it shall come to pass if ye shall hearken* [Deuteronomy 11:13-21], and the *And the Lord spake unto Moses* [Numbers 15:7-41]. They pronounced three Benedictions[8] with the people: 'True and sure', and 'Abodah', and the Priestly Blessing; and on the Sabbath they pronounced a fur-ther Benediction for the outgoing Course of priests.[9]

This second temple was at first a restoration of the former one; but over the years it was made increasingly elaborate. When

Herod the Great expanded and refurbished it just before the time of Jesus, beginning in 20 B.C., it reached the height of its glory. Now the outer court included space earlier occupied by Solomon's palace and according to Jewish tradition covered an area of 750 feet square. This court of the Gentiles was paved with marble and bordered by wide "porches" (actually halls supported and bounded by high columns) large enough for gatherings of different sizes. Archaeologists have discovered the foundations of a synagogue in the outer court, which indicates the new relationship between temple and synagogue. Here also would be found stands for selling and keeping animals for sacrifice as well as tables for money changers, who saw to it that worshipers had Jewish currency for their temple offerings. Also, in plain view, there was a marble screen warning, in Greek and Latin, that Gentiles were not permitted in the inner courts.

Just as the temple had been built with attention to intricate detail, so the services of worship were worked out in great detail. There were now 26 courses of priests, so each group had to do its week of temple duty only twice a year, although they were all needed on festival occasions (Passover, Pentecost, Feast of Weeks, and Day of Atonement [*Yom Kippur*]). During other times they were responsible for some aspects of synagogue services and other duties among the people. The temple musicians were chosen from the number of the Levites, who also did much of the cleaning and maintenance work around the temple.

In the Gospels we find Jesus teaching both in local synagogues and in the temple area. We find him also in contact with many synagogue leaders—Pharisees and their scribes—some of whom became his followers and others who turned against him. In the end it was the high priests who were most adamantly against him as they had been against the prophets earlier. So in this period leading up to the Roman destruction of Jerusalem in A.D. 70 we find a much more varied picture of worship, with more of what we would call "lay leadership" than was true during the first temple period. This sets the scene for the development of the structure and worship practices in the early church.

Worship in First-Century Synagogues

The synagogue that is so often referred to in the Gospels seems to be something new in Judaism. As we noted above, the Jewish synagogue appears to have been developed during the Babylonian exile, since the institution does not appear in the canonical Old Testament, nor do its accompanying officers: the Pharisees and rabbis. Thus the synagogue was developed independent of the temple and to some extent as its surrogate. Each synagogue was a relatively small assembly of Jewish men and their families. The tradition is that 10 men were necessary for the establishment and maintenance of a synagogue. Scholars can only guess at how these assemblies spread throughout the Mediterranean world and when they began constructing special buildings for worship. The earliest synagogue buildings thus far identified by archaeologists are dated in the first century B.C.[10] The destruction of the temple by the Romans in A.D. 70 catapulted the synagogue to the position as the only gathering place for Jews for worship and study of scripture. Therefore, the synagogue became much more important in the development of Christian worship than did the temple.

The primary purpose of the development of the synagogue appears to have been to preserve the major elements of the faith of Israel through the continual study of the law *(Torah)* and (perhaps later) worship/prayer. This was accomplished by means of four important activities. The reading of Hebrew texts was a regular and fundamental act. The leaders developed lectionary readings, which included systematic lists of texts to be read in a prescribed order, These texts came from the *Torah* and *haphtarah*. The *haphtarah* reading came from prophetic texts, which in the Hebrew Bible included the historical books of Joshua, Judges, Samuel, and Kings.[11] It is impossible to determine whether each synagogue had its own sequence of readings or whether the lists were codified and used commonly by many synagogues. However this worked, the synagogues were apparently careful to make the whole *Torah* (Genesis through Deuteronomy) heard, understood, and applied systematically over a three-year period.

The second element of synagogue worship included *targum*. Synagogue leaders developed the practice of orally translating the readings into the local languages. These translations were called *targumim*. The first *targum* was probably in the Aramaic language that was used by most Jews in Palestine after the return from exile. It was not long, however, until the Hebrew Bible was translated in writing into Greek, Syriac, and other common languages. In addition to a *targum*, which helped the people understand the weekly texts, a form of preaching was developed to help the people apply the text to their individual, family, and communal lives. This sermon form was called *midrash*, and many of such expositions have come down to us in book form. The general organization of a *midrash* began with a *Torah* text, and then followed by another (*haphtarah*) text, which was then related to the first. The two were then explained in such a way as to be helpful in dealing with an ethical or religious issue in the hearer's life. One can find examples of *midrash* in Romans 4 and Galatians 3, as well as other places in the New Testament.

The third element of synagogue worship was and is the recitation of the *Shema*. This fundamental confession of faith of all observant Jews is found in Deuteronomy 6:4-5: "Hear, O Israel: The LORD is our God, the LORD alone. You shall love the LORD your God with all your heart, and with all your soul, and with all your might." Sometimes just verse 4 is used, sometimes other verses are added (6:6-9, 11:13-21, and Numbers 15:37-41), but this statement is both the central confession of the oneness and sovereignty of God and the call to Israel to worship, love, and serve that God. It gets its name from the first word of the call in Hebrew: *Shema* = Hear. The *Mishnah* (*Tamid* 5:1) claims that the *Shema* was used as part of the Temple rites, connected with certain benedictions. Thus it appears

to be an ancient element of Jewish worship tradition adapted probably for synagogue services after the destruction of the first
Temple.

The fourth element of synagogue worship was and is the
prayers. The primary example of ancient Jewish prayers is the
Shemoneh Esreh (18 benediction prayer, sometimes called
amidah—prayer recited standing up—or the more general *Tefilla*).
Most scholars contend that the original 18 benedictions would have
been in use during the time of Jesus, although one of the later list of
19 (number 12, marked below with an asterisk) was likely added at
the time of the separation of Christians from the synagogue. The
Mishnah (*Berakoth* 4:1) stipulates that these prayers are to be recited three times a day (and see Dan 6:10), which some have seen as a
reminder of the two sacrifice times plus the "closing of the doors"
ceremony of the old Temple. A reading of these prayers is beneficial for our understanding of the way the Jews praised God and
provides insight for our own prayer life as well. Note the use of
Adonoy as a term for addressing God. The Jewish people do not try
to pronounce the name of God as revealed to Moses (what we
write as Yahweh), but instead even when reading it in Scripture
substitute the word for Lord—Adonoy.

SHEMONEH 'ESREH: 18 BENEDICTIONS

My Master, open my lips and my mouth will
declare Your praise.

1. Blessed are You, Adonoy, our God and God of
our fathers, God of Abraham, God of Isaac, and God
of Jacob, the Almighty, the Great, the Powerful, the
Awesome, the most high Almighty, Who bestows
beneficent kindness, Who possesses everything, Who
remembers the piety of the Patriarchs, and Who
brings a redeemer to their children's children, for the
sake of His Name, with love. King, Helper, Deliverer
and Shield—Blessed are You, Adonoy, Shield of
Abraham.

2. You are mighty forever, my Master; You are the Resurrector of the dead, the powerful One to deliver us. Sustainer of the living with kindliness, Resurrector of the dead with great mercy, Supporter of the falling, and Healer of the sick, and Releaser of the imprisoned, and Fulfiller of His faithfulness to those who sleep in the dust. Who is like You, Master of mighty deeds, and who can be compared to You? King Who causes death and restores life, and causes deliverance to sprout forth. And You are faithful to restore the dead to life, Blessed are You, Adonoy, Who restores the dead to life.

3. You are holy and your Name is holy and holy beings praise you every day, Selah. Blessed are You, Adonoy, the Almighty, the Holy one.

4. You favor man with perception and teach mankind understanding. Grant us from Your perception, understanding and intellect. Blessed are You, Adonoy, Grantor of perception.

5. Cause us to return, our Father, to Your Torah and bring us near, our King, to Your service; and bring us back in wholehearted repentance before You. Blessed are You, Adonoy, Who is pleased with penitence.

6. Pardon us, our Father, for we have erred, forgive us, our King, for we have sinned; because You are Forgiver and Pardoner. Blessed are You, Adonoy Gracious One, Who pardons abundantly.

7. Look, please, upon our affliction, and defend our cause: and redeem us speedily for the sake of Your Name; because You are a Mighty Redeemer. Blessed are You, Adonoy, Redeemer of Israel.

8. Heal us, Adonoy, and we will be healed, deliver us and we will be delivered; for You are our praise.

Grant complete healing to all our wounds, because You Almighty King, are a faithful and merciful Healer. Blessed are You, Adonoy, Healer of the sick of His people Israel.

9. Bless for us, Adonoy our God, this year and all the varieties of its produce for good; and bestow bless- ing upon the face of the earth; satisfy us from Your bounty and bless our year like the good years. Blessed are You, Adonoy, Blesser of the years.

10. Sound the great *shofar* for our liberty, and raise a banner to gather our exiles, and gather us together from the four corners of the earth. Blessed are You, Adonoy, Gatherer of the dispersed of His people Israel.

11. Restore our judges as before and our coun- selors as at first, remove from us sorrow and sighing, and reign over us, You, Adonoy, alone, with kindness and mercy, and make us righteous with justice; Blessed are You, Adonoy, King, Lover of righteousness and justice.

*12. Let there be no hope for the informers and may all wickedness perish instantly; may all Your ene- mies be swiftly cut off, and the insolent may You quickly uproot, crush, rout, and subdue speedily in our days. Blessed are You, Adonoy, Crusher of enemies and Subduer of the insolent.

13. Upon the righteous, upon the pious, upon the elders of Your people the House of Israel, upon the remnant of their scholars, upon the full proselytes, and upon us, may Your mercy be aroused, Adonoy our God. Grant perfect reward to all who truly trust in Your Name; and place our lot among them forever, and may we not be put to shame, for we have put our

trust in you. Blessed are You, Adonoy, Support and Trust of the righteous.

14. And to Jerusalem, Your city, return in mercy, and dwell therein as You have spoken; and rebuild it soon, in our days, as an everlasting edifice and the throne of David may You speedily establish therein. Blessed are You, Adonoy, Builder of Jerusalem.

15. The sprout of David, Your servant, speedily cause to flourish and exalt his power with Your deliverance, as we hope for Your deliverance all day. Blessed are You, Adonoy, Who causes to sprout the power of salvation.

16. Hear our voice, Adonoy, our God; spare us and have compassion on us, and accept our prayers mercifully and willingly, for You are Almighty Who heeds prayers and supplications; and from Your presence, our King, do not turn us away empty-handed, for You heed the prayers of Your people, Israel, with mercy. Blessed are You, Adonoy, Who heeds prayers.

17. Be pleased, Adonoy, our God, with Your people Israel and their prayer and restore the service to the Holy of Holies in Your abode and the fire-offerings of Israel; and accept their prayer, lovingly and willingly. May You always find acceptable the service of Your people, Israel. And may our eyes behold Your merciful return to Zion. Blessed are You, Adonoy, Who returns His Divine Presence to Zion.

18. We are thankful to You, Adonoy, that You are our God and the God of our fathers forever; You are the Rock of our lives, the Shield of our deliverance, in every generation. We will give thanks to You and recount Your praise, for our lives which are committed into Your hand, and for our souls which are entrusted to You, and for Your miracles of every day

with us and for Your wonders and benefactions at all periods—evening, morning and noon. You are the Beneficent One—for Your mercy is never withheld; And You are the Merciful One—for Your kindliness never ceases; we have always placed our hope in You. And for all the foregoing blessed and exalted be Your Name, our King, continually, forever and ever. And all the living shall thank You forever and praise Your Name with sincerity; Almighty Who is our deliverance and our help forever. Blessed are You, Adonoy, "The Beneficent" is Your Name and You it is fitting to praise.

19. Grant peace, goodness, and blessing, favor, kindness and mercy upon us and upon all Israel, Your people. Bless us, our Father, all of us as one with the light of Your countenance. For by the light of Your countenance, Adonoy our God, You gave us a Torah of life and the love of kindliness, righteousness, blessing, mercy, life, and peace. And may it be good in Your sight to bless Your people Israel, at all times and at every moment with Your peace. Blessed are You, Adonoy, Who blesses His people Israel with peace.

Although we have no direct evidence that these prayers were used regularly in synagogue worship, they are generally accepted as coming from this period and reflecting accurately the worship of the Jews of the time of Jesus. They were codified and specified as part of the regular synagogue service shortly after the destruction of Herod's temple (around A.D. 90 in Jamnia), and even then their exact wording and sequence was not hard and fast. They were stipulated for twice daily use in Jewish households, taking the place of the twice daily sacrifices in the temple. It is possible that the Judean synagogues, since they were close to the temple and thus to the services of prayer and praise, specialized in the teaching of *Torah* and not the other activities of worship, while synagogues farther away from Jerusalem offered a fuller experience of worship to those believers who could not regularly participate in the temple services.

There appears to be one more act of synagogue worship practiced at least occasionally—a priestly benediction when a priest was present. This benediction was likely the one embedded in Numbers 6:22-27:

> [22]The LORD spoke to Moses, saying: [23]Speak to Aaron and his sons, saying, Thus you shall bless the Israelites: You shall say to them,
>
> [24]The LORD bless you and keep you;
>
> [25]the LORD make his face to shine upon you, and be gracious to you;
>
> [26]the LORD lift up his countenance upon you, and give you peace.
>
> [27]So they shall put my name on the Israelites, and I will bless them.

We might wonder abut the use of music in the synagogue, but wondering is about all we can do. There is now no known evidence that even the Psalms were sung in synagogue services. Music was certainly part of Jewish life in first-century Palestine—both at the Temple and in family and community celebrations; but the sources are silent about music in the synagogues.

Worship at Qumran

The discovery of the Dead Sea Scrolls in the mid-twentieth century and their subsequent translation and explanation have been enlightening in many ways. Not least among these ways is the light they shine on practices of worship. Scholars are always careful to point out that the documents relate to a relatively small sect of Judaism, but the sect was a group of believing Jews active during the time of Jesus. The monastery-like settlement at Qumran, near the Dead Sea in southern Palestine, was destroyed by Roman armies in A.D. 68, so what has been discovered there is dated in the early first century and before. In fact, most of the scrolls discovered in the hillside caves above Qumran are likely much older than that since they appear to have been well used (often badly worn) when put into the pots that preserved them.

In addition to copies of Hebrew Bible books and commentaries on them, there are also documents that tell us about life in the Qumran community, including their worship patterns and their criticism of the temple hierarchy. They include set daily prayers, daily ablutions (baptisms) in water, instructions for worship during the primary Jewish festivals, and perhaps most important, songs to be sung at various occasions.

The music at the temple was performed by choirs and instrumentalists from among the Levites. This means that it was mostly professionally done. Some of the psalms are obviously designed for antiphonal use, so there were some times when the people in general could join in to respond to calls from the priests or Levites. There is no evidence that singing was part of the worship of first-century synagogues. However, the Dead Sea Scrolls introduce us to a community singing tradition more like the congregational singing that developed among Christians. There is a whole series of thirteen Songs of the Sabbath Sacrifice.[12] These songs describe the heavenly temple and the worship of the angels and other heavenly beings in the presence of God. In addition, the Community Rule document includes these lines in a psalm:

> I will sing with knowledge and all my music
> Shall be for the glory of God.
> My lyre and my harp shall sound
> For his holy order
> And I will tune the pipe of my lips
> To his right measure.[13]

We have no way of demonstrating a direct connection between the Essenes of the Qumran community and early Christians, but this evidence indicates the presence of musical practices in at least one other religious community at the time and in the place where the Christian traditions were being formed.

There were, of course, other groups in the broader culture using music in worship or education. The Jewish philosopher Philo describes the singing of a group called the Therapeutae.[14] Philo gives us the only description we have of this group who lived an ascetic life near Lake Mareotis, not far from Alexandria, Egypt, in the first century and who held Jewish worship services each Sabbath day. Philo's description reads:

> Then the President rises and sings a hymn composed as an address to God, either a new one of his own composition or an old one by poets of an earlier day who have left behind them hymns in many measures and melodies, hexameters and iambics, lyrics suitable for processions or in libations and at the altars, or for the chorus whilst standing or dancing, with careful metrical arrangements to fit the various evolutions. After him all the others take their turn as they are arranged and in the proper order while all the rest listen in complete silence except when they have to chant the closing lines or refrains, for then they all lift up their voices, men and women alike.[15]

Thus we have evidence that the New Testament's interest in song would not have seemed overly strange in its home environment. In fact, during this time of primary orality, when not more than one out of ten adults could read or write, all public reading of scripture or other literature would be done rhythmically, in what we would call a chant. Thus in most public gatherings of Jews the primary speakers would often break into a musical cadence while quoting scripture or just speaking.

Summary

Worship as described and prescribed in the Hebrew Bible is an extremely variegated experience, ranging from very formal, controlled actions in the temple to very informal and locally managed actions in synagogues. However, it can all be summarized under the heading: continual corporate participation in God's acts in history. Deuteronomy 5:2-3 pictures Moses telling the people, only a few of whom had actually been with him at Sinai (Horeb), "The Lord our God made a covenant with us at Horeb. Not with our ancestors did the Lord make this covenant, but with us, who are all of us here alive today." That kind of reliving of the great acts of God was what the people of Israel did as they participated in the great festi-vals of their worship calendar. Their participation in this history was accomplished in two main cultic ways: historical recital, as in Deuteronomy 26:5-9, and dramatic re-presentation, as in Exodus 1–19, esp. 12:1ff. (Passover), Joshua 2–6 (conquest), and Psalms 2, 18, 20, 21, 28, 45, 72, 89, 101, 110 (enthronement of David).

As complicated as this worship might seem, the meaning of Old Testament worship is relatively simple. It is always tied to ethics: the Holy of Holies contained the tablets of the commandments and restitution was necessary before presenting a guilt offering. Also worship is always rooted in God's initiative in history, which means it is basically a religion of grace. And it always reflects the God who is the ultimate power and reality at work in the creation. This means that worship was designed to bring people into a covenant relationship with God or to maintain them in that relationship so that their lives, both individual and communal, would show forth the praises of their God.

When compared to the temple rites, worship in first-century synagogues was quite informal, focusing on Scripture and prayer. As we shall see, the early church adopted this general pattern.

On the other hand, what we can see of worship in the Qumran community (and among other enthusiastic sects) was heav-ily participatory and employed music, including congregational singing, to good effect.

Thus we see broad variety of worship practices in the Jewish backgrounds to early Christianity.

For Further Reading

Albertz, Rainer. *A History of Israelite Religion in the Old Testament Period*, Volumes I and II. Trans. by John Bowden. Louisville, KY: Westminster John Knox Press, 1994.

Balentine, Samuel E. *The Torah's Vision of Worship*, Overtures to Biblical Theology. Minneapolis: Fortress Press, 1999.

Bradshaw, Paul F. *The Search for The Origins of Christian Worship: Sources and Methods for the Study of Early Liturgy*. New York/Oxford: Oxford University Press, 1992.

Danby, Herbert, trans. *The Mishnah: Translated from the Hebrew with Introduction and Brief Explanatory Notes*. Oxford: Oxford University Press, 1933 (1980 repr.).

Davila, James R. *Liturgical Works*. Eerdmans Commentaries on the Dead Sea Scrolls. Grand Rapids: Eerdmans, 2000.

Edersheim, Alfred. *The Temple: Its Ministry and Services as They Were in the Time of Christ*. Grand Rapids: Eerdmans, 1976.

Levine, Lee I., ed. *The Synagogue in Late Antiquity*. Philadelphia: The American Schools of Oriental Research, 1987.

Petuchowski, Jakob J. "The Liturgy of the Synagogue: Its History, Structure, and Contents." Ed. by William Scott Green. *Approaches to Ancient Judaism, Volume IV*. Brown Judaic Studies 27. Chico CA: Scholars Press, 1983.

Rowley, H.H. *Worship in Ancient Israel*. London: SPCK, 1987.

Webber, Robert E., ed. *The Complete Library of Christian Worship. Volume I: The Biblical Foundations of Christian Worship*. Peabody, MA: Hendrickson Publishers, 1993.

⸙ ——— ⸙

[1]*The New Revised Standard Version* (Nashville, TN: Thomas Nelson Publishers, 1989). Unless otherwise noted, all biblical quotations are from this version.

[2]Brevard S. Childs. *The Book of Exodus: A Critical, Theological Commentary* (Philadelphia: Westminster Press, 1974) 482-485.

[3]See the essay by John D. Witvliet, "The Former Prophets and the Practice of Christian Worship" in his *Worship Seeking Understanding* (Grand Rapids: Baker Academic, 2003) 23-38.

[4]Compare also Psalm 51:16-17, Proverbs 21:3, and Hosea 6:6.

[5]Rainer Albertz, *A History of the Israelite Religion in the Old Testament Period,* trans. by John Bowden (Louisville, KY: Westminster/John Knox Press, 1994) 128.

[6]These measurements are only approximate, since scholars differ on the length of a cubit. However, it seems certain that the temple was no smaller than these lengths indicate.

[7]See the drawings of Solomon's Temple on the College Press website: http://collegepress.com/GenOfPraise/index.html.

[8]See the Eighteen Benedictions under Worship in First-Century Synagogues on pages 24-28.

[9]Herbert Danby, trans., *The Mishnah* (Oxford: Oxford University Press, 1933) 586-587.

[10]See the helpful information in Lee I. Levine, ed., *The Synagogue in Late Antiquity* (Philadelphia: The American Schools of Oriental Research, 1987) especially his chapter, "The Second Temple Synagogue," 7-31.

[11]This *haphtarah* reading is sometimes counted as a separate rite, which gives us a count of five elements of synagogue worship. Paul F. Bradshaw, *The Search for the Origins of Christian Worship: Sources and Methods for the Study of Early Liturgy* (New York/Oxford: Oxford University Press, 1992) 21-22.

[12]James R. Davila, *Liturgical Works,* Eerdmans Commentaries on the Dead Sea Scrolls (Grand Rapids: Eerdmans, 2000) 83-167.

[13]Geza Vermes, trans. *The Dead Sea Scrolls in English* (London: Pelican Books, 1962) *The Community Rule* 10:9.

[14]Philo, *De Vita Contemplativa (On The Contemplative Life),* trans. by F.H. Colson, in Volume IX of Philo in the Loeb Classics series (Cambridge, MA: Harvard University Press, 1967) chs. 80–90, pp. 162-169.

[15]Ibid., ch. 80, p. 163.

CHAPTER TWO

Worship in the New Testament

$\mathcal{S}$ince Jesus and his disciples were Jews living in Palestine, we are not surprised to find recorded in the Gospels several visits to both the temple and synagogues. There are forty references to the temple in the Gospels and Acts and thirty-five occurrences of the word "synagogue." It appears that Jesus and his followers were all faithful adherents of the synagogue and that they did their expected occasional temple worship. Luke 4:16 indicates that it was Jesus' custom to attend synagogue on the Sabbath day. Acts also makes it clear that the early church in Jerusalem continued to worship in the temple— probably until its destruction in A.D. 70. It should not be surprising, therefore, to find the worship pattern of those earliest Christians reflecting their Jewish background. Since temple worship was based on animal sacrifices and the death of Jesus was early seen as God's ultimate sacrifice for human sin, the only aspect of temple worship we see developed in the early church is music. The rest, as we shall see, comes from the synagogue or elsewhere.

Three Major Patterns

We can identify three distinct patterns of worship described in the New Testament. We shall call them synagogue, charismatic, and apocalyptic styles. We have no worship bulletin-type documents from the first century, but the New Testament does give us some rather clear descriptions of these three, so we shall look at them one at a time.

Synagogue

Synagogue-style worship is described in Acts 2:42-47:

> [42]They devoted themselves to the apostles' teaching and fellow-ship, to the breaking of bread and the prayers. [43]Awe came upon everyone, because many wonders and signs were being done by the apostles. [44]All who believed were together and had all things in common; [45]they would sell their possessions and goods and dis-tribute the proceeds to all, as any had need. [46]Day by day, as they spent much time together in the temple, they broke bread at home and ate their food with glad and generous hearts, [47]praising God and having the goodwill of all the people. And day by day the Lord added to their number those who were being saved.

Here we get a glimpse of the worship and life of the earliest church and their similarities to the synagogue. These early Christians worshiped both by themselves and in the temple. When they were by themselves, they were taught first by the apostles and later by those who passed on the teachings of the apostles. This teaching program appears to have taken the place of the reading and expo-sition of *Torah* in the synagogues, although if we can judge by the sermons recorded in Acts, the apostles must have taught from texts of the Hebrew Bible.

"The apostles' teaching" is mentioned first, followed by "the fellowship." This Greek word, *koinōnia*, appears in the New Testa-ment in reference to the general nature of relationships in the church (Gal 2:9), to the church's offerings for the poor (see Rom 15:26; 2 Cor 8:4; 9:13), and even to the participation with Christ at the Lord's Table, from which we get the term "communion" (1 Cor 10:16). Such close relationships, connected with the giving of alms, have deep roots in the life of Jewish synagogues, where worship is community oriented and linked with works of charity.

Then is listed "the breaking of bread," which in Luke's writings appears to be a reference to the Lord's Supper (see Luke 24:35; Acts 20:7,11; 27:35). The Lord's Supper is a peculiarly Christian event, although sacred meals were certainly not strange to Jewish people.

The Passover meal itself was usually celebrated in families, with the ritual (*Seder*) as an important component. However, the under-standing of "family" was quite often broadened to include a group of disciples with their teacher. This was certainly the pattern for Jesus and his followers—a pattern that was brought to a climax "on the night when he was betrayed" (1 Cor 11:23).

After this comes "the prayers." Some versions (NIV, NASB) translate this generally ("prayer") and others (KJV, NKJ) have it "in prayers," but the Greek has it in the plural and with the definite arti-cle. This certainly indicates some sort of set prayers in use here, which could be prayers from the synagogue, perhaps the 18 bene-dictions we looked at in chapter one or a Christian adaptation of them. So this earliest record of Christian worship points to Jewish Christians worshiping in a pattern similar to synagogue worship, with the addition of the Lord's Supper as an adaptation of Jewish ritual meals at home.

Charismatic

Charismatic-style worship was found among the Hellenistic churches founded by Paul and others outside Palestine, where wor-ship experiences differed radically from those of the synagogue. Some pagan temples practiced animal sacrifices, as did the Jeru-salem temple, but judging from the apparent problem in Corinth about meat sacrificed to idols (1 Corinthians 8) Christians were never tempted to add such sacrifices to their worship. On the other hand we do find parallels in early Christian worship with those in the eastern mystery religions. Some of these cults practiced baptism in blood. Others staged a dramatic reenactment of a dying and ris-ing god. They worshiped primarily in a highly emotional, even ecstatic, state. A third interesting cultural parallel is in the schools of philosophy, in which a teacher instructed students in both ways of thinking and ways of communicating. Thus the early converts in the Hellenistic world were surrounded by concepts of divinity and sacrifice, as well as practices ranging from the ecstatic to the intellectual.

Not surprisingly, it wasn't long after the gospel spread to non-Jewish lands that Christian worship began to change from its Jewish roots. In Paul's first letter to the Corinthian believers (written about A.D. 54) he is led to deal with disruption in their worship services. Chapters 10–14 record his pastoral instructions to them. What he describes here looks like a radical shift from the education-centered style of the synagogue. It looks more like what we would call charismatic, with full participation of men and women and with enthusiastic reception of prophecies and other spirit-prompted experiences.

In chapters 10 and 11 Paul deals with some misunderstandings and blatant misuse of the Lord's supper. It is interesting to see that the only time the term "the Lord's supper" appears in the New Testament is in this discussion, and it is negative. First Corinthians 11:20 reads, "When you come together, it is not really to eat the Lord's supper." He then points out that their banquets appear to be contests to see how much and how fast individuals can eat and drink, and during this process the poor are neglected. He points out in 10:14-17 that the single loaf of bread at the table indicates the singleness of the church as Christ's body and that our eating and drinking is actually a *koinōnia* of the blood and body of Christ—an intimate participation. This is where the word *communion* was first connected with the Lord's supper, since the Latin (Vulgate) followed by the King James version translated *koinōnia* here as communion. Paul then goes on to point out that participating at this table rules out participation at pagan religious feasts, since "You cannot drink the cup of the Lord and the cup of demons. You cannot partake of the table of the Lord and the table of demons" (10:21). His instruction just before the familiar words of institution are that the Corinthian Christians, if they cannot control their selfish behavior at the Lord's table, should eat at home before gathering with the church (11:17-22). The significance of this table, then, is not in the feasting but in the remembrance and renewal of the covenant relationship with God through Christ (11:23-26,33-34). This exhortation closes with a dire warning against eating and drinking in an unworthy manner (11:27-32).

With this instruction about the central focus of worship behind him, Paul in chapters 12–14 turns to the basics of Christian relationships and worship. "Now there are varieties of gifts, but the same Spirit; and there are varieties of services, but the same Lord; and there are varieties of activities, but it is the same God who activates all of them in everyone" (12:4-6). He adds to this the teaching that the Spirit of God gives different abilities to different people, but they all come from the same God, which leads him into his teaching about the nature of the church as a body with different members playing different roles (12:7-31).

This is followed by his description of "a more excellent way" in chapter 13, a chapter that is too often left out of the discussion of Christian worship, in spite of the fact that it appears right in the middle of Paul's instructions on worship. Without love for one another in the church our disagreements about worship can wreck the church. That has become all too apparent in the many divisions over worship practices during the history of the church. So Paul, in 14:12, says, "So with yourselves; since you are eager for manifestations of the Spirit, strive to excel in building up the church."

This leads him to some very specific and important advice:

[13]Therefore, one who speaks in a tongue should pray for the power to interpret. [14]For if I pray in a tongue, my spirit prays but my mind is unproductive. [15]What should I do then? I will pray with the spirit, but I will pray with the mind also; I will sing praise with the spirit, but I will sing praise with the mind also. [16]Otherwise, if you say a blessing with the spirit, how can anyone in the position of an outsider say the "Amen" to your thanksgiving, since the outsider does not know what you are saying? [17]For you may give thanks well enough, but the other person is not built up. [18]I thank God that I speak in tongues more than all of you; [19]nevertheless, in church I would rather speak five words with my mind, in order to instruct others also, than ten thousand words in a tongue (14:13-19).

Then he comes to a description of the activities of these services:

[26b]When you come together, each one has a hymn, a lesson, a revelation, a tongue, or an interpretation. Let all things be done for building up. [27]If anyone speaks in a tongue, let there be only two or at most three, and each in turn; and let one interpret. [28]But if there is no one to interpret, let them be silent in church and speak to themselves and to God. [29]Let two or three prophets speak, and let the others weigh what is said. [30]If a revelation is made to someone else sitting nearby, let the first person be silent (14:26b-30).

This sort of participation and spontaneity apparently characterized the worship of Paul's Hellenistic churches, a radical departure from the sedate-sounding worship of the Jewish Christians. No longer do we see a rational reading and exposition of the Bible accompanied by set prayers and the breaking of bread. Now we have hymns, lessons, revelations, unfamiliar and unlearned tongues, and interpretations of tongues. Apparently all this was happening at times in a chaotic way; so Paul calls not for a cessation of these activities, but for an ordering of them. His concern here appears to be not just orderly worship, but the reputation of the worshiping community among outsiders. He is especially concerned that outsiders be able to understand what is going on so that they can add an "amen" to the thanksgiving (14:16). His climactic statement about this is, "I thank God that I speak in tongues more than all of you; nevertheless, in church I would rather speak five words with my mind, in order to instruct others also, than ten thousand words in a tongue" (14:18-19). By "in church" he means not in a special building but in a Christian assembly—a meeting of persons for whose edification he feels himself responsible. His final word on the subject here is "So, my friends, be eager to prophesy, and do not forbid speaking in tongues; but all things should be done decently and in order" (14:39-40).

So what we are designating as charismatic worship is a departure from the more pedantic Jewish pattern. It is highly participatory, touching the spirits and emotions of participants. It is, furthermore, charged with the dynamic presence and work of God's Spirit—a Spirit that inspired utterance and action, but a Spirit open to and even requiring order. And this charismatic worship style is not just tolerated but also encouraged by the apostle Paul, as long as there is some order and understanding around it.

Apocalyptic

Apocalyptic-style worship is a bit harder to locate geographically. What the New Testament gives us in this regard are two texts that hint at worship on earth modeled after heavenly worship and the Apocalypse itself (Revelation) that is full of worship descriptions. Other Jewish apocalyptic documents seem to parallel Hebrews 12:18-24 and 2 Corinthians 12:4, where worship in Heaven is similar to that on earth. Note the picture of Christian devotion in the Hebrews text:

> [18]For you have not come to what may be touched, a blazing fire, and darkness, and gloom, and a tempest, [19]and the sound of a trumpet, and a voice whose words made the hearers entreat that no further messages be spoken to them. [20]For they could not endure the order that was given, "If even a beast touches the mountain, it shall be stoned." [21]Indeed, so terrifying was the sight that Moses said, "I tremble with fear." [22]But you have come to Mount Zion and to the city of the living God, the heavenly Jerusalem, and to innumerable angels in festal gathering, [23]and to the assembly of the firstborn who are enrolled in heaven, and to a judge who is God of all, and to the spirits of just men made perfect, [24]and to Jesus, the mediator of a new covenant, and to the sprinkled blood that speaks more graciously than the blood of Abel.

The 2 Corinthians text is harder to connect with corporate worship since it is Paul's description of the experience of one individual ("a person in Christ," presumably himself) shown something in heaven: "was caught up into Paradise and heard things that are not to be told, that no mortal is permitted to repeat."

Both of these texts have some parallels to two documents produced by Jews in the intertestamental period. The Testament of Levi 3:4-9 reads:

In the uppermost heaven of all dwells the Great Glory in the Holy of Holies superior to all holiness. There with him are the archangels who serve and offer propitiatory sacrifices to the Lord in behalf of all the sins of ignorance of the righteous ones. They present to the Lord a pleasing odor, a rational and bloodless oblation. In the heaven below them are the messengers who carry the responses to the angels of the Lord's presence. There with him are thrones and authorities; there praises to God are offered eternally. So when the Lord looks upon us we all tremble. Even the heavens and earth and the abysses tremble before the presence of his majesty.

And 2 Enoch 20, with all its textual problems, reads:

And the men lifted me up from there, and they carried me up to the seventh heaven. And I saw a great light, and all the fiery armies of the incorporeal ones, archangels, angels, and the shining *otanim* stations. And I was terrified, and I trembled.

And the men picked me up with their . . .

And they said to me, "Be brave, Enoch! Don't be frightened!"

And they showed me from a distance the Lord, sitting on his throne.

And all the heavenly armies assembled, according to rank, advancing and doing obeisance to the Lord. And then they withdrew and went to their places in joy and merriment, in immeasurable light but gloriously serving him. . . .

Even though the 2 Enoch text comes with many gaps, it is clear that both of these apocryphal documents, which could easily have been familiar to the apostle Paul and other early Christian writers, deal with heavenly or apocalyptic worship. Thus, the early church had worship traditions that went far beyond the practices of the temple and the synagogue.

Therefore we should not be surprised that the book of Revelation offers a surprising number of depictions of Christian worship.[1] This book seems strange to readers early in the twenty-first century, partly because it attempts to describe a reality that we do not experience directly. Of course, most of the people to whom the book was originally addressed did not experience that reality either, but our modern educations have conditioned us to be suspicious of any mention or description of "things not seen" (Heb 11:1), therefore, when we read a description of dragons and other strange creatures battling, we switch to the mode of science fiction or fantasy, both of which we might be interested in, but which we also definitely categorize as fiction and therefore not reality.

Another reason for our dismissal of Revelation is the inordinate amount of space/time given to worship. Twelve of the twenty-two chapters of the book of Revelation contain direct references to or descriptions of worship. It is too easy to dismiss those references along with the more fantastic descriptions in the book as belonging to the general genre of apocalyptic, thus sounding erudite and in this way not having to deal with worship in heaven. However, if we are to take the book seriously at any level, we must come to grips with the dominant role of worship in it.

Can we read the accounts of worship in Revelation as reality? Might they not describe much more of the reality of Christian worship than the social scientist would? In this book the curtain that normally hides the heavenly reality from our eyes is pulled back. Here, perhaps better than anywhere else, we can see the reality of Christian worship.

Chapters 4 and 5 of Revelation lay a firm foundation for an understanding of the reality of worship. This passage begins with the presence of God, the object of all true worship. It is the first glimpse the book gives us of heaven. John is finished now with the hortatory letters to the seven churches to which the book is addressed. "After this I looked, and there in heaven a door stood open! And the first voice, which I had heard speaking to me like a trumpet, said, 'Come up here, and I will show you what must take place after this'" (4:1). The door is open, and what does he see? He sees God.

> ²At once I was in the spirit, and there in heaven stood a throne, with one seated on the throne! ³And the one seated there looks

like jasper and carnelian, and around the throne is a rainbow that looks like an emerald. ⁴Around the throne are twenty-four thrones, and seated on the thrones are twenty-four elders, dressed in white robes, with golden crowns on their heads. ⁵Coming from the throne are flashes of lightning, and rumblings and peals of thunder, and in front of the throne burn seven flaming torches, which are the seven spirits of God; ⁶and in front of the throne there is something like a sea of glass, like crystal (4:2–6a).

Here is the center of Christian worship—God enthroned; God more captivating than fine jewels; God framed by a jewel-like rainbow; God surrounded by people crowned, clothed in white, occupying other thrones; God with lightning and thunder emanating from the throne; God with seven torchlike spirits alongside, with a calm-as-glass crystal sea reflecting the divine glory. Light, pure and beautiful, dominates the description of God. These descriptive elements appear elsewhere in the Bible, but here John brings them together in a deeply impressive way to draw our attention to the central figure—God.

Who are the worshipers? We have already mentioned the twenty-four elders. The number is probably the sum of the twelve tribes of Israel and the twelve apostles of Jesus. They appear to represent God's people throughout human history. At any rate, they appear to be closest to the divine throne. Then we find further descriptions.

⁶ᵇAround the throne, and on each side of the throne, are four living creatures, full of eyes in front and behind: ⁷the first living creature like a lion, the second living creature like an ox, the third living creature with a face like a human face, and the fourth living creature like a flying eagle. ⁸And the four living creatures, each of them with six wings, are full of eyes all around and inside. Day and night without ceasing they sing,

"Holy, holy, holy,
the Lord God the Almighty,
who was and is and is to come" (4:6b–8).

Here we meet some strange creatures, full of eyes, so as not to miss anything. The first resembles a lion, the creature we connect with majesty. The second is like an ox, the symbol of strength. The third has a human face, exhibiting wisdom. The fourth is like an eagle, the swift creature. The majesty, strength, wisdom, and mobility of God's creation are worshiping here.[2] Their worship is unceasing adoration of the holy Lord God Almighty. And as they express their worship, the twenty-four elders fall down before God, throw down their crowns, and sing:

You are worthy, our Lord and God,
to receive glory and honor and power,
for you created all things,
and by your will they existed and were created (4:11).

In the words of Eugene Peterson:

In worship every sign of life and every impulse to holiness, every bit of beauty and every spark of vitality—Hebrew patriarchs, Christian apostles, wild animals, domesticated livestock, human beings, soaring birds—are arranged around this throne center that pulses light, showing each at its best, picking up all the colors of the spectrum in order to show off the glories.[3]

And then (5:1-4) the word of God—the scroll—becomes visible, but it is securely closed.

This scroll has a lot of information in it—"written on the inside and on the back"—but nobody can open it. Nobody can explain or apply it. The information is useless because it is inaccessible. "Then one of the elders said to me, 'Do not weep. See, the Lion of the tribe of Judah, the Root of David, has conquered, so that he can open the scroll and its seven seals'" (5:5). The conquering Christ can open it. Only with the help of Christ can the word of God become accessible. But who is this victorious Lion of the tribe of Judah?

⁶Then I saw between the throne and the four living creatures and among the elders a Lamb standing as if it had been slaughtered, having seven horns and seven eyes, which are the seven spirits of God sent out into all the earth. ⁷He went and took the scroll from the right hand of the one who was seated on the throne (5:6–7).

The Lion is a Lamb—a slaughtered Lamb, no less. Here worship is flavored with the kind of oxymoron that characterizes the gospel of Christ.⁴ Paul learned the hard way that God's "power is made perfect in weakness" (2 Cor 12:9). So in heaven the ability to make God's word accessible to God's people belongs only to the seven-horned, seven-eyed lamb that has been killed. Not only can he open it, he can take it from the strong right hand of God Almighty.

Now comes the singing of the main congregation. First the elders and the four creatures sing a new song:

> ⁹You are worthy to take the scroll
>> and to open its seals,
>
> for you were slaughtered and by your blood you ransomed
>> for God
>>
>>> saints from every tribe and language and people and
>>> nation;
>
> ¹⁰you have made them to be a kingdom and priests serving our
>> God,
>
>> and they will reign on earth (5:9–10).

Then the angels join the singing:

> ¹²Worthy is the Lamb that was slaughtered
> to receive power and wealth and wisdom and might
> and honor and glory and blessing! (5:12).

And finally,

> ¹³Then I heard every creature in heaven and on earth
> and under the earth and in the sea, and all that is in
> them, singing,
>
>> "To the one seated on the throne and to the Lamb
>> be blessing and honor and glory and might
>>> forever and ever!" (5:13).

Let your imagination play with the scene. Twenty-four white-robed elders and four mighty creatures begin the music by singing praises to the Christ; they are joined by myriads of angels; and finally, every creature made by God joins in the singing of praises to both Christ and God.

Music is the most appropriate response available to the sensate creatures of God. Music continues to be a primary medium of praise in the rest of the book. Revelation 7 describes a scene in the presence of a great multitude of people.

> [11]And all the angels stood around the throne and around the elders and the four living creatures, and they fell on their faces before the throne and worshiped God, [12]singing,
>> "Amen! Blessing and glory and wisdom
>> and thanksgiving and honor
>> and power and might
>> be to our God forever and ever! Amen" (7:11–12).

Chapter 11 presents another song:

> [17]We give you thanks, Lord God Almighty,
>> who are and who were,
> for you have taken your great power
>> and begun to reign.
> [18]The nations raged,
>> but your wrath has come,
>> and the time for judging the dead,
> for rewarding your servants, the prophets
>> and saints and all who fear your name,
>> both small and great,
> and for destroying those who destroy the earth
>> (11:17–18).

That song is followed by the opening of heaven, the appearance of the ark of the covenant, and "flashes of lightning, rumblings, peals of thunder, an earthquake, and heavy hail" (11:19).

Chapter 15 shows the victorious army of God's people with harps, singing the song of Moses and of the Lamb:

> ³ᵇGreat and amazing are your deeds,
>> Lord God the Almighty!
> Just and true are your ways,
>> King of the nations!
> ⁴Lord, who will not fear
>> and glorify your name?
> For you alone are holy.
>> All nations will come
>> and worship before you,
> for your judgments have been revealed (15:3–4).

Chapters 16 and 19 also present poetic ascriptions of praise without the mention of singing, although in the first century the normal way of reading to a group of people was to chant or sing the words, and thus even those passages would have been heard by their original audiences as songs.

And at the conclusion of all this worship in song, "the four living creatures said, 'Amen!'" Whether or not one feels comfortable in a charismatic style or an apocalyptic style worship experience, one must recognize that they were both among the primary ways of worshiping during the apostolic period and that none of these ways was inappropriate. On the other hand, it appears that the synagogue style and the charismatic style have been developed and practiced throughout church history, while the apocalyptic style has been less noticeable. There are glimpses of it in the worship of Eastern Orthodoxy and a hint of it in Calvin's understanding of the Lord's Supper, but otherwise it appears to have been forgotten.

Common Elements

Amidst all the diversity we find in the New Testament about worship, there are some common elements that appear in descriptions of all three patterns. One of these is the day of worship—**The Lord's Day** or the first day of the week. This was the day of the resurrection of Jesus. It was not the Jewish Sabbath day, nor was it a special day in the Hellenistic world. It was the day the Christians set aside for remembering the death of Jesus and celebrating his victory over death. Acts 20:7 informs us, "On the first day of the week, when we met to break bread, Paul was holding a discussion. . . ." Then Paul himself in the final instructions of 1 Corinthians (16:2) writes, "On the first day of every week, each of you is to put aside and save whatever extra you earn, so that collections need not be taken when I come." And the seer begins his report of visions in Revelation 1:10 with these words, "I was in the spirit on the Lord's day, and I heard behind me a loud voice like a trumpet. . . ." Although there is no direct mandate to meet on Sunday, we shall see that the practice of Christians has always been to set aside the first day of the week for our special worship.

The Lord's Supper is also a common element. It appears to have been so common that we have no detailed description of it—only numerous mentions and its roots in the tradition of meals Jesus had with his disciples. The tradition of the last supper is tied with the ongoing practice of the Christian community by Paul in 1 Corinthians 10–11. We have noted a variety of approaches to worship services already in the apostolic church. We see also a variety of ways the Lord's supper was done—from being part of a common meal (banquet?) to a more focused ritual, where the bread and cup were more representational than physically nourishing.[5] On the other hand, there appears to be no doubt that some form of the supper was common to all early congregations.

Scripture reading, with teaching and exhortation also appears to have been common. This would stem from the synagogue practice where during a Sabbath service a leader (scribe or rabbi) commented on the Scripture lessons of the day. First Timothy includes the instruction, "Give attention to the public reading of Scripture, to exhorting, to teaching" (4:13). Paul also assumes that his letters are read aloud to the assembled churches to which they are addressed. Colossians 4:16 instructs, "And when this letter has been read among you, have it read also in the church of the Laodiceans; and see that you read also the letter from Laodicea." The book of Acts is concerned more to record evangelistic preaching than the exhorting and teaching within the church, so we have very little indication of the content or form of this. We do have, in Acts 20:18-35, a speech of Paul to the assembled elders of the church in Ephesus, but it is mostly biographical—a farewell address that commissions them to their work in Paul's absence. He does quote the Lord Jesus at the end ("It is more blessed to give than to receive").

Prayer is also an assumed regular part of early Christian worship. In addition to examples in Acts and references in 1 Corinthians, we have the direct command in 1 Timothy 2:1, "First of all, then, I urge that supplications, prayers, intercessions, and thanksgivings be made for everyone." We also have the great prayers and praise in Revelation 4:8 and 11:16-18. But perhaps most important are the prayers of Jesus in the Gospels. The disciples were so impressed with the practice of prayer they saw in Jesus that they asked him to teach them to pray (Luke 11:1). He gave them a model prayer, that has become known as the Lord's Prayer and that we find in use in every subsequent period of church history (Luke 11:2-4 and Matt 6:9-13).

And finally, we find **music**. Jesus and the disciples, we are told, sang a hymn after supper before going to the Mount of Olives (Matt 26:30). This was probably the "Egyptian Hallel" (Psalms 113-118) that usually accompanied the Passover meal. The singing of psalms, hymns, and spiritual songs is recommended in both Ephesians 5:19 and Colossians 3:16. The former connects it with being filled with the Spirit and giving thanks to God, while the latter specifies that the songs are to be sung to God. The examples of songs of praise in the book of Revelation are to a great extent compilations of statements from the biblical psalms. Hymns might have been a more Greek style of music since there are also hymns to the Greek gods. Spiritual songs, or odes, might be more akin to what we call praise choruses. At any rate, we have here again a variety of ways to sing God's praise. It is also quite likely that the reading of Scripture, exhortation, and set prayers would have been vocalized in a metric, rhythmic way, similar to later traditions of chant.

Other Traces of Worship Forms

There are many traces of worship forms recorded in the New Testament. They are usually not labeled as statements recited (chanted) or songs sung in Christian worship, but they are recognizable from their poetic form and their subject matter.

One of these forms is **confessions of faith**. Romans 1:3b-4 is a powerful statement about the identity of the Christ: "who was descended from David according to the flesh and was declared to be Son of God with power according to the spirit of holiness by resurrection from the dead, Jesus Christ our Lord." It employs terminology not normally used by Paul, so many scholars take it to be a confession of faith of the early church to which Paul was referring as common ground between him and the Christians in Rome. Romans 10:9 is even clearer, since Paul labels as a confession (with the lips) the statement, "Jesus is Lord." First Corinthians 12:3 and 2 Corinthians 4:5 repeat the Romans 10 confession. A longer, more detailed confession of faith in the resurrection of Jesus is given by Paul as something he received (presumably from earlier believers) in 1 Corinthians 15:3-5. The statement labeled "the mystery of our religion" in 1 Timothy 3:16 is such a neat, poetic formulation that it could be hymnic:

> "He was revealed in flesh,
> vindicated in spirit,
> seen by angels,
> proclaimed among Gentiles,
> believed in throughout the world,
> taken up in glory.

There are other possible confessions, but these are enough for our purposes.

We also find some specific **prayer formulas** in the New Testament. The Aramaic terms *Abba* and *Maranatha* appear from time to time where Aramaic, the language of Palestine in the time of Jesus, was rarely spoken. This indicates that these terms ("father" and "come, Lord") were in use in prayers of Christians who didn't normally speak Aramaic. The "Our Father," or "The Lord's Prayer," was recalled in the oral tradition of those early believers so well that it was written down in two of our Gospels. The versions in Matthew 6:9-13 and Luke 11:2-4 are similar enough to convince us that they both go back to the Lord himself, the familiar closing doxology having been added later. In addition to these texts, Paul customarily begins his letters with a prayer of thanks and blessing for the believers to whom he is writing. It is interesting that we have even a prayer position or posture described in 1 Timothy 2:8, where people are encouraged to "pray, lifting up holy hands without anger or argument."

One worship form that seems to be plentiful in the New Testament is texts that look very much like **hymns**. In fact, many of them have been put to music in more modern times. For instance, Luke 1:46-55 is the song of Mary at the time of the annunciation of her pregnancy with Jesus. This beautiful text of dedication, often called the *Magnificat*, from its first word in Latin, is modeled after the prayer of Hannah in 1 Samuel 1:11; 2:1-10. In Luke 1:68-79 we find the response of Zechariah on the occasion of the circumcision of John (later: the Baptist). This *Benedictus* (again from the Latin) would have been chanted as it praises God and prophesies the role of the forerunner of the Messiah. In Luke 2:14 we have the brief song of the angels at the birth of Jesus, usually referred to as the *Gloria*. Paul gives us two great songs about the Christ in Philippians 2:6-11 and Colossians 1:15-20. Most commentaries point out the structure, meter, and poetry of these passages, but one cannot be sure whether they were original with Paul or quoted by him as reminders to his readers of the faith they had in common. Worked into the prose of the opening paragraph of Hebrews is the beautiful and concise statement, "He is the reflection of God's glory and the exact imprint of God's very being, and he sustains all things by his powerful word. When he had made purification for sins, he sat down at the right hand of the Majesty on high, having become as much superior to angels as the name he has inherited is more excellent than theirs" (1:3-4). And as we pointed out earlier, Revelation 15:3-4 gives us what is called "the song of Moses, the servant of God, and the song of the Lamb."

There is another text that resembles a song that could be used for a very specific purpose. For this reason I call it a baptismal formula. It is found in Ephesians 5:14. Paul introduces it with words that indicate that the Ephesian Christians would be familiar with it:

Therefore it says,
"Sleeper, awake!
Rise from the dead,
and Christ will shine on you."

It is not hard to imagine this being shouted or sung by a congregation as a new believer is raised from the baptismal pool to enter the new life with Christ.

The texts recording the last supper of Jesus with his disciples that became what we variously call **the Lord's Supper** or Communion or the Eucharist are Matthew 26:17-30, Mark 14:12-26, Luke 22:7-23,and 1 Corinthians 11:17-34. Each of these texts records the event in its own way, but the basic elements of bread and wine and the actions of blessing, breaking/pouring, giving, receiving, and eating/drinking are common to them all. John's Gospel lacks a last supper episode, but many scholars take John 6:41-58 as referring to the supper, since here Jesus talks about people eating his body and drinking his blood.

In addition to general prayers, the New Testament also gives us special prayers we call **benedictions and doxologies**. Benedictions are found as writers close their documents. First Corinthians 16:23 contains the simple, "The grace of the Lord Jesus be with you." Second Corinthians 13:13 states the very familiar, "The grace of the

Lord Jesus Christ, the love of God, and the communion of the Holy Spirit be with all of you." Revelation 22:21 closes this work with the general, "The grace of the Lord Jesus be with all the saints. Amen."

Doxologies appear quite often, especially in Paul's letters. These are ascriptions of praise to God. A very brief one, yet quite typical of Jewish practices, is Romans 1:25, where Paul refers to the Creator and immediately adds, "who is blessed forever! Amen." Then in Romans 9:5 he refers to "the Messiah, who is over all, God blessed forever. Amen." Another similar short ascription is in 2 Corinthians 11:31, "The God and Father of our Lord Jesus (blessed be he forever!) knows that I do not lie." A similar formulation is found in Galatians 1:5. Ephesians includes several such doxologies. The letter begins (1:3) with, "Blessed be the God and Father of our Lord Jesus Christ, who has blessed us in Christ with every spiritual blessing in the heavenly places. . . ." We see other examples in Ephesians 3:20, Philippians 4:20, and 2 Timothy 4:18.

The **Amen** is an interesting study. It appears both in the apocalyptic literature and in Paul's instructions to the Corinthians. Amen means "truly"; it is a congregational "yes" to whatever is being said or done. This is no period at the end of a prayer. "Amen" in the New Testament is not the end of anything; it is a resounding affirmation. The apostle Paul indicates in 1 Corinthians 14:16 that it makes sense only when people can understand what is being said, and then in 2 Corinthians 1:20 he connects it with the affirmation God has made in Christ: "For in him every one of God's promises is a 'Yes.' For this reason it is through him that we say the 'Amen,' to the glory of God". Then in Revelation we find it used as a collective affirmation: God is truly Lord of all—yes! Christ is thoroughly worthy—yes! We find the center of our lives at the throne of God—yes! God will help us live our throne-centered lives in this world. Amen.

More complex is the picture of other rites in the New Testament, such as baptism, the laying on of hands, anointing with oil, and foot washing.

There is no scholarly disagreement about the original meaning of the word *baptizō*, to immerse, from which we get baptism, although there is plenty of disagreement about how and on whom the act was performed. The Gospels report on the baptizing ministry of John, which forms the background for the later Christian practice. We find it commanded, but not described, in Matthew 28:19 and mentioned in Mark 16:16, part of an ending probably not in the original of the Gospel, but reflecting early practice. It appears often in Acts, although again without detailed descriptions. According to Acts 2:38 Peter declares repentance and baptism as the means to forgiveness of sins, and in verse 41 we are told, "So those who welcomed his message were baptized." The next mention of baptism is in chapter 8, where Philip is preaching in Samaria. Verse 12 tells us, "when they believed Philip . . . they were baptized, both men and women." Even Simon the sorcerer was baptized there. Here is where things get complicated. Peter and John go from Jerusalem to Samaria and find that these people had been baptized only "in the name of the Lord Jesus," and had not yet received the Holy Spirit. The apostles laid their hands on the new believers, who then received the Holy Spirit. Without an explanation, we cannot know what this looked like. Something happened that called attention to a change in these people, but the author does not describe it. Then later in the chapter we find Philip explaining Isaiah to the Ethiopian, who then asked to be baptized, indicating that Philip's teaching included baptism. Here we get more of a description, with the statement, ". . . both of them, Philip and the eunuch, went down into the water, and Philip baptized [immersed] him. When they came up out of the water . . ." (vv. 38-39). The next mention is in 9:18, where Saul of Tarsus is baptized apparently by Ananias in Damascus. Then we find Peter at the home of Cornelius. Peter mentions the baptism of John (Acts 10:37) in his presentation of the gospel, after (or during) which "the Holy Spirit fell on all who heard the word" (10:44). Here we find the people speaking in tongues as in Jerusalem on Pentecost; so Peter said, "'Can anyone withhold the water for baptizing these people who have received the Holy Spirit just as we have?' So he ordered them to be baptized in the name of Jesus Christ" (10:47-48). In chapter 16 we find the baptism of Lydia and her household in Philippi (v. 15) and then the jailer and his household (v. 33). Acts 18 records the baptisms of people in Corinth (v. 8) and then in 19:5 the enigmatic story of the baptism of twelve disciples who had known only the baptism of John. They also showed signs of the reception of the Holy Spirit. The final mention of baptism in Acts is in 22:16, in the retelling of the conversion of Saul/Paul, and here it is connected, as at Pentecost, with the washing away of sin.

In addition to the Gospels and Acts, baptism is dealt with in Romans, 1 Corinthians, Galatians, Ephesians, Colossians, Hebrews, and 1 Peter—a formidable list. A quick look at all these texts indicates both the importance of baptism as one step toward what we call salvation and the great variety of ways the early Christians understood baptism. It is connected with the gift of the Holy Spirit, the new birth, the new life, and union with Christ. It appears to have been an act expected of all new believers and performed wherever and as soon as possible when people came to believe. The experience was so rich that it could be described as a change from death to life, slavery to freedom, and burial to resurrection (Romans 6) nearly all in one breath.

But how does **the laying on of hands** connect with baptism? Twice in Acts we see it following baptism for the reception of the Holy Spirit, but both of those instances (Peter and John in Samaria and Paul in Ephesus) can be understood as special circumstances, as can the case of Cornelius, where the Holy Spirit comes before baptism—to convince Peter and the other Jewish believers to permit Gentiles to be baptized. First Timothy 4:14 tells the young leader, "Do not neglect the gift that is in you, which was given to you through prophecy with the laying on of hands by the council of elders." To what rite does this refer? We are left in the dark about this act that sounds like what we call ordination, but about which we have only clues.

The same questions remain about **anointing and confession of sins**, as dealt with in James 5:13-16:

> ¹³Are any among you suffering? They should pray. Are any cheerful? They should sing songs of praise. ¹⁴Are any among you sick? They should call for the elders of the church and have them pray over them, anointing them with oil in the name of the Lord. ¹⁵The prayer of faith will save the sick, and the Lord will raise them up; and anyone who has committed sins will be forgiven. ¹⁶Therefore confess your sins to one another, and pray for one another, so that you may be healed. The prayer of the righteous is powerful and effective.

Are these instructions for regular rites of worship or for special occasions? We just are not told.

Similar questions arise about foot washing. According to John 13, Jesus washed the feet of the disciples and told them, "So if I, your Lord and Teacher, have washed your feet, you ought to wash one another's feet" (v. 14). Some Christian traditions have foot washing services regularly. Others have decided that since we have no record in Acts or the epistles of the early church's participation in it, we are not expected to treat it as an ordinance (a command to be followed regularly), and so they treat it as an example of humble service that we are to emulate.

Summary

We find a great variety of worship forms in the New Testament—none of which offers an exact pattern for our worship today, but all of which give us glimpses of worship as the earliest Christians experienced it and as we can adapt to our services of worship. One can identify traces of each of the primary New Testament patterns in many services today—the reading and teaching/preaching of Scripture, the prayers, singing hymns and praise choruses directed to God on the throne and the lamb, the Lord's supper, offerings of food and money, fellowship in all sorts of configurations, testimonies of God's working in life. In other words, even though no one church does everything we find in the New Testament, we need not search long to find most of them in action in the churches. This variety of acts of worship should encourage us to be at least tolerant of, if not encouraging of, changes in worship styles and patterns in our own congregations.

For Further Reading

Barker, Margaret. *The Great High Priest: The Temple Roots of Christian Liturgy.* London: T. & T. Clark, 2003.

Bartels, Ernest. *Take Eat, Take Drink: The Lord's Supper through the Centuries.* St. Louis: Concordia Publishing House, 2004.

Bradshaw, Paul F. *The Search for the Origins of Christian Worship.* New York: Oxford University Press, 1992.

Hieronymus, Lynn. *What the Bible Says about Worship.* Joplin, MO: College Press, 1984.

Marshall, I. Howard. *Last Supper and Lord's Supper.* Grand Rapids: Eerdmans, 1980.

Martin, Ralph P. *Worship in the Early Church.* Grand Rapids: Eerdmans, 1974.

Smith, Dennis E., and Hal E Tausig. *Many Tables: The Eucharist in the New Testament and Liturgy Today.* Philadelphia: Trinity Press International, 1990.

꒰ ——— ꒱

[1]This section was published originally in a longer form as an article by Bruce E. Shields in *Leaven* 8/2 (Winter 2000) 32-35.

[2]Eugene H. Peterson, *Reversed Thunder: The Revelation of John and the Praying Imagination* (San Francisco: Harper San Francisco, 1988) 62.

[3]Ibid.

[4]For a good discussion of this dialectic, see M. Eugene Boring, *Revelation,* Interpretation (Louisville, KY: John Knox, 1989) 108–111.

[5]Dennis E. Smith and Hal E. Tausig, *Many Tables: The Eucharist in the New Testament and Liturgy Today* (Philadelphia: Trinity Press International, 1990), deal in detail with the variety of forms.

CHAPTER THREE

The First Three Centuries

*I*t is evident that the Church of the Apostolic and early Postapostolic periods was eagerly awaiting the imminent coming of Christ in glory—what is called the *parousia*. The enigmatic word(s) *"Maranatha!"* found in the earliest worship texts, can be translated not only as a prayer —"Come, Lord [Jesus]!"—but also as an acclamation—"Our Lord is coming!" Obviously, these earliest believers were not so much concerned with crafting and promulgating a formal worship structure that would survive indefinitely. After all, Christ was coming, and "soon" was implied! It is understandable, then, why worship in this period remained rather simple (or at least documented simply— where it was documented at all). As we saw in the previous chapter, it was modeled to a large extent on the worship of Yahweh which was already being practiced by the majority of Jewish communities at the time.

A generous amount of data also exists that indicates the worship of the earliest Christians was multiform and adaptive. Communities, scattered throughout the Roman Empire, expressed their corporate worship in ways which often reflected their local surroundings. Worship texts were most often those that were readily available by means of the preexistent Hebrew corpus, or other documents which were authenticated by their regular usage by the worshiping assembly. Convenience prevailed as small gatherings of Christians within a particular city adapted older traditions of

Judaism to the radically newer circumstances of Gentile Christianity, especially after the predictable break of the Christians with the worship tradition of the synagogue.

But each of these characteristics: multiformity, simplicity, convenience, and expectancy, carried both positive and negative aspects. Take convenience, for example. A modern Evangelical might appreciate the improvisational (*ex tempore*) style that must have characterized many of the public prayers of this time. But this common practice was not without its problems. Evidently, not every presider was adequately gifted to compose an acceptable prayer "on the spot," since at least one early document provides a model prayer for less-gifted presiders to follow while making the allowance that others may compose a prayer according to their ability.

For Christian worshipers who have not yet ventured past the New Testament, the first introduction to these extrabiblical writings of the first three centuries of worship is an understandably exciting event. Many expect to find the singular and original pattern of Christian worship in its purest form. Others hope to have their own contemporary worship practices confirmed by the witness of the earliest believers. At the very least there is a reasonable curiosity as to how the information gaps within the biblical material might have been realized among these early apostolic communities. We need to be aware, however, that in this period there are just as many (if not considerably more) gaps in historical data, especially now that Christianity was beginning to cover a larger geographic area. This means that locations other than Palestine are now becoming increasingly more important. One should bear this in mind when looking at the specific evidence at hand: just because a certain ritual is popular in the worship of Milan does not mean that it is practiced by the church in Rome (even though the latter was not an insignificant neighbor). We will eventually be able to track some of the developments of worship forms by way of liturgical "families" that share common roots in a particular geographic region.

Furthermore, we are dealing with roughly the same period of

time in which our present-day New Testament was being compiled. That some documents of the early Church later became canonized while others did not is beyond the scope of this book, but we should remember that both the formation of the New Testament and the later development of the worship/liturgy of early Christians had concurrent beginnings in this historical period. After all, included in the canon of the New Testament were those written texts that were being used with some degree of regularity in the worship of various local communities. In other words, it was actually the *worship texts* of these earliest Christians that factored into the formation of the Christian Bible. This means that unwritten tradition was possibly as important—or even more important—at this time than at any other period of Christian history since relatively little was being written down for the sole benefit of worship historians. This should rightly make anyone nervous who appeals solely to the New Testament for information on the worship practices of the early Church. Writing only 200 years after this period in question, Basil the Great (d. 379) legitimates the stability and pure transmission of liturgical practices by means of oral tradition:

> Concerning the teachings of the Church, whether publicly proclaimed (*kerygma*) or reserved to members of the household of faith (*dogmata*), we have received some from written sources, while others have been given to us secretly, through apostolic tradition. . . . For instance (to take the first and most common example), where is the written teaching that we should sign with the sign of the Cross those who, trusting in the Name of Our Lord Jesus Christ, are to be enrolled as catechumens? Which book teaches us to pray facing the East? Have any saints left for us in writing the words to be used in the invocation over the Eucharistic bread and the cup of blessing? As everyone knows, we are not content in the liturgy simply to recite the words recorded by St. Paul and the Gospels, but we add other words both before and after, words of great importance for this mystery. We have received these words from unwritten teaching. We bless the baptismal water and the oil for chrismation as well as the candidate

approaching the font. By what written authority do we do this, if not from secret and mystical tradition? . . . Are not all these things found in unpublished and unwritten teachings, which our fathers guarded in silence, safe from meddling and petty curiosity? They had learned their lesson well; reverence for the mysteries is best encouraged by silence.[1]

We also need to be cautious when reading extrabiblical documents about worship, realizing that there is a larger context that surrounds the text and may possibly be the reason for the text having been written in the first place. We will begin our study of this period with the historical context that influenced early Christian worship.

Context

Christian worship was not a novel invention of the followers of Jesus. Rather, it was a process of adopting and adapting worship forms that would have been available to the first disciples. As we have seen in the last chapter, Jewish Christians of this period by some accounts not only modeled their worship on that of the synagogue, but may have even been considered by other Jews to be a synagogue of their own (cf. Jas 2:2). The obvious differences, of course, would have been the primacy of meeting together on the Lord's Day—Sunday rather than the Jewish Sabbath—and the celebration of the sacraments, particularly the Lord's Supper. The apostle James betrays a growing antagonism between Gentile and Jewish Christians and so it may be safe to assume that the Gentiles are becoming the more numerous adherents to Christianity at least in Jerusalem. However, no matter where in the Greco-Roman world we may look, especially as this concerns Rome and East Syria, it may be safe to assume that any Jewish elements of Christian worship appearing anywhere in the Diaspora came from these predominantly Palestinian sources.

Influences other than the obvious connections with the contemporary forms of Judaism can account for some characteristics of early Christian worship, but scholars continue to be cautious so as not to read anachronistically into the data. So while Judaism is the major contributor to Christian worship, the Greco-Roman Mystery Religions, Gnosticism, and various Eastern Religions had some degree of impact as well, although there is some question about feeling Gnosticism's effects this early. As for the Mystery Religions (also called Mystery Cults), many, if not all, had secretive initiation ceremonies, purification rituals, and highly developed systems of symbols and rituals that offered something of an explanation to the cosmic order and to humanity's place in that order. Common Mystery Cults of the time would have included those of Mithras, Serapis, Isis, and Dionysus among others. In a similar way, Gnosticism emphasized mysticism, cosmic dualism, cultic secrecy, and supernatural "knowledge" (*gnosis*). The effects that Gnosticism had on the Christian sacraments are still discernable as one sees almost two thousand years of theological and ecclesial explanations and debates about the nature and essence of baptism, eucharist, and ministry.[2] Eastern Religions, as a final category, were also present to some degree in Greco-Roman times, but historians in general are agreed that their influence is eclipsed by Judaism and the Mystery Cults.

Sources

There is no surviving manual for worship leaders during this period, no church bulletins, and no service transcripts. What information we can piece together must come from a variety of sources: letters written from one church leader to another; written homilies that make reference to a specific worship practice; hymns that allude to a particular ritual; and documents that condemn particular practices (yes, even heresies can be valuable sources of historical information). The highlights which follow can be easily obtained in modern translations (most are available online). We wish to remind the reader that while the sources we will mention in this section might have unfamiliar names and seem confusing, the historical study of worship in this period is as dependent upon them as the study of the previous period depends on the letters of Paul. At best, these sources only indirectly yield information about worship, but one type of document: the *Church Order* (*ordo* in Latin) provides the most abundant data. An *ordo* typically provides general instructions on a number of ministry topics that would have directly concerned a specific community. The authorship of the *ordo* would often have been associated with (or later attributed to) a church hierarch who, if not actually known by the recipient, would have been influential enough among a wider readership for the order to actually carry some weight. While the documents that will be cited in this chapter are not lengthy tomes, they are too long to be printed here in their entirety. As we later proceed to categorize these various elements of worship, we should make it clear that there is no substitute for reading each document as the singular unit that it is, and to pay close attention to its historical context and provenance. Only then do the parts and the whole remain in their delicate balance, and only then can one make better guesses about the specific practices of worship that lie behind the text.[3]

Perhaps the earliest of the church orders, and one of the most noteworthy, is the *Didache* which, in Greek, simply means "teaching." A manuscript copy, written completely in Greek, was discovered in a library in Constantinople and is dated around the year 1056. The date of the original document, however, ranges somewhere between A.D. 60 and the end of the second century (with scholars favoring the latter).[4] The material in the *Didache* is divided into two major sections. The first is an instruction on the "Two Ways" which is essentially a moral teaching about the "Way of Life" versus the "Way of Death." The second section is completely devoted to worship matters. Here is found information on baptism, on the *agape* (love-feast)/eucharist, on the Sunday celebration, on fasting days, and on the ministry structure of the particular community in question. We are even provided a few, brief prayer texts.[5] In this one document we are already faced with the need to see worship as something that is much larger than the Sunday morning gathering. Indeed, the categories mentioned in the *Didache* and those mentioned in other documents encompass a holistic life of worship: daily prayer, special feast days, catechetical instruction, initiation, visitation of the sick, reconciliation, and the celebration of the saints, to name a few.

Another church order known as the *Apostolic Tradition* comes to us from Rome. For a long time its authorship was attributed to Hippolytus, a schismatic bishop of the early part of the third century. But this theory of Hippolytan authorship is not generally accepted among scholars. It is even difficult to believe that the worship described by the document was actually what was going on in Rome at the time (some scholars think the author is describing an "ideal" or "imaginary" liturgy).[6] In any case, the influence of this document became widespread and, even as recently as the 1960s, played a major part during the liturgical reforms of both Catholic and Protestant churches. The contents are roughly divided into three parts: (1) ordination rites and other information about bishops, presbyters (priests), and deacons; (2) responsibilities and regulations for the laity, with special attention given to catechetical instruction and the initiation of converts; and (3) a section that deals with a variety of topics that range from blessings upon produce to the *agape* meal.[7]

The third church order we should mention here is the *Didascalia* which can often be confused with the *Didache* since both words stem from the Greek word for *teaching*. The *Didascalia* has its origins in the early third century. Like the *Didache*, the *Didascalia* was originally written in Greek, but the only extant copy that contains the complete text comes down to us in the Syriac language. This particular *ordo* is a compilation since the editor seems to rely heavily on the material from the *Didache*. The *Didascalia* contains expanded information on the weekly liturgy, the celebration of Easter, the Sunday eucharist, and a few references to church architecture.

Other than the church orders, data on worship and liturgy can

be found in letters written by early church leaders, more specifically: in the epistles of bishops—those who were responsible for the
oversight of the "local" church in a particular city. Names that
should become familiar to students of worship are Clement of
Rome, Ignatius of Antioch (scholars often refer to the author of
these letters as "Pseudo-Ignatius"), Polycarp of Smyrna, Clement of
Alexandria, Cyprian of Carthage, Tertullian, and Hippolytus. From
Clement's letters we gain insight into the ministerial offices, and
how Jewish prayer forms were obvious models for this particular
bishop's supplicatory prayers. In Pseudo-Ignatius we glimpse a vision
of the Church as a unity of worshiping congregations. The author
also provides us with his understanding of eucharist and orders
(divisions of ministry roles). Polycarp writes beautifully and poignant-
ly about martyrdom as an imitation of the *pascha* of Christ (Easter)
with its dual themes of suffering (*paschein*) and passing-through
(*pesach*). The letter of Polycarp is also an early attestation of the
early development of a cycle by which saints would be commemorated on their "birthday" (*natale*: the day of their martyrdom).

One can look to other writings from this early period for still
more indirect data about worship. The following sources, whether
from preachers, martyrs, heretics, or Roman government officials
are often mentioned in more comprehensive histories of worship:
The Shepherd of Hermas, The Odes of Solomon, and the works
of *Melito of Sardis, Justin, Pliny, Origen*, are just a few. These are
often new names to those who are venturing for the first time
beyond the confines of the New Testament to see the shape of
Christian worship in the early Church.

For the rest of this chapter, we have chosen to provide information topically (eucharist, daily prayer, ministry, etc.), using the
wide range of these documents which, although separated by many
miles and even many decades, should give a general shape of worship in the first three centuries of Christianity. Hopefully this bare
minimum will convey the essence of each topic at hand.

Worship and Space

It may be reasonable to say that some local synagogues would have even served as primitive Christian meeting places, but larger private homes—at least those that could have adequately accommo- dated those assembled—would have eventually become the norm. The Diaspora contributed to the proliferation of synagogues in areas other than Palestine since, as with Judaism, the God of the Christians' assemblies needed no special structure or locale in order to be duly worshiped. In fact, the Greco-Roman religious system whereby a specific god "resided" in a particular place and exercised jurisdiction within certain boundaries was both a point of contrast and contention as Jewish and Christian groups coexisted alongside those who practiced pagan worship. Rather than being subjected to the building of special temples or shrines, Christians, like Jews, were free to make use of whatever space was most conducive to meeting together for worship. In eastern Syria at Dura-Europos, the remains of one of these house-churches were found.[8] The largest room measured 39 by 16 feet, so the reasonable size of the assembly must have topped at fifty people. Another room in the same struc- ture was most likely used for baptisms, since the paintings near what must have been the baptistery convey the rich symbolism of the women on their way to the tomb of Christ, bearing myrrh to anoint his body.

Worship and Time

1. Daily Prayer

It is not in the first three centuries that one finds a developed schedule of daily communal prayer, but at least morning and evening prayer is attested by Tertullian (*De orat. 25*), by Cyprian (*De or. dom. 29, 34, 35, 36*), and evidence can also be found in the *Apostolic Tradition* (35, 41). These prayer times were naturally carried over from morning and evening prayer as found in the Gospels of Mark (1:35; 6:46) and Luke (10:27). Later sources help us to imagine something of the structure of this daily prayer. There were most likely short sentences of Scripture (later called *versicles*) that would have been integrated in a musically appropriate way along with Psalms (perhaps several of these) sung antiphonally, that is, alternating from one group or individual to another. The continuity with the synagogue style of worship would have made the antiphonal singing of the Psalms a likely element of daily prayer. Intercessions and thanksgivings would have been included along with the Lord's Prayer as the *Didache* has preserved it with its final doxology: "For thine is the kingdom, etc." It is noteworthy that not all ancient biblical authorities include this doxology in Jesus' prayer in Matthew 6:9, Mark 11:25, and Luke 11:2-4, so this element may already be thought of as "extrabiblical."

While it may seem obvious to the reader now, the following important point is often overlooked by modern Christians: these two times of prayer would have been governed cosmically, rather than chronologically—that is, the times to meet would have depended on the rising of the sun and its setting. Thus, it would have been unlikely that a specific time like six o'clock in the morning and six o'clock in the evening would have been a regular time set apart for prayer, although this might have been the case in larger communities that required a more consistent organization. The *Apostolic Tradition* (25) preserves the text of the *lucernarium*, the blessing for light, when the lamp was brought into the place where evening worshipers would have already gathered. It reflects the Jewish light ceremony at the beginning of the Sabbath which, likewise, would have been governed by the darkness of evening rather than the hour of the day. Other extrabiblical hymn texts like the *Phos Hilaron* ("O Gracious Light") which survive to modern times in various liturgies of daily prayer and in countless musical settings can be traced back to the practice of daily worship in this period of the liturgy.

It is possible that other "hours" of the day were kept in addition to the morning (Lauds) and evening prayer times (Vespers), but it is unlikely that these would have been communal gatherings. The "lesser" hours: the third hour (approximately 9:00 in the morning), sixth hour (~noon), ninth hour (~3:00 in the afternoon), before sleeping (Compline) and during the night (Vigils/Matins) might have been observed on an individual basis depending on how zealously a person regarded devotional prayer. No strong evidence for this, however, will appear until the Peace of the Church in the fourth century.

2. Weekly Feasts and Fasts

It is difficult for contemporary Christians to think of every Sunday as qualifying for the designation of "festival"—a *feast day*—but such was certainly the case in the Early Church. There is no lack of evidence in the source material for the first day of the week becoming for the earliest Christians a day of remembrance of the resurrection of Christ (see *Didache* 14:1; *Ign. Mag* 9:1; Tertullian; Justin; Hippolytus; *Didascalia*). The first day also became, in light of the seven-day structure of the week, an "eighth day" which later was embedded into the symbolism and numerology of the Church. There was already in the Jewish Sabbath a strong theme of the coming "Day of the Lord" (Day of Yahweh) that linked the Passover theme of deliverance from Egyptian bondage to the deliverance ushered in by Yahweh at the end of time. For the early Christians, however, the focus of this eschatological expectation was shifted to Christ the Lord whose "Day" encompassed all of time; past, present, and future. In other words, both the past event of Christ's resurrection and his second coming at the end of time could be brought into the present Sunday celebration by continuing to use the familiar Jewish theme, "The Day of the Lord." However, the process by which the Jewish Sabbath on Friday evening became the Christian Lord's Day on Sunday morning (or beginning as a vigil on Saturday evening) is a complicated one.

Tension certainly existed between Jewish and Gentile Christians regarding the importance of the Sabbath, and we should expect that for many Jewish Christians, the Sabbath may have been observed alongside Sunday until eventually the older custom was forsaken. In extreme cases, some Christians, whether Jew or Gentile, may have even viewed the *"sabbatizontes"* (Sabbath-observers) as non-Christians.[9] For the most part, however, it would have been difficult for Jewish Christians to sustain both practices, particularly because Sunday, the first day in the week, would have been an ordinary workday in the weekly calendar and not the day off that is currently enjoyed by contemporary Americans.

There is, among others, one very compelling theory as to the origins of the Sunday celebration: The regular practice of the Lord's Supper may have been more strongly linked with the meal Christ shared with his disciples *after* the resurrection than with his "last supper" *before* his crucifixion. In other words, the meal *after* the resurrection was more symbolically appropriate for Christians celebrating Christ's resurrection than was the Passover meal, the last supper. Worship historian, Herman Wegman explains:

> Perhaps the meal of the Lord (*kuriakon deipnon*) influenced the origin of Sunday (*kuriake hemera*). The community gathered for the meal on the day on which, according to the testimony of the disciples, the Lord had held a meal with his followers after his resurrection. The term *kuriakon,* indicating that which pertains to the *Risen One,* was transferred from the meal to the day on which the meal was celebrated, and later evoked a theology of the Day of the Lord: the fulfillment of the Day of Yahweh is realized in the resurrection of the Son, the Risen One, the *kurios,* Christ.[10]

One early account of this Sunday celebration is provided in an official government report written sometime around the year 111. Pliny, the Governor of Bithynia and Pontus, wrote a letter to his superior, Trajan, to clear up some rumors about what the secretive Christians were doing in their meetings. His findings were the result of interviewing (or rather, torturing) those who professed to be Christians but "weren't any longer." He found out that they gathered before dawn on a fixed day, sang a hymn to Christ as though to a god, and bound themselves by an oath to abstain from certain criminal practices. Then they would disperse and reassemble later for a community meal. We should be reminded that it would have been necessary to meet before dawn since a Sunday morning meeting would have required the assembly to dismiss early enough for their daily work. The "off peak" worship schedule, then, might have been celebrated in two installments: (1) morning prayer, and (2) evening meal/eucharist. "This evening meal, however, soon came to be forbidden by governmental authorities (or so it appears; see Pliny's letter) because such horrible rumors had circulated concerning it or because 'clubs' were generally forbidden. The meal was then shifted to the morning—certainly evidence that Christians held the celebration of the meal of the Lord to be the heart of Sunday."[11] The community meal would not only have been politically suspect for being an unlawful assembly in the evening, but the economics of such a meal would have been a direct threat to a system of government that depended on reinforcing the divisions of socioeconomic classes. Outside Bithynia and Pontus, however, Justin gives us early evidence that the eucharist was already being celebrated on Sunday in the morning for some time (Rome, ca. 150, *Apol.* 1:65-67).

Apart from Sunday, Wednesdays and Fridays also held some degree of significance. In the *Didache* (8), in the *Shepherd of Hermas,* and in numerous places in Tertullian's writings there is reference to Wednesdays and Fridays being special days of fasting. On these "station" days, the practice was to fast until the midafternoon meal. Then the fast was ended by communing from the bread that had been taken home from the communal celebration of the eucharist. That this bread came from the Sunday eucharist or whether Tertullian knew of a daily eucharist is unclear, but the possibility remains that the eucharist was not celebrated on these station days (*De orat.* 19; and also *Apostolic Tradition* 37).[12]

3. Pascha as Annual Celebration and Season

At this stage of the development of a yearly cycle of worship, only one annual feast is attested—and unfortunately it is *not*, as Charles Dickens would have liked it, Christmas. In the *Didascalia*

(5:19-20), in the *Apostolic Tradition*, and in Tertullian (*De Bapt.* 19) we have the earliest references to what we now call "Easter." The material in these documents does not concern itself directly with the details we would like to know about this annual feast, although a few early homilies (Melito of Sardis *On the Pascha*, in Origen, and in the paschal homily of Pseudo-Hippolytus) provide us with a variety of theologies and several explanations for the symbolism of this day.

We have already seen that the resurrection of Christ was celebrated as a weekly feast by the early Church. Still, these early Christians were well acquainted with the obligatory nature and significance of the annual celebration of the Passover by their Jewish neighbors, not to mention those adherents to Christianity who still kept one foot in Judaism. In any event, the transition from Jewish Passover to Christian Easter could not have been a more schismatic one. One could begin by examining how difficult it is to harmonize a solar calendar with a lunar one:

Passover is determined by the birth of the new moon and always occurs, according to the (lunar) Jewish Calendar, on the 14th day of the month Nisan. However, 14 Nisan does not always occur on Sunday—the first (eighth) day of the *solar* week and temporal symbol *par excellence* among the early Christians. Put another way, the question for the postapostolic Church was: Should the calendar date of the Jewish Passover hold more significance and symbolic weight than a celebration on the day of Christ's resurrection (Sunday)? The historian Eusebius tells us that this was no small controversy and, if not for the intervention of Bishop Irenaeus of Rome, would have resulted in the Church's first schism. The debate has since become known as the *"Quartodecimen* Controversy" from the Latin word for *fourteen*. We will cut to the chase and remind the reader that, obviously, the Sunday celebration won out and the Quartodecimen tradition eventually disappeared (certainly by the council of Nicea where the debate was ecumenically put to rest once and for all). Although the Quartodecimen controversy is now settled, modern scholars are ironically divided as to the particulars of how this annual event of Easter might have evolved during the first and second centuries, and it is important for us to look at their arguments since in them lies an insight into the relationship between biblical interpretation and the ecclesial theology of the Liturgical Year.

On the one hand, some scholars focus on the general Christian understanding of Judaism and the particular interpretation of the Hebrew Bible (Old Testament) that was developing throughout Asia Minor during the first three centuries of Christianity. For Christian interpreters of the Bible in this part of the world it was not a great intellectual leap to find Christ prefigured in the Hebrew Scriptures. Clearly, the Passover lamb that was to be slain, according to Exodus 12, was none other than Christ himself. Therefore, a Christian could keep the Passover celebration on 14 Nisan with a specific understanding that the Christian celebration was both derived from this Jewish narrative and, concurrently, had superseded it.

On the other hand, some historians believe that the early Christians in Palestine would have followed the tradition of keeping the Christian *Pascha* on the Sunday following the Jewish Passover, a tradition they claim would have been reasonably confirmed by apostolic precedent, since Sunday celebrations are so widely attested. This camp of scholarship can also imagine that before the year 135 an annual celebration of Easter was probably unknown in either Rome or Palestine, the tradition having caught on more slowly after that year (cf. Eusebius). This line of reasoning, while not confirming the apostolic initiation of an annual Easter feast, would reaffirm the importance of the widely attested weekly Sunday celebration that would have eclipsed even the Jewish Passover celebration of 14 Nisan. What basically remains are two explanations of the significance of this first and greatest feast of Christianity: (1) Easter celebrated Christ as the Passover lamb of the Hebrew Bible; and (2) Easter broke with the Jewish tradition by proclaiming the resurrection of Christ on its own day—a day instituted by the apostles, and a *new* day for all believers. Certainly, the material of the first three centuries can be read in the light of both of these theories.

Further insights about the theology of Easter are related to the variety of mutations of the words used to describe Passover. In the Hebrew, *Pesach* means simply to *pass over.* When the Hebrew was translated into Greek, however, the noun used, *Pascha,* was also commonly associated by Christians with the verb *paschein:* to suffer. This form is also reflected in the Latin: *passio,* which we now employ directly when we speak of the *Passion* of the Christ. While the Greek connotations of "suffering" in *Pascha* never disappeared, in the first few centuries a wonderful blend of metaphors began to crop up around this word. *Pesach/Pascha* and its context in the book of Exodus became the fountainhead for some rather interesting interpretations of both the Jewish *and* the Christian feasts.

Philo of Alexandria (ca. 20 B.C.–ca A.D. 40) already had known of a second emphasis for the Jewish celebration of *Pascha:* that of *passage* (Greek: *diabasis,* Latin: *transitus*) through the Red Sea. Already one can see that the historical context of the death angel passing over the homes of the Israelites has nearly been lost! (We should also caution the more informed reader that although in later centuries, Easter will be the feast centrally associated with the rites of initiation, particularly baptism, at this time, according to the data available, the connections between Easter and baptism at sunrise are not yet conclusive.) At any rate, the hermeneutics of Philo of Alexandria came to have a great amount of influence on the Christian theologian, Origen (also of Alexandria), who in turn influenced the theological thought of Gregory of Nazianzus, Basil the Great, and Gregory of Nyssa in Asia Minor (together, the three are known as the "Cappadocian Fathers") as well as Ambrose of Milan in the west.[13] The Cappadocians would add more substance to the analogies of the Israelites' journey from Egypt to Canaan, and the passage of the Jordan will come to represent yet another *transitus* effected by the resurrection of Christ.

Before we piece together a description of the celebration of

Easter, we should be aware that this feast would not likely have taken place on a single day. Here we find the beginnings of a *season* within the year, and not an isolated 24-hour period of celebration. In the case of Easter, there are three distinct divisions to this season: (1) a fast equivalent of a day's duration or longer, (2) the actual day of the festal celebration, and (3) an extended period by which the feast would have been reiterated as if to ensure it were only *one* celebration.

There was a period of arduous fasting that preceded Easter that, according to a variety of sources, ranged from one or two days, to forty hours, to a week. At the conclusion of this fast was a vigil service that possibly lasted throughout the evening, and consisted of Scripture readings. It is clear, at least, from Melito's homily that Exodus 12 was the preferred text to have been read. Most likely, some type of harmonization of the passion narratives in the Gospels was also included. The communal celebration of the Lord's Supper (in the morning?) powerfully signified the breaking of the fast as it ushered in the reality of resurrection with the new day that was just beginning to dawn. Over the next fifty days—the *"Pentecost"*— themes of the resurrection would then be developed: the giving of the Spirit, the ascension of the Lord, and the return of Christ in glory. (At this point, Pentecost is not a specific Christian feast day of its own.) Tertullian refers to this protracted feast as a *laetissimum spatium;* a "most joyful space,"[14] and it seems a far cry from the simple 24-hour period that our modern secular calendars have made it to be. So it is clear that, possibly as early as the mid-second century, Easter had become an entire season celebrated annually on the Sunday following the 14th day of Nisan. This cyclical sanctification of time, conveniently corresponding with springtime in the northern hemisphere, elevates the weekly celebration of the resurrection to the genera of a *season* which is to be prepared for, joyously commemorated, and drawn out as long as possible.

Ministry

In the sections on Initiation and Eucharist we will be introduced briefly to the presence of ministers who function in specific roles within the assembly gathered to celebrate the eucharist. It is important to note, however, that ministry as an administrative/governmental element of the Church has never been, in theory, separated from its *liturgical* function within the corporate *worship* of the Church. We can go so far as to assert that how the Church has worshiped throughout history speaks volumes about its real hierarchical identity. Since it is the hierarchical element (as this is expressed in both *worship and* church leadership) that is arguably the strongest reason for the divisions within Christianity today, we feel it important to draw attention to its historical roots here in this volume, taking care not to confuse or separate the liturgical role from the institutional one.

A hierarchical structure is not distinguishable in the time immediately following the New Testament, and the designation of *episcopos* (overseer) is *not* to be confused with the later role associated with *bishop*. Rather, the oversight of the local community was given to a group of *presbyters* (elders—later *priests*) along with the service of other ministers, the *diakonia* (deacons). Wegman explains:

> At the beginning leadership in the communities was democratic and collective (but not precisely structured). Perhaps it paralleled the makeup of civil government in the cities. It seems certain that office was adapted to the congregation, the house church, the brotherhood and sisterhood. With the consolidation of the "church" a single-headed leadership began to develop, with the elders acting as counselors. The elders' task remained vague, however, and slowly became meaningless. In the west the presbyter would not begin to operate in any modern sense [i.e., that of a modern parish priest] as an independent officeholder in a local congregation until the twelfth century.[15]

However, we notice that in the city of Rome in 250 there is already a threefold ministry of bishop, presbyter, and deacon. From several of the letters of Ignatius of Antioch (Pseudo-Ignatius?) we see the bishop's three primary roles pushed to the fore: (1) that of preserver of the true faith (apostolic function), (2) the sign of unity within his congregation—the church in one particular city (episcopal function), and (3) that of a bridge between his and other congregations (pontifical function, catholicity-universality). It is important to note in the Ignatian epistles, however, that the writer is responding to the dual crises among the churches: external persecution and internal schismatic teachings. So the bishop as the *locus* of absolute authority in these documents should be tempered with the less emphasized passages that situate the bishop within a larger web of ecumenical authority. The role of the diaconate (deacons) is equally intertwined with assisting the bishop in liturgical rites (as one who publicly reads the Scriptures and instructs the congregation during the liturgy—especially during corporate prayers), assisting the bishop in various capacities during larger rituals (at baptism, the distribution of bread and wine at communion, etc.), and in the arrangement of the bishop's practical affairs (which would have included the finances of the local church). In a nutshell, the deacons remained directly connected to the bishop as ministers, whereas the function of the elder/presbyter is difficult to determine at this time. Later, the elders will represent the teaching/preaching body of the local church, while the bishop would be the guarantor that this teaching would be "orthodox" (right) and "catholic" (universal). The divisions between the bishop (with his deacons), and the elders (who can now be thought of as a "college of presbyters") will become even more pronounced when, during the exchange of the "kiss of peace" in the liturgy, the two groups will honor the other's office by greeting only those within their particular order.

We should remember that this particular structure is specific to the city of Rome, although it is likely that it was normative elsewhere. In most cases during this period there was a great degree of flexibility and the structure of the local churches would have been commensurate with the immediate need. Some scholars have tried to differentiate between two divisions of leadership roles in the churches of Palestine based on data from the New Testament: (1) Apostles, prophets, and teachers as being the missionary and evangelistic movement of early Christianity and (2) Bishop (overseer), presbyter(s) and deacons as the hierarchical structure of the local worshiping assembly within a city. Whether or not the expectancy of an immediate return of Christ (*parousia*) was in any way diminished throughout the first three centuries is difficult to say, but given the dynamics of a new and growing religion, and an empire that was often hostile to Christianity, a visible, streamlined, and ubiquitous structure of authority would not have been of primary concern.

Those of the modern "Free Church" ilk look to this as a golden age of church government and the "pure stream" of biblical worship. What is often forgotten is the historical context: a close proximity to the earthly ministry of Christ and the apostles, various degrees of real (not simply "felt") persecution, and few precedents to consult unless these were carried over from Judaism or borrowed from local culture. We must also admit that while we do not possess a great amount of historical data, we do know that unity was perhaps as much a problem then as now. "Independent" Christians (so-called) would be well-served to remember that the relative independence of churches in this period may be a misnomer based on lack of evidence and overgeneralizing—a risk that is common in any historical study. Certainly, to think of small, independent congregations as a *pattern* would be to also ignore the well-attested *pattern* of one bishop per city.

Baptism (Initiation)

We have noticed in our study of the Quartodecimen controversy that geographic location is beginning to account for much of the difference in theology and worship forms among the early churches. If the churches of Asia Minor can be grouped into a category that favored three days from the Jewish Passover to determine the date of Easter, then when it comes to the early rites of initiation we will have to look at two other liturgical "families:" (1) Rome and North Africa, and (2) Syria and eastward. We will use the term "initiation" to refer to the amalgam of rites associated with the making of Christians, since baptism in water was a part (albeit a significant one) of a larger whole. Initiation in most cases included some form of proclamation of the Scriptures; a period of instruction—*catechesis*—that varied widely in form and content; a special period of preparation immediately preceding the water bath that involved fasting, exorcism, keeping vigil, and scrutiny by church leaders; water baptism proper with associated anointings with oils; reception of the newly baptized by the eucharistic assembly and the celebration of the Lord's Supper. The details of the initiation rites vary widely during this period, as do the explanations given by our indirect sources. If nothing else, this tells us that our categories of simplicity and pluriformity hold especially true during this period. Local churches, under the direction of the local bishop, may have performed the initiation rituals based on need/convenience (as might have been determined by number and personal history of catechumens, available water sources, availability of the local bishop to administer one or more of the rites, etc.); or initiation may have adopted the customs and discretions particular to the locale (anointings, renunciation of former occupations, bathing etiquette, white apparel, offerings at the eucharist, receiving milk and honey, etc.).

The extent of the influence that the pagan environment had on the local rites of Christian initiation still remains a topic in dispute. We mentioned earlier that the mystery cults of the Greco-Roman period had elaborate initiation rituals, and even a form of water baptism for proselytes to Judaism is attested. Furthermore, the baptism of John, and the pluriformity of the baptisms that the writer of Acts records, make it impossible to follow a golden thread that leads us to *the* primitive pattern. For now, it can be safe to assume that the early Christians would have tried to avoid imitating their pagan neighbors, no matter how appealing the latter's initiation rituals

might have appeared. Later on, when churches were well established and could exert some degree of influence within the Empire,
Christians may have tried their hand at transforming pagan culture
by attaching Christian significance to their rituals.[16]

For a record of the earliest descriptions of the rites of initiation, we now turn to Rome and North Africa, the first of the two
liturgical traditions we will examine. The *Didache* (7:1) and its
expansion of the initiation rites in the *Apostolic Tradition* (15-21)
give us a fair amount of information as it concerns this region.[17]

As was mentioned earlier, the first part of the *Didache* is a
moral teaching on the "Two Ways." While it has been suggested
that this is the work of an editor, there is a consensus among scholars that this may in fact be a type of baptismal catechesis.[18] Less
convincing is the evidence that in Pliny's letter to Trajan, the oath to
which Christians bind themselves in their meetings is a type of baptismal vow. With similar scholarly reservations some have believed
"the hymn sung to Christ as to a god" might have been a baptismal
vow (although this is still a possibility since Pliny seems to be looking
for information about initiations in general).[19] The best evidence
for a prebaptismal time of instruction comes down to us in the
Apostolic Tradition (20). Here it is described how those seeking to
convert to Christianity are enrolled in the catechumenate. This was
no "come one, come all" format. There was a rather long list of
occupations that might exclude one from being accepted as a catechumen, some of which are not immediately obvious; for instance,
teachers would have been viewed as unworthy candidates for the
catechumenate since they may have been required to teach pagan
religion to their students. Soldiers, likewise, while discouraged from
their occupation, might have been able even to remain in military
service, provided they took an oath not to kill while on duty.[20]

During this time, catechumens were admitted to regular worship services, but since they were not yet initiated they would have
been excluded from participating in the celebration of the Eucharist.
They were permitted to stay for the proclamation of the Word in

the reading and preaching of the Scriptures, but then they were formally dismissed from the assembly, hands having been laid upon
them by their catechists and the assembly of the remaining "faithful"
having publicly prayed for them. It is reasonable to assume that they
would have been dismissed from the assembly in order to continue
their catechetical training. Closer to the time chosen for baptism,
there was an even more intense period of instruction that might
have involved daily exorcisms even up until the baptismal night.
Clearly, the making of a Christian was seen to a large extent to be
one of a contest with Satan (including, per several ancient sources,
"his pomp and his works").[21] Throughout all of this process, the candidates' lives were examined by all of the faithful to see whether
Christianity had indeed become an ethic: Had they taken care of the
poor? Had they helped the widows? Clearly there was an integra-
tion of faith and praxis in this historical era.

We have now arrived at the vigil when baptism would have
been administered. At this point, the catechumens would have been
fasting more rigorously, and their status would now have become
that of *competente*—ready for baptism. In the first three centuries
a unified time in the liturgical year when baptism was most likely
administered was not yet widespread. However, it is not unreason-
able to believe that baptism was administered both at Easter and,
after that, at Pentecost. This was not only because it added a major
dimension to an already important event, but because the theology
of dying and rising was already in place at the Easter celebration as
was, likewise, the giving of the Holy Spirit on Pentecost. In fact, the
return of the newly baptized with the bishop from the location of
the baptism, often a considerable distance from the worshiping
assembly, was itself a symbol of the promise of the death and rebirth
promised by the resurrection of Christ. It is important to note that,
at this time, there is not yet a three-day period between Good Friday
and Easter, so what is best imagined here is a Saturday evening
vigil, possibly lasting all night, before sunrise on Sunday. Within this
vigil is a multiplicity of rites that, while varying slightly from source

to source, shows a cohesiveness and unity when practiced together. We shall see later that some rites began to be separated from the rest, sometimes with the intervening period being several years.

What later became known as "the scrutinies" took place at the beginning of the vigil: The bishop, who would have been in attendance, blew on the candidate (*exsufflation*) and looked for a response that might suggest the lingering presence of demonic activity. The text suggests that the bishop is actually expecting to *see* something—just what this may have been is not indicated. Then follows a blessing over the baptismal water which most likely included the pouring of consecrated oil on or into the water. The unique situation of the "house churches" apparently required that baptism be done elsewhere. Natural sources of water seem to have been preferred since the reference to "living water" in Jesus' dialogue with the Samaritan woman has survived to modern times in the pre-Easter tradition of reading this scriptural pericope. The public baths are also well attested as having been suitable for baptism before the construction of church baptisteries (usually a separate building). After the blessing of the water there would either be another exorcism, or a threefold renunciation by the candidate of the devil, his pomp, and his works. The candidates, having already removed their clothes, entered the baptismal pool with the assistance of a deacon or deacons. For the sake of propriety, deaconesses assisted the women. A threefold immersion by a *presbyter* (i.e., an elder or what liturgical traditions know as a priest) followed. This was creedal in structure: "Do you believe . . . in the Father?" Candidate: "*Credo* (I believe)"—first immersion. "Do you believe . . . in the Son?" etc.

After the water bath, in this geographic region, there is an anointing, possibly of the entire body, with scented oil since, according to one source, the newly baptized (*neophyte*) is to refrain from the daily baths for a week. Others stipulate that the bishop is to lay a hand on the neophyte (or trace the sign of the cross over the brow of the baptizand—also called *sphragis* or "sealing") while a prayer is made for the descent of the Spirit. There may even be a final anointing by the bishop which may indicate that any previous anointings would have been administered by a presbyter. The neophyte would have been greeted by the bishop with the kiss of peace and brought into the eucharistic assembly for a "first communion." Honey mixed with milk may have also been presented in a chalice to the newly baptized, symbolizing the entrance into the promised land of Canaan, or it may have been the case in some places that the initiates would have been the ones who presented these offerings of milk and honey at the eucharist.

Whatever the specific variations on this ceremony may have included—the giving of a white garment, the use of candles or lamps, prebaptismal anointings, facing the west and turning eastward (*ad orientam*), renouncing and adhering—there was no simple, clear-cut, moment where the believer's "card was punched" and the magic moment of salvation occurred. Rather, there appears to have been an organic progression that symbolized both a forward movement of the Spirit with a recognition that the Spirit had brought the believer to the earlier stages as well. Herman Wegman also notes that the candidate was far from passive in the whole process: "The personal decision of the candidate was important, even determinative of many of the components of the ritual; happily, ritual and faith within a community went hand in hand."[22]

A few loose ends have yet to be tied up with regard to initiation. The designation as to who does the baptizing is still unclear in some sources. Tertullian provides that the authority to baptize can be assigned to someone other than a bishop—even a lay person. Ignatius makes it clear that nothing is to be done without the supervision of the bishop. In the *Apostolic Tradition* the presbyter (priest) performs the immersion along with the pre- and postbaptismal anointings while the bishop gives a final anointing and imposes hands. At least in the early rites of Christian initiation it appears that there is a web of authority that is at work that includes lay persons (catechists may or may not have been specifically ordained to their role), clergy (deacons, presbyters, and bishop), and, surprisingly, women ("deaconesses" who, although performing what we might see to be commonplace services, would have necessarily been ordained to function in any capacity).

Furthermore, the question of infant baptism, or the baptism of small children (paedobaptism), still looms large. While adult baptism is normative, infant baptism is also attested in this period. The *Apostolic Tradition* dictates that children ("little ones" can include infants) are to be baptized first, then the men, then the women. Tertullian is opposed to the practice, but this only confirms the fact that it must have been rather widespread.

The problem of the double postbaptismal anointing by both presbyter and bishop seems unique to Rome and North Africa, and later we shall see the complications that resulted when some bishops were not able to be present to function as this ritual required. We should mention that no evidence of this practice can be found in the rites of initiation associated with Syria and the East. The primary sources in this second grouping come from the *Didascalia*, the Syriac version of the *Acts of Thomas*, and the *Apostolic Constitutions*—another important church order. In this family of rites, baptism begins with anointing and imposition of hands, but whereas in the West this prebaptismal anointing had exorcistic connotations (the oil, in fact, was referred to as the *oil of exorcism*), the eastern rite assigned to the ritual the Old Testament metaphors of a prophetic or kingly anointing. In the West, the well-known practice of anointing one's entire body before athletic events—which included the custom of wrestling before entering the public baths—eventually found its way into the mystagogy of the prebaptismal anointing: the baptizand would be doing battle with the devil, the oil serving as a prophylactic. This meaning was not assigned in the East where there is very little evidence for even a public renunciation of Satan. Rather, the focus in much of the Syriac literature is on sonship (*huiothesia*) since the Gospels tell of the audible voice at Jesus' own baptism announcing that he was the Son, the Beloved. In the West, the confession of faith, or creed, was spoken by the baptizand in the water in response to a threefold interrogation: "Do you believe?" "*Credo.*" In the East, however, the Syriac tradition has a much stronger emphasis on the Holy Spirit, on the appearance of light at the Baptism of Christ, and on the opening of the heavens. Baptisteries (or the other places where baptism would have occurred) were amply decorated with lamps and candles, and a few records of baptisms attest to the appearances of angels and blinding light. One early hymn that might have been sung, perhaps repeatedly while the baptizands were being immersed, would have been the "Holy, Holy, Holy" from Isaiah 6 and its later versions in the apocalyptic literature of the intertestamental period. Gabrielle Winkler, the forerunner of liturgical scholars concentrating on the Syriac tradition has, in the last century, translated many texts from this and later periods that have opened up this relatively new and promising area of research to serious students of historical worship.

Eucharist

In Pliny's letter to Trajan (ca. 111–112), the word *sacramentum* makes its first appearance as the "oath" (*sacramento*) to which this relatively small enclave of Christians bound themselves each meeting. There is not as yet the understanding of a "sacrament" in the scholastic or modern sense of the word, but in this period we will see the meal take on more symbolic ballast, moving further away from a direct or simple imitation of the Last Supper.

At the outset, it would be beneficial to ask two important theological questions that will focus the lenses through which we read this part of worship history. (1) If historicity and its accurate preservation is of primary importance, why, then, did the early Church deliberately move away from an imitation or re-creation of the Last Supper event? (2) What values can be assigned to ritual language and action that can withstand the test of time, bridging the historical gaps throughout the centuries? Therefore, whatever the practical reasons that influenced the historical shift from communal meal to ceremony, it is important that we not undervalue the power of symbol not only to "make present again" (re-present) what can be remembered of the past, but also to do so in a way that allows for present and future meaning to be *endlessly* assigned. In other words, simply imitating the Lord's Supper as an historical event or doing so because the Lord commanded Christians to "do this" is to fall into a repetitive and legalistic paradigm—the very thing that prejudices many people against what they *think* to be ceremony or "ritual." It should be emphasized that in this period of history ritual was rarely, if ever, separated from reality. In fact, to participate in the ritual was to *assent to the reality* it made present—without the pressure that Medieval theologians would later feel to "scientifical-ly" explain or justify the process. This is not to say that theological explanations of the eucharist were not attempted in the postapos-tolic and patristic periods, but the marriage of Christian ritual and Christian lifestyle/ethic was alive and flourishing in this dynamic period of history and the reality of the bread and wine mysterious-ly being the Body and Blood of Christ was quite taken for granted.

In this milieu we see the vestigial Jewish table prayers with their telltale verse-refrain structure serving as blessings over the bread and the wine. The nature of these blessings—the *berakoth* as well as the *birkat ha-mazon*—is one of thanksgiving to God who, as the ruler of the universe, has provided gifts of his creation and sanc-tified the process of human productivity in cultivating and properly using them. This theme of thanksgiving (*eucharist*) becomes ger-mane to the entire rite, so much so that a verb—"eucharistized"— was created to refer to the bread that had been blessed. In moving away from the simple imitation of the Last Supper, the tradition began to focus on the activity of Christ as having (1) *taken* bread, (2) *given thanks/blessed* it, (3) and *distributed* it. This tripartite divi-sion of the rite is *the* common theme that is preserved from almost all of the special meals recorded in the New Testament, both pre-and postresurrection, and it is this focus that was initially preserved, even to the exclusion of the institution narrative, linking the rite to the Last Supper (or Paul's version of it to the Corinthians).

Thus, only a few decades after the Pauline epistles were composed, the components of blessing the bread and the wine may have evolved, with some ease, into an abbreviated ceremony which could have been celebrated within or without the context of a larger meal. There is no way to neatly pin down the exact reason for the change from the larger *agape* feast to the ceremonial meal, but a combination of pressure from secular authorities who were suspicious of larger common meals and the growing number of converts may have played respective parts in this process. [23]

The sources available for information on the eucharist at this time are found in short comments made in the epistles of Ignatius to the Ephesians (13), to the Smyrneans (8), and to the Magnesians (6). Justin, in his first *Apology* (65, 67), has a complete description of an early form of the rite that shows the primitive roots of a worship service with a dual focus: Word and Table.[24] He wrote the following from Rome, most likely around A.D. 150:

> On the day named after the sun, all who live in city or countryside assemble.
>
> The memoirs of the apostles or the writings of the prophets are read for as long as time allows.
>
> When the lector has finished, the president addresses us and exhorts us to imitate the splendid things we have heard.
>
> Then we all stand and pray.
>
> As we said earlier, when we have finished praying, bread, wine, and water are brought up. The president then prays and gives thanks according to his ability, and the people give their assent with an "Amen!" Next, the gifts over which the thanksgiving has been spoken are distributed, and everyone shares in them, while they are also sent via the deacons to the absent brethren.
>
> The wealthy who are willing make contributions, each as he pleases, and the collection is deposited with

the president, who aids orphans and widows, those who are in want because of sickness or some other reason, those in prison, and visiting strangers—in short, he takes care of all in need.

It is on Sunday that we all assemble, because Sunday is the first day: the day on which God transformed darkness and matter and created the world, and the day on which Jesus Christ our Savior rose from the dead. He was crucified on the eve of Saturn's day, and on the day after, that is, on the day of the sun, he appeared to his apostles and disciples and taught them what we have now offered for your examination. (*Apologia* I, 67)[25]

We get a fuller description of the eucharist from Justin's description of the baptismal liturgy:

After we have thus cleansed the person who believes and has joined our ranks, we lead him in to where those we call "brothers" are assembled.

We offer prayers in common for ourselves, for him who has just been enlightened, and for all men everywhere. It is our desire, now that we have come to know the truth, to be found worthy of doing good deeds and obeying the commandments, and thus to obtain eternal salvation.

When we finish praying, we greet one another with a kiss.

Then bread and a cup of wine mixed with water are brought to him who presides over the brethren.

He takes them and offers prayers glorifying the Father of the universe through the name of the Son and of the Holy Spirit, and he utters a lengthy eucharist [i.e., prayer of thanksgiving] because the Father has judged us worthy of these gifts.

When the prayers and the eucharist are finished, all

the people present give their assent with an "Amen!" "Amen" in Hebrew means "So be it!"

When the president has finished his eucharist and the people have all signified their assent, those whom we call "deacons" distribute the bread and the wine and water over which the eucharist has been spoken, to each of those present; they also carry them to those who are absent.

This food we call "eucharist," and no one may share it unless he believes that our teaching is true, and has been cleansed in the bath of forgiveness of sin and of rebirth, and lives as Christ taught. For we do not receive these things as if they were ordinary food and drink. But, just as Jesus Christ our Savior was made flesh through the word of God and took on flesh and blood for our salvation, so too (we have been taught) through the word of prayer that comes from him, the food over which the eucharist has been spoken becomes the flesh and blood of the incarnate Jesus, in order to nourish and transform our flesh and blood.

For, in the memoirs which the apostles composed and which we call "gospels," they have told us that they were commissioned thus: Jesus took bread and, having given thanks, said: "Do this in memory of me; this is my body." And in a like manner he took the cup and, having given thanks, said: "This is my blood." And he gave these to the apostles alone (*Apologia* I, 65-66).[26]

We shall conclude this section with what has now become the most well-known of all ancient eucharistic prayers. Whether the text of the *Apostolic Tradition* can be attributed to Hippolytus or not, the following is often referred to as the "Prayer of Hippolytus." Notice that, since this is in the genre of a church *ordo*, there is an instruction to those who preside at the eucharist. The option is made available for the prayer to be composed by the presider *ex tempore* (on the spot), but it is apparent that some did not have the ability to do this well, and so a model follows. The context here is that of a worship service in which a bishop has been newly ordained:

> *Then the deacons shall present the offering* [i.e., bread and wine] *to him* [who has been made bishop]; *and he, laying his hands on it with all the presbytery, shall say, giving thanks:*

The Lord be with you.

And all shall say:

And with your spirit.
Up with your hearts.
We have (them) with the Lord.
Let us give thanks to the Lord.
It is fitting and right.

And then he shall continue thus:

We render thanks to you, O God, through your beloved child Jesus Christ, whom in the last times you sent to us as a savior and redeemer and angel of your will; who is your inseparable Word, through whom you made all things, and in whom you were well pleased. You sent him from heaven into a virgin's womb; and conceived in the womb, he was made flesh and was manifested as your Son, being born of the Holy Spirit and the Virgin. Fulfilling your will and gaining for you a holy people, he stretched out his hands when he should suffer, that he might release from suffering those who have believed in you.

And when he was betrayed to voluntary suffering that he might destroy death, and break the bonds of the devil, and tread down hell, and shine upon the righteous, and fix a term, and manifest the resurrection, he took bread and gave thanks to you, saying,

"Take, eat; this is my body, which shall be broken for you." Likewise also the cup, saying, "This is my blood, which is shed for you; when you do this, you make my remembrance."

Remembering therefore his death and resurrection, we offer to you the bread and the cup, giving you thanks because you have held us worthy to stand before you and minister to you.

And we ask that you would send your Holy Spirit upon the offering of your holy Church; that, gathering her into one, you would grant to all who receive the holy things (to receive) for the fullness of the Holy Spirit for the strengthening of faith in truth; that we may praise and glorify you through your child Jesus Christ; through whom be glory and honor to you, to the Father and the Son, with the Holy Spirit, in your holy Church, both now and to the ages of ages. Amen. (*AT*, 4)

> . . . *And the bishop shall give thanks according to what we said above. It is not at all necessary for him to utter the same words that we said above, as though reciting them from memory, when giving thanks to God; but let each pray according to his ability. If indeed he is able to pray sufficiently and with a solemn prayer, it is good. But if anyone who prays, recites a prayer according to a fixed form, do not prevent him. Only, he must pray what is sound and orthodox.* (*AT*, 9.3-5) [27]

The difficulties associated with "what is sound and orthodox" prayer will carry over into the fourth century where the Church, free from persecution, will fight a more formidable foe: prosperity and governmental status.

Conclusion

Although we have not been able to locate a pristine or singular formula for Christian worship in the first three centuries, we can nevertheless conclude that the newest religion on the scene had identifiable characteristics that distinguished it from all the others. If the socially and politically disruptive table fellowship of Jesus and his disciples marked the first Jewish Christians, certainly the emphasis on the Lord's Supper as part of the assembly's new practice of worship was a distinctly Christian addition to the Jewish synagogue liturgy of prayer and Scripture. Although the forms varied from community to community, the further evolution of the Supper from a ceremonial blessing of bread and wine situated within an actual meal to a ritual component of the assembly's regular worship was another pivotal development in the history of Christian liturgy. This new addition to Jewish worship successfully blended the ancient reverence for the Word of the Lord as experienced in the liturgy of the synagogue with a specific community action powerfully imbued with the theology of incarnation, of salvation history, of mysterious transformation by the Spirit, and of mission to the world. What is especially beautiful is how the addition of the Supper did not eclipse or obscure the potency of the proclamation of the Word. On the contrary, the one enhanced the other and, in time, a fertile interdependence would become firmly established. Thus it is important to note the emergence of a new worship structure with two foci: Word and Table. The Supper could rightly be called "Eucharist" now since it was a response of thanksgiving for Christ who had been made present in the public proclamation of the Word, and then became re-presented to the faithful in a "second advent" in the mystery of eucharistic bread and wine.

During this period clandestinity was an important feature of Christian worship, especially as it concerned the eucharistic meal. It is especially curious, however, that the church of this age thrived in spite of an officially low profile and an ever-present threat of persecution. The concern for the integrity of the community, an integrity and unity symbolized by the eucharistic meal itself, resulted in a general secrecy—the *Disciplina Arcani*—that guarded the Supper from not only catechumens and pagans but even from benignly inquisitive individuals who were not yet interested in making a full commitment to the Christian community. This priority on community was reinforced with the prerequisite of catechesis and baptismal initiation for anyone wishing to participate in the eucharist. It may actually be this restriction which acted as a catalyst for attracting converts to the Christian movement; a movement that, as far as worship was concerned, was now beginning to pull away from its Jewish forbears with increasing resolve.

The governmental structure of the local assemblies was more than *ad hoc* and yet had not fully achieved the hierarchical divisions that would be widely known in the fourth century. Apostolic authority held sway, especially because the transmission of the faith through an unbroken chain of local bishops would have been easily calculable. The president of the eucharistic assembly was commonly the bishop, but his role was interwoven—both liturgically and functionally—with presbyters, deacons, and an active laity so as to reflect the diversity and interdependency of ministerial roles. It is especially notable that the daily, practical, and pastoral responsibilities associated with any leadership role were also reflected in the worship organization of the local churches. Everyone had a specific part in the worship order that more or less corresponded to one's ecclesiastical function.

Sunday was considered the day *par excellence* for common worship, but daily gatherings for prayer and eucharist are also attested from very early on. This daily prayer and praise spoke of a lifestyle of common worship that in this period would have taken a considerable commitment to sustain since the demands of living in the contemporary culture would not have left much room for the luxury of daily assemblies. As a complement to the Sunday and daily gatherings, and in response to the inherited religious significance of the Jewish Passover, an annual celebration of the Paschal mystery of Christ took primacy of place within an emerging festal cycle. Details of preparatory fasts and particular commemorations before Easter Day and the length of the season following it still varied from region to region, but it was clear that the beginnings of a church calendar can be traced to this period of Christian history.

In everything, the return of Christ—thought to be imminent in the first few centuries—provided the appropriate impulses that encouraged multiformity, simplicity, convenience, and expectancy. The Church had only begun to consider the notion of worship "for the long haul" and, accordingly, Christians would have never expected the political and social turn of events that were to happen in the year 312. It is this pivotal period in the history of the Church that is our subject for chapter 4.

For Further Reading

Primary Documents

Apostolic Tradition (pseudo Hippolytus): Cuming, Geoffrey J. *Hippolytus: A Text for Students.* Bramcote, 1976.

Clement of Alexandria: Deiss, Lucien. *Springtime of the Liturgy: Liturgical Texts of the First Four Centuries*, pp. 111ff. Trans. by Matthew J. O'Connell. Collegeville, MN: The Liturgical Press, 1979.

Clement of Rome: Lake, Kirsopp, ed. *The Apostolic Fathers,* vol. 1, pp. 1-121. *Sources chrétiennes* 167.

Didache: Audet, J., ed. *La Didaché, Instructions des Apôtres* (Paris: 1958). Lake, Kirsopp, ed. *The Apostolic Fathers,* vol. 1., pp. 303-333. Cambridge & London: 1912. Rordorf, W., ed., *Sources chrétiennes* 248.

Didascalia: Deiss, Lucien. *Springtime of the Liturgy: Liturgical Texts of the First Four Centuries*, pp. 165ff. Trans. by Matthew J. O'Connell. Collegeville, MN: The Liturgical Press, 1979.

Eusebius: Lake, Kirsopp, ed. & trans. *Eusebius, Ecclesiastical History,* vol. 1, pp. 503-513. Cambridge & London, 1926.

Ignatius of Antioch (Pseudo-Ignatius?): Lake, Kirsopp, ed. *The Apostolic Fathers,* vol. 1, pp. 165-277. *Sources chrétiennes* 10, pp. 66-181.

Justin: Richardson, Cyril C., ed. *Early Christian Fathers.* Vol. 1 of *Library of Christian Classics* (Philadelphia: Westminster Press, 1953).

Melito of Sardis: Hall, Stuart George. *Melito of Sardis. On Pascha.* Oxford: Clarendon Press, 1979.

Polycarp of Smyrna: Lake, Kirsopp, ed. *The Apostolic Fathers,* vol. 2, pp. 307-345. *Sources chrétiennes* 10, pp. 242ff.

Historical Development of the Liturgy

Bradshaw, Paul F. *The Search for the Origins of Christian Worship: Sources and Methods for the Study of Early Liturgy.* New York: Oxford University Press, 1992.

Dalmais, Irénée Henri. "History of the Liturgy: Liturgical Rites and Families." In *The Church at Prayer: An Introduction to the Liturgy,* pp. 12-44. Ed. by Aimé Georges Martimort. Trans. by Matthew J. O'Connell. One-volume ed. Collegeville, MN: The Liturgical Press, 1992.

Deiss, Lucien. *Springtime of the Liturgy: Liturgical Texts of the First Four Centuries.* Trans. by Matthew J. O'Connell. Collegeville, MN: The Liturgical Press, 1979.

Finn, Thomas M. *From Death to Rebirth: Ritual and Conversion in Antiquity.* Mahwah, NJ: Paulist Press, 1997.

Jasper, Ronald C.D., and Geoffrey J. Cuming. *Prayers of the Eucharist: Early and Reformed.* 3rd ed. Collegeville, MN: The Liturgical Press, 1990.

Johnson, Maxwell E. *The Rites of Christian Initiation: Their Evolution and Interpretation.* Collegeville, MN: The Liturgical Press, 1999.

Jones, Cheslyn, et al. *The Study of Liturgy.* Rev. ed. New York: Oxford, 1992.

Mazza, Enrico. *The Origins of the Eucharistic Prayer.* Trans. by Ronald E. Lane. Collegeville, MN: The Liturgical Press, 1995.

Metzger, Marcel. *History of the Liturgy: The Major Stages.* Trans. by Madeleine Beaumont. Collegeville, MN: The Liturgical Press, 1997.

Nocent, Adrian. "Christian Initiation in the First Four Centuries." In *Handbook for Liturgical Studies.* Vol. 4, *Sacraments and Sacramentals,* pp. 1-29. Collegeville, MN: The Liturgical Press, 2000.

Wegman, Herman. *Christian Worship in East and West: A Study Guide to Liturgical History.* Trans. by Gordon W. Lathrop, 1985. Collegeville, MN: The Liturgical Press, 1990.

ⅰ ——‥— ⅱ

[1]Basil the Great (ca. 329–379), *On the Holy Spirit* 27.65-66, trans. by David Anderson (Crestwood, NY: St. Vladimir's Seminary Press, 1980).

[2]D.H. Tripp, "Gnosticism," in *The Study of Liturgy,* ed. by Cheslyn Jones, et al. (New York: Oxford University Press, 1992) 81.

[3]For a list of these primary texts, please refer to the section entitled "For Further Reading."

[4]Cf. Paul F. Bradshaw, *The Search for the Origins of Christian Worship: Sources and Methods for the Study of Early Liturgy* (New York: Oxford University Press, 1992).

[5]An example of a prayer text giving thanks after eating: "We give thanks to thee, O Holy Father, for thy Holy Name which thou didst make to tabernacle in our hearts, and for the knowledge and faith and immortality which thou didst make known to us through Jesus thy child. To thee be glory for ever. Thou, Lord Almighty, didst create all things for thy Name's sake, and didst give food and drink to men for their enjoyment, that they might give thanks to thee, but us hast thou blessed with spiritual food and drink and eternal light through thy child. Above all we give thanks to thee for thou art mighty. To thee be glory forever. Remember, Lord, thy Church, to deliver it from all evil and to make it perfect in thy love, and gather it together in its holiness from the four winds to thy kingdom which thou hast prepared for it. For thine is the power and the glory for ever."—from the *Didache*: Kirsopp Lake, ed., *The Apostolic Fathers* (Cambridge & London: 1912) 1:322-325.

[6]Cheslyn Jones, et al., Chapter 7, "The Apostolic Tradition," in *Search for Origins*, 88.

[7]Cf. Bradshaw, *Origins*.

[8]See the picture from Dura-Europos on the website.

[9]Herman Wegman, *Christian Worship in East and West: A Study Guide to Liturgical History*, trans. by Gordon W. Lathrop, 1985 (Collegeville, MN: The Liturgical Press, 1990) 26. Originally published in Dutch as *Geschiedenis van de Christelijke Eredienst in het Westen en in het Oosten*, ©1976 Gooi en Sticht bv, Hilversum.

[10]Ibid., 26-27.

[11]Ibid., 27.

[12]Ibid.

[13]Ibid., 33.

[14]Cf. Tertullian, *De Baptismo* 19.

[15]Wegman, *Christian Worship*, 48.

[16]Geoffrey Wainwright, in *The Study of Liturgy*, referring to J.A. Jungmann, *The Early Liturgy to the Time of Gregory the Great* (Notre Dame: 1959; Darton, Longman & Todd, 1960).

[17]To a lesser extent Justin's *Apology* (61, 65), Pliny's letter to Trajan, and Cyprian's epistles (64, and 74:1) are also helpful. It is Tertullian, however, who provides a lengthy sacramental treatise *On Baptism*, but a few background details about this document are necessary here. First, this treatise, written around the year 200, is a polemical work defending baptism against a specific Gnostic group (identified in the very first part of the work). While it is not the ideal analytical piece we might hope it to be, scholars still consider his descriptions of the rites to be accurate since Tertullian made many references to initiation in his other works (particularly: *On the Resurrection of the Flesh, On the Crown*).

[18]K.W. Noakes, "From New Testament Times until St. Cyprian," in *The Study of Liturgy*, 119.

[19]Tripp, "Gnosticism," 81.

[20]This list of excluded professions leads some to the conviction that Hippolytus, himself a rigorist, might still be a candidate for the authorship of the *Apostolic Tradition*. In any event, there appears to follow a quite lengthy catechumenate: several years.

[21]One must bear in mind the *taken-for-grantedness* of the presence of demons and their influence on the human person in Greco-Roman culture. Our modern entertainment industry has painted demonic activity as belonging exclusively to the realm of "fantasy" and "science fiction." Hence, one cannot speak of an exorcism in contemporary culture without conjuring up the image

of levitating children spewing split-pea soup. The progress of the candidate towards the new ethical life of Christianity during the catechumenate, however was, in any event, a matter for the corporate prayer and the discernment of the entire ecclesial assembly, with the exorcism being something more than a *formal*, presidential expression. Later, exorcists, along with catechists, will be included in the list of the Church's diverse ministerial roles, accentuating the corporate nature of initiation. Prebaptismal exorcisms still survive in the modern rites of Christian initiation for many liturgical churches, but nuances in language have been introduced that make this component of the catechumenate and the baptismal rite itself more intelligible to modern cultures. At the same time, the older formulas have been preserved to be used locally where a particular culture still ascribes to a pre-Enlightenment understanding of the demonic.

[22]Wegman, *Christian Worship*, 35.

[23]Ibid., 42.

[24]Ibid.

[25]Lucien Deiss, *Springtime of the Liturgy: Liturgical Texts of the First Four Centuries*, trans. by Matthew J. O'Connell (Collegeville, MN: The Liturgical Press, 1979) 93-94.

[26]Ibid., 92-93.

[27]R.C.D. Jasper and G.J. Cuming, *Prayers of the Eucharist: Early and Reformed*, 3rd ed. (Collegeville, MN: The Liturgical Press, 1990) 34-36.

CHAPTER FOUR

Worship in the Empire: 312–600

*T*hus far we have organized our study of worship history in the somewhat tidy divisions of Old Testament, New Testament, and Early Church. For church historians, the events surrounding the victory of the Roman emperor Constantine in 312 form a pivot-point, dividing the whole of early Christianity into two epochs: (1) The Postapostolic Era (associated with the pre-Constantinian Roman Empire) when Christians were marginalized, relatively few in number, and frequently persecuted; and (2) The Patristic Era, or the age of the Church Fathers (*Patres*), when the influence of Christianity grew from its origins as a tolerated religious sect to become the official religion of the empire. Still, in regard to worship, changes at this time were not altogether sudden and unprecedented. Despite the many obvious differences in the two periods there remains an identifiable thread of continuity in worship, and it is this continuity that will be the lens through which we study this subject.

There are a few generalities we can bear in mind during this chapter. To begin with, there is no reason to assume that multiformity and creativity in worship slackened any more than it had in the previous three centuries. That is to say, simply because Christianity became a legally recognized religion does not mean that a particular form of worship became standardized everywhere. We will see some healthy degree of diversity, organized by locality. Of the sources that have come down to us there are certainly patterns and trends that could be considered to be normative and common to most of the larger communities, but there also existed those communities on the fringes of society whose theology and praxis did not meet the qualifications for what would later be considered *orthodox* Christianity. It is these communities that, even if we are not able in this brief history to give our attention to them, are nevertheless a silent witness to the dynamic nature of Christian worship in this period of 312–600.

Furthermore, early Christian missionary efforts outside the political influence of the Byzantine Empire resulted in established worship forms unlike those within the more prominent cities. The oral traditions surrounding the characters of the New Testament (hagiographies) tell that some followers of Christ had established churches in the far East, sub-Saharan Africa, or the British Isles during this period. While difficult to confirm with great historic certainty, these traditions are valuable to see how specific rites developed differently in all of these places.[1] In any case, one should also consider that there were remote places within the borders of the empire that were largely unaffected by "official" Christianity. Of primary significance during this period was the movement of ascetic men and women from the city centers to the wilderness where they felt they could better pursue a life of worship and prayer. This contributed to a worship trend that had a very different evolution than those forms found within the urban centers.

Lastly, although Jewish elements of Christian worship continue to be found in the liturgy of the Empire, there was no way a contemporary could have recognized this. Such elements would have been unintelligible, having been severed long before from their moorings in Judaism. All worship practices, whether Jewish or secular in origin were now thoroughly baptized as "Christian" worship, even though Christianity was beginning to move away doctrinally from its Jewish influence.

Context

If in the previous historical period we witnessed the blood of the martyrs having become the seed for the Church, we see in this period a veritable springtime where that seed was watered and the Church was able to flourish theologically, aesthetically, culturally, and in relative peace. However, this peace resulted in both gains and losses. The visibility and popularity that characterized theological discussions within this period, while having moved light years away from the persecuted underground Church, also bred divisions between orthodox and heretical adherents. As it concerned the clergy, they were happily exempted from paying taxes or fulfilling the governmental obligations for military service, but it was not always to good ends that bishops held the pastorally precarious role of civil magistrate. And while the use of many governmental buildings (basilicas) had now been transferred to the numerically burgeoning Church, so also the pomp of imperial ceremony had become commingled with the humbler, beginning forms of early Christian worship. And while ecclesial language filtered slowly into the everyday speech of the Byzantine citizen, so too had civil language (both Greek and Latin) been introduced into the speech of the Church. Let us take, for example, the word *liturgy* (literally, *the people's work*). The origins of this word are found in the description of the people's public role in the civil ceremony of the Empire. The convening of the Church's first Ecumenical Council (Nicea, 325) marked a watershed ecclesial event for Byzantine bishops and theologians alike, but the fact that it was the Emperor who both convened and presided over this assembly would alarm many bishops and theologians of our day. Finally, conversion to Christianity was not only a popular trend for the average citizen, it was also a requirement if one wished to climb the political ladder.

Here, in spite of Constantine's desire for a doctrinally unified (*ecumenical*) Church, it is possible to see the beginnings of a divided Church on geographical and linguistic grounds. Constantine moved the administration of his empire from Rome to the city of

Byzantium on the straits of the Bosphorus in modern-day Istanbul, Turkey. The city quickly assumed the stature properly befitting an imperial capital, and its name was changed to Constantinople—Constantine's City. This left the "Eternal City" of Rome culturally, politically, and militarily weakened. As it concerned the Church, however, Rome retained its honorable position as the see of the apostle Peter and the place of Paul's martyrdom. The bishop of Rome remained *first among equals*—the "equals" being all the other bishops throughout the Christian world. Each bishop was concerned with the administration of the local church in the units geographically determined by the civil government. These units were basically significant city-centers that incorporated the surrounding countryside. Of all these local churches, Rome retained the most venerable status of all. Nevertheless, the emperor incited not a little nationalistic disapproval when he decreed Constantinople to be the "New Rome." Constantinople—with its flourishing Hellenistic culture, its official language of Greek rather than Latin, and its geographical distance from the Eternal City—stripped the latter of much of its significance except as it concerned the Church. This may possibly explain the reason why the authority of the Bishop of Rome (the Pope) began to increase in the Church from this period onward and may perhaps explain why Latin was to remain the authoritative and liturgical language of the Church in the West until as late as the 1960s!

By the time of emperor Honorius (395–423) it is admissible to speak of two geographic "churches." These were united generally in doctrine by the ecumenical communion visible in the councils of all the bishops but, culturally, beginning to polarize. Rome would forever be synonymous with "The Western Church" and would later only exert jurisdiction over those localities in the East who would choose to remain loyal to the Pope in the face of schism (e.g., the Maronite Church in Lebanon). As it concerns the study of worship, these churches will represent various liturgical "families" whose structure aptly incorporates both Byzantine and Roman elements. Altogether, these churches would later become known as the "Roman Catholic Church" from the word in the Nicene Creed *katholikos*—worldwide. Geographic regions associated with the Church in the West during this time are Rome (with nearby Milan and Ravenna, both of which became important ecclesial and governmental centers), Old Gaul, Spain, Portugal, and North Africa (particularly Carthage and Hippo).

Among the Byzantine churches in the East—to be known later as the Eastern Orthodox—a variety of languages and cultures exerted their influence on local expressions of worship. The most notable languages relevant to worship in this period are Greek, Syriac, Coptic, and Old Slavonic. The Byzantine Church covered much more territory than did the Church in the West, which seemed, by the end of the fourth century, to be perpetually under attack from various waves of barbarian invasions. The Church in the East had the benefit of a stronger military and, until its containment under Islamic rule, its territory extended from Asia Minor and the Balkan Peninsula to the north, and eastward around the Mediterranean Sea encompassing Syria, Lebanon, Jordan, Iraq, Palestine, and Egypt. Its theological centers included the patriarchates of Alexandria in Egypt, Jerusalem in Palestine, Antioch in Syria and, naturally, Constantinople in Asia Minor. We will say more of the history of the eastern churches in Chapter 5. In the pages that follow we will turn our attention to the worship data of this period when the Byzantine Empire reached its apogee and the Church, visibly unified, began to embellish many of those forms that were foundational in the first three centuries.

Sources

We have been introduced to the document known as the *Church Order* in Chapter 3. In this period another Church Order known as the *Apostolic Constitutions* takes center stage. Not to be confused with the *Apostolic Tradition* (formerly attributed to Hippolytus), the *Constitutions* comes to us from Syria at some point

during the late fourth century. The original, written in Greek, survives and is replete with direct material about worship in this century. Because the document is in part a reworking of the *Didascalia,*
the *Didache,* and the *Apostolic Tradition,* it is often enlightening to
sift through the textual layers to determine which material is older
and which reflects the situation at the time of its compilation. Book
7 closely resembles the *Didache* but with several liturgical additions.
Book 8 has a detailed description of the Eucharist that has often
been attributed to pope Clement I.

Another Church Order, the *Testamentum Domini* (Testament
of Our Lord Jesus Christ) is most likely of 5th-century Syrian origin.
In the tradition of most documents of this genre, the author's community attributes its provenance to a recognized Church authority—in this case, none other than Christ himself! The contents are
useful to us in that it describes the church building in addition to the
usual topics of initiation, eucharist, and ordination.

We introduce the reader here to a new category of document:
the *euchologion,* or *euchology.* Unlike the Church Order that usually offers general directions about worship, a euchology resembles
more closely a modern worship text, complete with prayers and
sometimes *rubrics*—instructions for gestures and actions or other
details that accompany the text to be spoken. The so-called
Euchologion of Serapion (traditionally and erroneously attributed
to the bishop of Thmuis in Egypt, c. 350) falls in this category. The
content includes the texts for ordinations, the blessing of oil, a burial prayer, and a prayer over the eucharist commonly known as the
Anaphora of Serapion (anaphora=offering, as in the "offering up"
of the eucharist).

Two documents also survive from this period that are classi-
fied under the category of *lectionaries.* A lectionary is a schema that
organizes the readings from Scripture (or other extrabiblical material) into a logical sequence, indicating when each text will be read
in the course of worship throughout a given period of time (usually
a year or longer). This, of course, necessitates some references to a

civil or Church calendar. In a few cases, these lectionaries indicate the particular church building where a certain liturgical service might have been celebrated. Two lectionaries survive from this period: The *Armenian Lectionary* (ca. 420–450) and the *Georgian Lectionary* (5th-century material most likely edited in the 8th–9th century).

One more category can be added to the documents of this period. We have preserved for us a *travel diary* of a nun named Egeria (also spelled Etheria in some modern editions). The particulars of her religious life are unknown but her community was probably located in Spain or Gaul. The text of the diary dates from somewhere in the beginning of the 5th century and tells of her pilgrimage to Jerusalem. She describes the liturgy there with a fair amount of detail and with a personal style that is delightful to read. Although her diary preserves no specific liturgical texts, we learn much of the daily and weekly worship life that must have been firmly in place in Jerusalem since before the end of the 4th century. Details that are included in this diary are the celebration of Easter (including the season of preparation), specific readings that accompany specific celebrations, and the liturgical function of the buildings situated on the venerated sites in the Holy City of Jerusalem.

The above are the most well-known representations among the direct liturgical sources. There are a multitude of sources that mention worship indirectly. This material, while not as descriptive as we might like it to be, is nevertheless of immense value as it concerns the theology of worship. Much indirect liturgical information is found in the *homilies* (sermons) of the notable preachers of this period. In the West these include from Rome the writings of the popes Vigilius and Gregory the Great; from North Italy: Ambrose and Pseudo-Maximus of Turin; in the East, from Syria (Antioch and Jerusalem): Cyril of Jerusalem, Theodore of Mopsuestia, John Chrysostom, Nestorius, Narsai, and Hesychius; from Asia Minor, the Cappadocians: Basil the Great, Gregory Nazianzen (Gregory the Theologian), and Gregory of Nyssa. Then there are *letters*, notably: the papal letters of Innocent I, Hilarius, and Felix II. From North Africa come the letters of Grennadius and Augustine; and from Egypt the Paschal letters of Athanasius and Cyril of Alexandria. Other categories of documents include *regulations* (by the Councils of Hippo in 393, Carthage in 397, and Mileve in 416); and an *historical account* (the *Ecclesiastical History* of Eusebius).[2]

Space

In the previous era we see that Christians met in whatever spaces were available to them. In the days before the Jewish-Christian tensions these may have included the local synagogue or, after separating from Judaism, a wealthy person's home or another space that was conducive to assembling a crowd under one roof. As yet there was no designated place that would have been considered *holy* (set apart, separated for divine use) in and of itself, although the concept of *holy* was inextricably woven into the fabric of the Greco-Roman culture and would have been unquestionably inherited from Judaism. Certainly, the graves of the martyrs would have been hallowed places, and the eucharist would have been celebrated there as if the deceased were present. Of other "holy" places we have little data until the reign of Constantine.

Aided by his mother, Helen, the emperor sought out those traditional sites of significant value to Christians. The endeavor was not guided by any method that we would call "scientific" by today's standards since there is some indication that where local tradition disagreed on the exact location of a site, the matter was quickly settled by the Emperor as arbiter. It is from this century that the traditional holy places in Jerusalem were established: the Garden of Gethsemane, Golgotha, and the holy sepulchre, to name a few of the places associated with Christ. Others focused upon the Holy Family, and the patriarchs/matriarchs of both Judaism and of Apostolic Christianity. While we can only speculate as to the extent of how politically serendipitous or potentially commercial these "discoveries" may have been we should remember that above all these were enhancements to an already thriving worship milieu in Palestine, Antioch, Rome, and elsewhere. While not at the core or essence of the Christian faith, the emphasis on holy things and holy places strengthened values that were uniquely Christian: namely, the incarnation of the eternal God within finite human time and history. Other doctrinal positions, such as the Communion of Saints, or the unity of all the churches of God, were more or less obviously related to holy things and places. This is specifically the case with the tradition that Constantine and Helen, having found the "True Cross," delivered pieces of it to all the churches of the empire so that it could be universally venerated. Such a relic was truly a tangible symbol of unity, but such a lesson may have been obscured by the opposing tendency of common people to assign more significance to the symbol than to the thing or event it symbolized.

The church in Jerusalem boasted those holy sites where Jesus had been born, lived, performed miracles, preached sermons, was crucified, rose from the dead, and ascended into heaven. Other cities boasted the houses of apostles, martyrs, and other saints, the places themselves being the chief storyteller to both locals and pilgrims. The preservation and the transfer of relics from one place to another also served to *consecrate* (make sacred) an altar of a particular church or other place of pilgrimage. Although magic coexisted with Christianity at this period of Christian history, there was a greater and theologically credible acknowledgment of the awesome mystery that connected person to thing, or person to place, and all to God.

Constantine, who by this time was regarded as Patron of the Church, assisted in the transference of governmental buildings to the Church and financed the building of impressive new edifices. The architectural structure of the basilica, once designated for official civic use, now became the normal or even preferred space for public worship. Although the basilica could range in overall size and infinitesimal detail, certain generalities germane to the liturgy of this period are important to note. Here, for the first time, a large number of people could be accommodated in a central space free of pillars. Furthermore, the central space could be expanded laterally by additional pillars, forming a wide corridor that could remain opened to the original space in the center. A Christian adaptation of this technique was the formation of a *transept* that gave the basilica its cruciform shape when seen from a bird's-eye view.

It was most common that a raised area existed at one of the four sides of the interior. Frequently this area was in the shape of an apse in which may have been placed the altar, the president's/ bishop's chair, or rows of seats for the presbyters/elders. It was common for churches built during this time and afterwards to have this raised area (known variously as the *sanctuary* or *synthronon*) in the easternmost part of the basilica; the symbolic point of the compass where light was born anew each day. In its worship organization the entire congregation would thus be "oriented", i.e. facing the East.

In some basilicas, a raised platform called the *ambo* was common in the middle of the large central space, the *nave*. This was a common architectural element in the Jewish synagogue. It was from the ambo that the Gospel or other readings would be proclaimed by the deacon and, at least in Antioch, where the preacher would have stood. Often connecting the ambo in the middle of the nave to the altar/table in the sanctuary on the eastern wall was a raised walkway called the *solea*. In these churches the dual foci of the worship service, i.e. Word and Table, would have been architecturally obvious. The Word and all that pertained to it would have been proclaimed from within the midst of the assembly, while the offering of the eucharist would have been made by everyone (led by the presider) facing the East.

It was both architecturally and socially difficult to avoid a distinction between clergy and laity in the basilica structure. Obviously, those with leadership roles sat, read, or sang from higher levels than the rest of the assembly, but this was important for both visual and acoustic reasons. Railings separating these spaces were necessary if one considers the large crowds that would have regularly gathered for worship at this period of time. In the larger churches, several presbyters would have been able to occupy seats in the raised *synthronon* within the apse, and in that same place the bishop's chair would have been visibly positioned near the altar. In such a setting the hierarchical structure of the worship service was readily apparent. However, in both this period and as it has continued in the Eastern Orthodox Church until the present, the liturgical and theological separation of clergy from the laity never achieved the severity of detachment that was the unfortunate evolution of western worship in the Middle Ages. One can only look to the more massive among the sacred buildings and wonder if there could have been any other architectural and liturgical options for preaching and leading. We speak here in generalizations; there existed a large variety of church buildings with the altar, ambo, and important seats rearranged in manifold positions. For the most part, two features common to modern evangelical churches were noticeably missing: (1) The baptistery was not incorporated into the main structure of the church. The preferred mode of "living water" for baptisms necessitated a trip to a natural river, lake, or spring. In many cities, public baths would have been reserved for a few days before the baptismal rite. (2) There was not any kind of modern seating as we know it within the central space. Worship would have necessitated all to stand or kneel. If there were provisions for the elderly or disabled, they are not mentioned.

With the advent of public financing for the Church and the popularity of Christianity among the wealthy or politically ambitious individuals, church buildings in the city centers became increasingly more opulent and awe-inspiring in their beauty and grandeur. The ceremony of the liturgy took its cues from the imperial culture and its elaborate processionals, majestic vestments, courtly gestures, and magnificent furnishings. The Church became the conservatory of the arts as attested in elaborate mosaics which still survive, rich frescoes, and costly building materials and accouterments. Far from being merely ostentatious in the shallow sense—but not so as to escape the possibility of excess—the basilica depicted foremost a God of majesty and grandeur, a *pantokrator*, i.e., an all-triumphant ruler, a God who dwells in the heights of heaven, and whose glory surpasses all. A country peasant, having walked into one of these churches, would have undoubtedly been overwhelmed by the splendor of the space and would have associated the God worshiped there as much more divine than human.

By contrast, pious men and women, now free from the threat of martyrdom because of the Faith, did not feel comfortable with the ease and luxury of a secularized Christianity. These, who could no longer die for their faith, chose the "white martyrdom" of poverty, of exile from inhabited areas, of rigorous fasting and prayer, and of various expressions of living in contrast-communities. Their worship space was, more often than not, within the confines of their monastic cell where they could pursue the quest for ceaseless prayer and experience the second baptism of renouncing the pleasures of the world. These monastics also gathered for a common celebration of the eucharist in the desert wilderness, but exactly where and how this took place is beyond history's written record. Most likely they left their desert retreat to join in a common eucharistic assembly on Sundays; or a priest from the nearby town might have brought the eucharist to them.

Time

1. The Daily Synaxes

The Church had progressed almost overnight from meeting in secret at "off-peak hours" to gathering publicly at significant times of the day. The daily Christian assemblies (synaxes) took different forms depending on the place. In the West, specifically Rome and North Africa, we see the Eucharist was a daily celebration whereas in the East it took place primarily on Sundays and major feast days. We will say more about this particular eucharistic liturgy below. In both East and West, however, a complementary service of daily prayer and praise began to propagate from its roots in the earlier centuries. It is in the light of the monastic movement of the fourth century that this daily practice of offering prayer and praise can best be seen. Morning and evening prayers continued from their Jewish and Christian sources in earlier times, but other times of the day were soon to be added. It is due largely to the movement of ascetics away from the cities—and then back to them—that the component parts of these prayer services would crystallize into two unique forms.

The first seems to be best suited for the mixed multitude; those individuals who most likely lived in the larger cities, whose level of piety and devotion was not particularly ascetic, and whose participation in congregational singing may have required the repetition of familiar texts and tunes. At evening prayer, Psalm 140 was commonly sung and, at morning prayer, Psalm 62. This type of assembly must have found such Psalmody easy to learn and sing.[3] Certainly the theological content of these few Psalms would have distilled into the worshiper with the result that only thoughtful repetition over a lifetime is capable of producing. Many Christians glimpse the profound effects of such repetition each time they pray the Lord's Prayer. The words of the prayer may remain the same, but the person who is praying and that person's world changes to some degree every day. Apart from the formative benefits of repeatedly singing the same psalm text, the practice allowed the entire assembly to participate actively in the psalmody rather than listen as spectators to an "expert" choir.

Concerning these praise and prayer meetings on ordinary weekdays we have no indication during this period of any required proclamation of the Word whether by way of reading, recitation, or preaching. However, it can be safely assumed that this practice would have followed logically from the synagogue tradition and the earlier apostolic period and would have been suited for the needs of the various local communities. As the service continued, there would have been a point at which those who were enrolled as catechumens, those who were "possessed by demons," those who were under discipline, and those who were immediately preparing for baptism would have been dismissed. These would have been categorically blessed by the presider, usually the bishop, often with the imposition of the bishop's hand and the accompanying prayers of the assembled "faithful" who would remain for further prayers. The latter took the form of intercessions by categories announced by a deacon, possibly following this structure: intercession on behalf of the whole Church, the world, the infirm, and the deceased. Following these prayers, the faithful would be instructed to bow for the bishop's blessing and then be dismissed.

The second form of this praise and prayer service is attested by the Jerusalem church of the 4th century where monks living in the city were apparently a unique attraction. These were no desert ascetics living miles away from inhabited areas! They may have returned to the more populated areas in order to propagate their spirituality, and it was in the larger churches—especially those in Jerusalem—that they imported their worship traditions. In her diary, Egeria notes that these monks are now leading the assembly's daily psalmody which has been expanded from the ordinary morning and evening psalms to include the entire Psalter—all 150 Psalms! She notes that the psalms are not necessarily read in canonical order, but the selection is governed by the references within a particular psalm to morning, evening, midday, or even at night. Basil the Great, bishop of Caesarea (ca.330–379) knows of prayer at night and mentions at least two styles of chanting the psalms. *Antiphonal:* The assembly is divided into two *choirs.* The verses or half-verses of the psalm would then be sung as if the chant were being thrown back and forth between the two groups. *Responsorial:* Basil also indicates that one person was entrusted with intoning the chant while all the others responded. Prayers were also interspersed among the psalms, and so the vigil night was spent in a diversified singing and praying of the Psalter.

This second form would develop into what will later be known as the *Liturgy of the Hours* or *The Daily Office* or *The Monastic Office*. The morning and evening offices, however, remained the climactic times ("hinges") of daily prayer, and in the larger cities like Jerusalem these were celebrated with the skilled voices of the monks and nuns that had given themselves to the rendering of ceaseless praise to God. The beautification, perfection, and leadership of this praise they held to be their calling.

2. Fasts and Feasts: The Emerging Liturgical Year

With Easter remaining the focal point of the entire year, and each Sunday being a reiteration of the Easter feast, the liturgical calendar began to congeal to accommodate an ever-widening logic of worship-in-time. Even with the tendency towards stability there existed regional variations. Easter, however, remained fixed to the lunar cycle, and was always the Sunday following the full moon after the spring equinox. The Great Week (Holy Week) that preceded Easter was celebrated with some variations from region to region, but the majority would have celebrated the most significant services on Thursday, Friday, and the vigil service on Saturday evening. In some places there was a celebration each day of this week from 3:00 in the afternoon to 6:00 in the evening, but special attention was always given to the commemoration of the Lord's last supper with his disciples (Thursday), his passion (Friday), and Saturday night's watchful expectancy of Sunday's resurrection.

The Great Feast of Easter was prepared for by a Great Fast: the forty days of Lent. Depending on whether the church in a particular region fasted on Saturdays or not, the number of weeks in Lent might vary from seven to eight, but always the thematic focus of this fast was on the commemoration of the earthly life and ministry of Jesus. On the Sunday following Easter—roughly the time proportionate to the scriptural account—most churches would have celebrated the appearance of Jesus to the apostle Thomas. With similar chronological integrity, Jesus' ascension into heaven forty days after Easter would have been celebrated on its prescribed day; always a Thursday. Pentecost Sunday was reckoned fifty days after Easter and symbolically closed the Easter/Paschal season with the birth of the Church and the giving of the Spirit as recorded in Acts 2.

Lent[4] was especially significant in the Jerusalem church, which had the upper hand when it came to linking liturgical time and space. After all, a specific event in the life of Christ could be celebrated "on location" and even the progression from one place to another could be symbolically represented. Thus began the *stational liturgies* of the church in Jerusalem. Egeria records that the bishop was quite busy during Lent with all of the daily assemblies for the catechumens and pilgrims. The multiplicity of services would have been necessary to accommodate the flood of worshipers at all of the holy sites, but how impressive it must have been to hear the scriptural account read while standing on the ground where it traditionally was believed to have happened! Prayer could truly take on new experiential dimensions in such places. Pilgrims, like Egeria, would experience the liturgies of Jerusalem and take reports of them back to their own communities which would, consequently, attempt an imitation.

The Holy City and its stational liturgy is credited as the birthplace of the formal *procession* that would be adapted and adopted by such influential cities as Rome and Byzantium. For instance, worshipers in Jerusalem would gather outside Jerusalem on the Mount of Olives on what is now known as Palm Sunday, and go in procession to the next stational church in the Holy City. Likewise, the processional on Ash Wednesday in Rome would find worshipers gathered at the church of St. Anastasia. From there they would walk in procession to the church of St. Sabina in which the eucharistic liturgy would have been celebrated. Certain common worship elements accompanied such processionals: psalmody, reading of Scripture, hymn chants (based on scriptural phrases or extrabiblical material), and prayers. One category of prayer that has a unique evolution since its origin in the stational liturgies is the *collect* (emphasis on the first syllable: *COL-lect*). This was originally the prayer of the bishop when all had gathered (collected) at the next stational church. The form survives in the modern liturgies of the eastern churches, but in this context: The deacon calls the congregation to pray at a certain point within the worship service (the prayer known variously as a *litany* or *ektenis*) After the deacon has spoken the *intention* of the prayer (e.g., "For this holy house, and those who have gathered in it . . . for the welfare of all the churches of God . . . etc., let us pray to the Lord), the congregation prays silently and/while the choir sings, "Lord, have mercy." At the conclusion of several such intentions, the bishop will pray a *collect*, and in this way the modern designation "collect" has become associated with "collecting" the prayers of the people into the one spoken by the bishop on behalf of all.[5]

All of the events surrounding Lent/Easter/Pentecost were determined by the annually variable date of Easter. Two fixed dates are found in the entries of two separate calendars of feasts found in the *Apostolic Constitutions*: December 25 marked the Feast of the Nativity of Christ, and January 6 denoted the Epiphany/Baptism of Christ.

Christmas was not merely a celebration of the birth of the "baby" Jesus, but of the cosmic entrance of Light into the world and of the incarnation of God as the Word that had become flesh and tabernacled among humankind. Its fixed date of December 25 corresponded to the winter solstice when the hours of daylight gradually increase in the northern hemisphere. Hence the season still carries many references to the advent of Light (see John 1:1-14). Scholars still disagree on the origins of the day, but many look to Constantine for having encouraged the christianization of formerly pagan holidays—in the case of Christmas, a Christian adaptation of the holiday celebrating the "Birth of the Sun." Similar cosmic references to light accompany the day of Epiphany (January 6) with certain Syriac sources telling of the blinding light that traditionally accompanied the baptism of Christ. January 6 was formerly celebrated in the East among pagans as the birth of Aion/Dionysius, and pagan feasts traditionally incorporated the stories of the revelations ("epiphanies") of the gods to humans. Christian Epiphany had, historically, two or even three emphases depending on the geographic location: the nativity of Christ, the baptism of Christ, and the "revelation" of Christ in his first miracle—the wedding at Cana in Galilee. Historians believe the Epiphany celebration is the older of the two traditional dates for the nativity of Christ, with at least one modern scholar (Thomas Talley) positing that both December 25 and January 6 can be historically linked to calculations from early celebrations of the Paschal celebration on 14 Nisan.[6]

Other fixed dates in the *Apostolic Constitutions* included the feasts of the apostles, the feast of St. Stephen, and the other martyrs. The greater number of these major feasts would remain *solemnities* throughout the next ten centuries and to them would be added other significant dates. At the same time, the calendar began to be filled with the memorials of other saints resulting in a calendar of feasts of greater and lesser universal import known as the *Sanctoral Cycle*.

Ministry (*Orders*)

So far in our study we have found it is impossible to pin down the exact organization of ministry within the Church. The New Testament evidence seems to show two patterns emerging. The first we might call "charismatic" in the etymological sense of persons having been given a special *grace* by the Spirit to perform specific ministerial roles. These are identified by the somewhat interchangeable titles of *prophet* and *teacher* and there is significant data in early extrabiblical sources to support that these ministries may have been of an itinerant nature. The second pattern appears to be one that is more stabilized in a particular local community and, indeed, may have grown out of it organically speaking. The characteristic titles for this second group include *bishop* (overseer<*episcopos*), *presbyter* (elder<*presbuteros*), and deacon (assistant, minister< *diakonos*).

History does not tell us why the first group (the charismatic pattern of *prophet* and *teacher*) appears to have moved behind the scenes rather early on, but historians are agreed that throughout the first three centuries and extending into the fourth and fifth, the concern of local bishops with doctrinal orthodoxy reached a significantly high level of intensity. Gnosticism, which had competed with Christianity since its beginning, held that an individual need only receive knowledge directly from the divine with no human intermediary. Of course, prophets and charismatic teachers fell within this category, claiming the Spirit as their highest authority. The apostle Paul, while not suppressing this activity of the Spirit (indeed, he is careful to affirm and even to encourage it), also dictates that there should be an order to such utterances, i.e., that people so gifted might be subjected to others in the community. Montanus, who began prophesying in 172, represents a stereotype of the self-proclaimed "spirit-filled" prophet who regarded the church leaders of his day as "animal-men" who had forsaken the fervor of the apostolic Church.[7] More likely, it was the schismatic effects of such divisive teaching and its associated worship practices that was destroying the truly spiritual unity of the churches, and the local bishops responded (ecumenically) as guarantors of that unity and orthodox teaching.

By the time of Constantine, however, the theological concerns of orthodoxy and the unity of the local churches came face to face with imperial systems of political hierarchy and pressure from the State to bring order to the affairs of the Church into a recognizable schema of ecclesial authority. The phenomenon of the charismatic leadership of the prophets and teachers was barely understood, much less easily controlled in such a systematic way. But a stable, hierarchical system of local church government could fit into a secular understanding of an institutional Church. So argue most scholars on the reasons for the establishment of the *episcopal* structure of the Church in the fourth century and onward. However, we should bear the following in mind as we continue our study of ministry.

Of primary importance is that we do not superimpose our contemporary ideas (most of them false dichotomies) of democracy, monarchy, chain-of-command, and institution as these are secularly understood. To do so with our modern conceptualization of demo-cratic elections, corporate or pyramidal chains-of-command, and a mechanical succession of leaders throughout each generation, would be to deny the activity of the Spirit that was invoked on all levels of the Church's governing processes. Furthermore, students of worship should be especially careful to note the liturgical func-tions associated with the leadership roles as the latter began to be crystallized. Ordination was not simply a pragmatic solution for an expeditious and efficiently governed Church. It was an acknowl-edgment and public affirmation of the Spirit's *prior* choice in select-ing shepherds for the flock of God. This is chiefly evident in that many who were elected as bishops did so under duress at times, with the idea of a personal discerning of an "inward calling" to min-istry flatly unattested in the historical record. That the role of the leader in governing the affairs of the local church went hand in hand with the presidential role during the liturgy indicates that the two are inextricable. Leading the flock gathered in the worship assembly cannot be extirpated from leading the flock in other con-texts. So while we may acknowledge the uneasy relationship between Church and State during the reign of Constantine and afterwards, we can look to the ordination rites themselves to see the faithful and high theology of ministry that is historically preserved in their prayers and rubrics.

As for the ordering of the assembly, two analogies are pro-posed in the *Apostolic Constitutions* and in the *Didascalia*. The first is an illustration of the church as a ship—headed east, of course—with a captain and crew in their assigned capacities all working together in an orderly fashion. The second is that of a sheepfold with each type of animal grouped together with its own kind. While both of these illustrations seem lacking on several aspects, we must remember these documents emerged in a culture that recognized diversity in Christ for what it was: a many-membered Body with each part having a specific function. Egalitarianism, strictly speak-ing, would have nearly destroyed any theological notion of a Holy

Trinity of distinct Persons, or the diverse distribution of the Spirit's gifts within the Church.

The Bishop

The *Apostolic Tradition*, upon which the majority of the church orders of the fourth century and later depend, first directs that the bishop must be chosen by the entire people. Here we see the importance of the entire community at work in the selection of a leader. After his nomination and unanimous acceptance, there is to be an ordination ceremony on a Sunday where not only the local presbytery, but other bishops (presumably from neighboring cities or dioceses) will be in attendance. This is an ecclesiological imperative, since the selection of a bishop that will govern a particular local church is, in fact, a matter of concern for the *entire, universal Church!* The issues at stake here are often confusing because the local bishop might appear to the local community—or, as history has too often shown, might actually behave—as a monarch who answers only to God, or as a liturgical "high priest" who oversteps the symbolic liturgical role of presider. It is in this sense that the presence of other nearby bishops is important. They guarantee the universal approval of what is being done, and bear witness to this universality by their presence in the local assembly. In later centuries, three bishops, at the very least, will be required to be in attendance at the ordination of a new bishop in order for it to be considered valid.

The college of presbyters, the elders of the local assembly, is also present at the ordination of the bishop and represent their own distinct order within the church. They attend in silence while one of the visiting bishops, chosen unanimously, lays hands on the one to be ordained bishop. All the other bishops and presbyters keep silence and pray "in their hearts" for the descent of the Holy Spirit. The bishop laying on hands prays:

> God and Father of our Lord Jesus Christ,
> Father of mercies and of every consolation,

you who dwell in the highest heaven
and lower your gaze to what is lowly,
you who know all things before they exist;
who have assigned the boundaries of your Church
by your word of grace;
who from the beginning have predestined
the race of just men descended from Abraham;
who have appointed leaders and priests
and have not left your sanctuary without its liturgy,
and whose delight it has been, since the foundation of
   the world, to be glorified by those you have chosen:

Pour out now the power that comes from you,
the sovereign Spirit whom you gave
to your beloved Child Jesus Christ,
and whom he handed on to the apostles
who built the Church, your sanctuary,
for the glory and ceaseless praise of your name.

Father, who knows the heart,
grant that your servant whom you have chosen bishop
may feed your holy flock and exercise your sovereign
   priesthood without blame,
serving you day and night.

May he always make you merciful to us
and offer you the gifts of your Holy Church.
In virtue of the Spirit of high priesthood,
may he have the power to forgive sins
as you have commanded.

May he distribute offices according to your order;
may he loose from every bond in virtue of the power
you bestowed upon the apostles.

May he please you
by his gentleness and purity of heart.

May he offer you a sweet fragrance
through your Child Jesus Christ, our Lord.

Through him, glory is yours, power and honor,
Father and Son, with the Holy Spirit,
in your holy Church,
now and always for ever and ever!
    Amen.[8]

Upon a close examination of the preceding prayer text one can ascertain a pastoral theology of the bishop's office. It is God who chooses the leaders for the Church and is glorified in those chosen to serve. It is the Spirit who was given to Christ, then to the apostles, then to all the Church, who now will empower the one being consecrated bishop. The ordinand is now standing in the line of servants, of whom Christ is first and head, to glorify God's name and to offer God unending praise. Then follows a description of the bishop's duties: "to offer you the gifts of your holy Church" may be a reference to both praise and the gifts of bread and wine in the eucharist; "to exercise your sovereign priesthood" in the sense of representing the people before God by speaking, in the prayers of the liturgical assembly, on their behalf; "to forgive sins" is a reference to the emerging penitential system of this era (but also a reference to the authority with which Christ invested Peter to remit and retain sins); and "to distribute offices" indicates that the bishop is the locus of authority for the other orders as concerns his local church.

After the consecratory prayer, all are to greet the new bishop with a "kiss of peace" which is not to be confused with the "kiss of peace" that later follows in the eucharistic liturgy. The entire assembly is then to acclaim him with the word: *Axios!* i.e., "He is worthy!" These two directions accentuate the participation of the assembly with a verbal reception of the ordinand. This is no longer a part of the selection process since it is rather late for that but, like the entire rite itself, it is a public affirmation and covenantal binding of the bishop to his people and the people to their bishop. All of this takes place just before the celebration of the eucharist at which the newly consecrated bishop will preside since this is now his new liturgical role.

In the *Apostolic Constitutions*, a further rite is mentioned; that of imposing the Book of the Gospels over the one being ordained bishop. The rite is tied to the Antiochene church at the end of the fourth century, and variations existed in later centuries—even to the extent that the book is placed on the head *and neck* of the ordinand, symbolizing the yoke and mantle of the Spirit. Another variation from East Syria is that the gospel is proclaimed by the deacon, the book of the gospel itself resting on the back of the new bishop so that he acts as a human lectern.[9] Various interpretations for each of these rites exist in contemporary homilies, but all show that it is the burden of the bishop to protect and submit to the gospel that he has received and from which the power of the Spirit flows. Such eastern rites would make their ways a few centuries later to the Church of Rome in the West.

Presbyter/Priest

In all likelihood it was common for the first bishop (overseer) in a community to have been chosen from among the college of presbyters (elders) unless this role was *de facto* assigned to the one who first evangelized the community and was now a permanent resident. It was the bishop who presided at the eucharist and who symbolically represented in his person the unity of all the churches. The bishop was the guarantor of orthodox doctrine, but he was not the solitary preacher. In the larger metropolitan churches it was the *presbyters* who were assigned the responsibility of teaching and preaching. Since the presbytery was a collective, the teaching role was a shared assignment. In fact, in Egeria's diary we learn that in Jerusalem at the appropriate place in the Sunday liturgy, there are several presbyters who comment/preach *in turn* on the Scriptures that had been read, the last of these preachers being the bishop himself. Multiple sermons on a Sunday morning! So we see the teaching/preaching role being the chief liturgical function of the presbyters.

While it was normative for the bishop to have presided over

the eucharist, there were provisions even in the second century that this responsibility could have been assigned by the bishop to a presbyter. In any event, this would not have been within the presbyter's ordinary duties.[10] Apart from their role in governing the church in various nonliturgical ways, we know little more about the role of the presbytery within the worship assembly of this period. By the end of the third century, the title of "priest" to describe presbyters is beginning to creep into the vocabulary of the church, and by the fifth century the designation of the presbyter as "priest" prevailed. Such a designation could only be understood if the presbyter were a priest under the aegis of his bishop, and the leader of a laity of priests. As most people know, however, it was popularly impossible to sustain this theological concept of a priesthood ministering to a priestly people. The integrity of the priesthood of all Christians continued to shift downward until the presbyters would occupy a priestly role that, at least in the West, became cleanly severed from the laity.

What might have begun as a collegial relationship between bishop and presbyters became, by the reign of Constantine, a more visually and liturgically separated hierarchy. This was such that at the time in the liturgy for the *kiss of peace,* it was protocol for presbyters to exchange the greeting only among themselves while the bishop would exchange the greeting with those deacons who had the role of being his personal assistants.

Deacon

The *Apostolic Tradition* makes the distinction that deacons are not included within the "priesthood" although the earlier reference in the book of Acts states that the deacons were responsible to "serve tables." Whether in Acts the definition of "serving tables" is a reference to the Eucharist, or whether it involves the same type of financial scenario that concerned the apostle Matthew (the tax collector who was sitting at his "tables" when Jesus called him), the author of the *Apostolic Tradition* makes it clear that the deacon does not have priestly responsibilities. The ambiguity was clarified within the era of Constantinian Christianity. Deacons were the min-isters of the bishop, and ranked under the authority of the pres-byters. Their liturgical function, however, was especially clear and has remained so in the eastern churches until today. Their role was to lead the congregation in prayer, instructing them when to kneel or stand, and to organize the assembly for an orderly execution of the communion rite which would have included dismissing the vari-ous groups of catechumens and penitents who would not have been able to participate in the "prayers of the faithful" or the eucharistic offering. Deacons were ordained solely by the bishop, and not as a presbyter who would have been ordained by the imposition of the bishop's hands with the other presbyters gathered touching him.

Confessors, Healers

During times of persecution, a Christian who had been impris-oned for the faith would have been able, upon release, to attain the status of deacon or presbyter without the imposition of the bishop's hands, since the word of their testimony was confirmation of the gift of the Spirit within them. Similarly, those who had the gift of healing needed no further endorsement by the imposition of the bishop's hands. The gift and the operation of the Spirit would have already been evident.

Readers, Subdeacons, Catechists/Exorcists, Singers, Doorkeepers

Each of these had some type of liturgical ministry and would not have been ordained, technically speaking, but would have been appointed within the context of Sunday (eucharistic) worship with an accompanying rite that involved being handed an object appro-priate to their ministry. To the readers would have been handed the Book of the Epistles; to the doorkeepers, keys. Whatever the specif-ic ministry, the ritual, performed in the presence of the eucharistic assembly, would have authenticated both the individuals and their service as something more spiritually significant than that of a mere functionary.

Virgins, Widows

Other groups would have remained under the financial benevolence of the church. In the earliest communities that were considerably smaller, it would have been the responsibility of the bishop to distribute from the collection to all who were in need. By the fourth century this group had grown to such a considerable size that the role of the deaconate in managing and dispensing the church's funds was a full-time affair (perhaps necessitating the *subdeacons* mentioned above).

Initiation

Introduction

To call this section "Baptism" would be a misnomer in this period when the earlier rites associated with Christian initiation would have become more organized and institutionalized. Far from an emphasis on the singular salvific act of the water bath, a collection of associated rites, each having its own significance in its symbolism and administration, deepened the mystery for those who dared to make the decision to become fully initiated into the Church. The act of participation in the mystery of baptism was no trivial matter in spite of the fact, as we mentioned above, that the contemporary culture was becoming more and more Christian. To accommodate the nominally Christian culture, there existed two general groups of worshipers: those who had been fully initiated, and those who were catechumens. Although larger metropolitan areas, such as Antioch and Jerusalem, would have witnessed up to a thousand baptisms on a particular Easter, this number was proportionately small considering that much of the city's population would have considered themselves Christian but had not as yet submitted to baptism. There are several explanations for this phenomenon.

The theologies associated with baptism were somewhat responsible. In North Africa, infant baptism, though not normative, was practiced and was encouraged by Cyprian (of Carthage) on the theological grounds that baptism remits original sin; a doctrine which later became fundamental to the theology of Augustine (of Hippo). Cyprian, too, did not accept the baptisms administered by heretical bishops who, he claimed, did not have the authority to impart the Holy Spirit, since these bishops had detached themselves from the unity of the Church. (That is to say, one cannot give what one does not possess.) Elsewhere in the West and in the East, previously baptized persons, even those whose baptisms were performed by schismatics or heretics, were accepted into the communion of "orthodox" assemblies without rebaptism. It sufficed that the bishop needed only to lay hands on these as a sign of both the giving of the Spirit and of the validation that the Spirit had already been at work in the candidate's previous baptism albeit by the hands of one not in fully catholic communion.

In spite of the teaching that original sin should be remitted as soon as possible after birth, the number of baptisms among infants and children was still small. An opposing theological view, particularly widespread in the East was responsible for this. Rather than the emphasis on original sin that was inherited from Adam, there prevailed the notion of original innocence; that children had not lived long enough to commit any sin for which they would suffer eternal damnation. Contrary to the modern evangelical "loophole" of an "age of accountability" which largely rests on the individual's ability to cognitively understand sin and choose salvation, the prevailing theological view in the East was that baptism represented the choice of a life of commitment, of asceticism, of joint heirship with Christ, and of becoming a participant in the divine nature by the anointing of the same Spirit who anointed Christ. One need only look to the rites themselves to see this theology substantiated by the language and content of the prayers associated with them. It was this theology that was predominant in Antioch and Jerusalem, and it was the liturgies of these churches that were the most influential throughout the Christian world during this period.

There was a third reason for the decline in the baptisms of infants and youth in this period: The question of postbaptismal sin that had arisen in the second and third centuries[11] now had evolved into a penitential system that punished grave sins committed after baptism by excommunication (denial of communion). Penance, as an emerging sacramental system, was still fairly young and varied greatly from region to region, but its roots are found in the fourth century. We will say more about this later on. For now, it is enough to know that baptism was delayed, often with the support of the clergy, so that sins more or less expected of youth would not be subject to the severity of the penance that was in place. (For instance, the penance for adultery was a lifelong ban on sexual relations, even with one's marital partner!)

Nevertheless, not everyone delayed baptism until the deathbed. Preachers such as John Chrysostom, Gregory of Nazianzus, and Augustine—themselves baptized in their late 20s and mid-30s—continually encouraged baptism as a radical but worthy commitment to a life of holiness. Nevertheless, an alternative existed for those who chose association with the Church but who rejected an immediate baptism: the *catechumenate*. Catechumens were enrolled as such, and thus were registered as Christians. They were able to participate with the worshiping assembly by staying for the initial portion of the liturgy where they would have heard the Word proclaimed in song and in public reading; and they would have heard the preaching which, by this time had achieved a renown that has marked this period as a "golden age of preaching."

Since the worship service was divided into two larger segments: first, the Liturgy of the Word (or, as it is often called, the Liturgy of the Catechumens) and, second, the Liturgy of the Eucharist; it was logistically simple to dismiss the catechumens just before the Liturgy of the Eucharist. The remaining baptized worshipers, the *Faithful*, would then do the things that they were theologically and liturgically ordained by baptism to do: (1) to intercede on behalf of the world (since they were, collectively, a laity of priests by virtue of their baptism and anointing); (2) to respond in ecclesial acclamations and to confess the creed of the Church (at this time the latter was being formulated by the first ecumenical councils); and (3) to participate in the threefold division of the eucharist (to offer bread and wine, to assent to the eucharistic prayer with a resounding "Amen," and to receive communion).

Thus we see within the Church of the Empire the two divisions which we mentioned earlier: the Catechumens and the Faithful (baptized). Both groups were considered Christians, but it was obvious that the majority of individuals were slow in accepting the Christian faith in its entirety. It is certain that paganism was not completely stamped out in this era, and the catechumenate allowed one to keep a foot in each world so long as one could ignore the call to holiness proclaimed by the preachers and evidenced by a growing monastic presence that modeled it.

1. The Catechumenate

Sources vary as to the actual length of the formal, prebaptismal catechumenate. Some indicate a period as long as three years (attested as early as the *Apostolic Tradition*), although it is reasonable to conclude that this prebaptismal period would have been much shorter considering that many were catechumens for most of their adult lives. Those who were already catechumens but desired baptism would submit their names to the local presbyters who, in turn, would present the list of names to the bishop. This was known as *enrolment* and it took place at the beginning of Lent. Egeria tells us about how this happened in Jerusalem:

> On the second day of Lent . . . one by one those seeking baptism are brought up, men coming with their [male sponsors] and women with their [female sponsors]. As they come in one by one, the bishop asks their neighbors about them: "Is this person leading a good life? Does [she] respect [her] parents? Is he a drunkard or a boaster?" . . . And if his inquiries show him that someone has not committed any of these misdeeds, he himself puts down [the person's] name; but if someone is guilty [that one] is told to go away. (Egeria, 45)[12]

This notion—that someone could be denied enrolment into the catechumenate—seems particularly foreign to the widespread practice these days of not requiring much moral accountability *before* baptism, but this was no new development. Its roots are strong in the previous era (cf. the *Didache* and the list of excluded occupations that would prevent one from becoming initiated into the early Christian communities).

Since the baptismal liturgies were replete with references to turning from the region of darkness to the region of light, this 40-day period of intense catechesis became known as *enlightenment*. The *illuminandi* (Latin) or *photizomenoi* (Greek)—the "Enlightened"—would be formally dismissed as a group before the eucharistic portion of the liturgy along with the catechumens, the excommunicated, and the demon-possessed. Unlike the other three groups, however, the Enlightened would retire with their catechists for further teaching. The teaching often began with the book of Genesis and highlighted the significant narratives and interpretations of salvation history throughout the entire Bible. During the period of enlightenment, regular exorcisms by the presbyters in the full assembly and by the catechists in their own meetings took place. In Jerusalem, these were *daily* throughout the 40-day period of Lent. These exorcisms were most likely nothing akin to the modern horror movie versions, although the acknowledgment of spiritual activity was much more taken for granted in this period than our contemporary intellectual sensibilities would admit. Here is found the relatively small category of prayers that are addressed to Christ (not to the Father), since it is traditionally by the sole authority of Christ himself that demons can be cast out. Whatever our understanding in the 21st century of these exorcisms, we can be assured that the crucible of the 40 days of enlightenment was unquestionably one of interaction between catechumen and catechist. Spiritual growth was expected.

In most places, during the three weeks before Easter, the themes of the catechumenate dominated the Liturgy of the Word for the entire assembly, the Gospels focusing on (1) the man born blind; (2) the woman of Samaria; and (3) the raising of Lazarus. All three were significantly symbolic for the particular stage at which the Enlightened stood. The pericope of the man born blind provided bishops (or priests) the opportunity to preach about the condition of spiritual blindness to all those who had not yet been "anointed" by Christ. (It is possible that we may have here, in this text, a reference to some kind of prebaptismal anointing.) The second narrative, the woman of Samaria, takes place around the central figure of Jacob's well, and Jesus' gift of "living water." Certainly the reference here is to water baptism proper, but also to the good news that has come through catechesis (Jesus' dialogue with/evangelism to the woman). That the woman is not a Jew, but an ethnically distant relative suggests the universal appeal of the gospel to any who encounter the Christ and choose to respond. The plot of the last text, the raising of Lazarus, is hard to miss.

Here is pictured one communal aspect of Lent that was ignored during the Middle Ages when this type of catechumenate was all but extinct: The entire assembly of the faithful would have been able to identify with the catechumens in their period of preparation for Easter. These three Sundays became known as the "Scrutinies" in the West, since the catechumens' lives would have been closely watched to see if they were, in fact, ready for baptism. Those who were approved, sometimes by a final exorcistic rite by the bishop (who then "scrutinized" the candidate to see any evidence of remaining demonic activity), were then considered as the *Elect*—those who were chosen for baptism. In Jerusalem this final stage took place in a separate gathering with the bishop, the candidates, and their catechists.

In addition to the exorcisms, prayers, sponsorship/accountability interaction, and the exposition of Scripture and salvation theology, the Enlightened were responsible for learning the Lord's Prayer and the Creed. These were "handed over" to them (some sources suggest on Palm Sunday) and they were then "returned" in the presence of the bishop on the Saturday before Easter, in close proximity to the vigil night where baptism would have been administered. In the final week, rigorous fasting was to be expected which, in addition to diet, also included refraining from the baths (except on the Thursday before baptism, for respectability), and sexual relations (even within the bond of marriage). Once again, the idea of the entire Church participating in a Lenten fast can be explained as a *community-wide event with all the faithful sharing in solidarity with the candidates on their journey to the baptismal font*, and not as it has commonly been understood to be; the practice of the few zealous and pious, "seasoned" Christians.

2. The Rites of Initiation Associated with the Easter Vigil

The procession to the baptistery: With the earlier preference for baptism in "living water" on the wane, the general availability and convenience of public baths that could be dedicated for the occasion, and the new architectural addition of the baptistery (normally a separate edifice accessible only from the exterior of the church building), processionals to the font began to constitute a ritual component of their own. Because of the especially large number of candidates at the Easter vigil, most of the ministry orders were involved in the baptismal process: bishop, presbyter, deacon, and deaconess. All of these would have had to leave the worshiping assembly which had already gathered in the church for the Easter vigil. The few remaining ministers and the laity would have been occupied in singing psalms, hymns, and perhaps even in hearing some of the readings of the vigil service while the baptisms were taking place elsewhere.

This is vastly different from the spectacle that baptisms have become today! It is almost impossible to think of a modern baptism without family and friends as spectators, or cameras flashing, or video recording, and—in the larger churches—digital projection of the event on the large screen. While it can be argued that baptisteries were designed for the purely practical purpose of baptizing without a plan to accommodate onlookers, there is a larger symbolism at work in the processional to and from the place of baptism.

The typology of Christ's death and burial begins to unfold to the faithful who are remaining within the church building while the bishop and other ministers are elsewhere with the baptismal candidates. Christ, in the person of the bishop, though absent from the assembly, has "descended to the dead" (the baptismal font) and is about to bring back from the grave the baptizands with him into the gathered assembly. What a powerful image of resurrection that is symbolically communicated not only to the baptismal candidates who have just been newly born (*neophytes*), but also to the gathered assembly who see them return "from the dead" with their bishop in resurrection glory!

The architecture of the baptistery and font reflected these themes. Most baptisteries were octagonal rooms, symbolizing the resurrection of Christ on the eighth day; the day of the new creation. The number eight also hearkens back to the number of persons within Noah's ark that were saved from the waters of the flood, as well as the eighth day after birth when Jewish males became part of the covenantal people of God through the rite of circumcision. Anterooms within the baptistery edifice served for the associated rites of stripping, anointing, and clothing. The font itself was the subject of a diverse artistic, practical, and theological approach. Early representations in this period ranged from a simple, rectangular trough, sunk into the floor with a few access steps on either side, to a cruciform design that might have accommodated several people who would administer the baptism. Another frequent design was that of a womb, an unmistakable symbol of new birth.

There is some archeological evidence that provision was made through inlet and outlet pipes for fresh, running water to have circulated throughout the baptistery. Through iconographic and mosaic evidence we see that the baptizand stood in the water which was at least up to the ankles but usually covered the waist. The smaller quantity of water in some fonts would have made effusion (pouring) a necessity.

The blessing of the baptismal water by the bishop took place immediately before the baptisms. The prayer would have had an exorcistic flavor to it, commanding that all evil spirits be driven out from the water so that its curative power might alone be present. Then the Spirit was invoked, in the form of a thanksgiving, to descend into the water (in the East it is the Word who descends into the water and fills it with the Spirit). Finally, the bishop would trace the sign of the cross either in the water with his hand, or he would dip his own cross into the water and make the sign, or would pour consecrated oil crosswise on top of the water.

Disrobing: For the anointings of the entire body which follow in almost every liturgical family, this would have been a necessity. As in previous centuries, the candidate was led naked to the font for baptism (deaconesses would have assisted the women so that propriety was observed). Cyril and Ambrose in their homilies explain the symbolism of nakedness as variously corresponding to the innocence of the garden of Eden, to the nakedness of Christ in his birth and death, and to the stripping of the candidate as symbolically "putting off the old man."

In chapter three we mentioned that nakedness, along with the anointing of the entire body with oil, had sociological connections with the contemporary bathing protocol of the Greco-Roman era.[13] In the rites we are studying (which find their prototype in the initiation rites of the church in Jerusalem) such sociological concerns pale in comparison with the biblical symbolism and metaphors that are now deliberately attached to them. In this stage of worship development, a detailed system of biblical interpretation is at work, some of which will be part of the catechumen's prebaptismal instruction (*protocatechesis*), and some of which will be explained to the neophyte during the season of Easter in subsequent catecheses that unpack the "mysteries" of baptism and eucharist that had been recently experienced (*mystagogical catecheses*).

Prebaptismal Anointing: It is during this period that important differences between eastern and western rites emerge. First of all, it is helpful to note that while some sources omit the *Effeta* rite, or say nothing of clothing the candidate in a white garment after baptism, or offering a chalice mixed with milk and honey, *all rites men-*

tion some type of anointing with oil at baptism. Two oils are important to distinguish. The first is olive oil that has been consecrated by the bishop at an earlier point in the week. It is variously called the *oil of exorcism,* or the *oil of the catechumens* depending on the source. The second oil is often scented with balsam (in the West) or with *myron* (in the East). This is referred to differently as *chrism* (from which the term *chrismation* begins to be used for anointing with this particular oil), or *the oil of thanksgiving,* or *unction.* Another term that is often confusing with reference to anointings is *sphragis* which in some contexts means "to sign" or "to seal" with oil but may also mean "to trace with the sign of the cross."

Source material for anointings is extremely complex, and the rites themselves are widely varied. Here we must refer the reader to the recommendations at the end of the chapter for further study. Having mentioned this caveat, the following material in this section represents broad generalizations for the purpose of finding a few themes that the student of worship history can grasp.

The mode of prebaptismal anointings can be categorized into the following: (1) Anointing the organs of sense; including the ears, nostrils, and chest (the heart is considered an organ of sense). The *Effeta* rite, practiced in Milan (attested by Ambrose in his treatise *On the Sacraments*), has the bishop touching the candidate's ears and nostrils and saying, *"Effeta,"* which in Aramaic means, "Be opened." The reference is to 2 Corinthians 2:15 and the application is that the candidate will be able to perceive with spiritual sense those things that are about to take place. We include it here in the "prebaptismal anointing" category, although there is no oil involved. It does focus, however, on a specific organ of sense. (2) Anointing the head; by pouring oil on the top of the head, or by laying a hand with oil on the head. The significance of hand-laying with oil is often confused with other hand-laying rites without oil; (3) Anointing the entire body from head to toe.

The significance of prebaptismal anointings is interpreted differently in eastern and western rites, but the following themes emerge: (1) anointing as a prophylactic: the oil serves as a shield against the assault of the devil whose defeat at baptism is assured, (2) anointing as the preparation of an athlete ready to wrestle with the devil, (3) anointing as exorcistic: in this medicinal sense, the candidate is freed from any remaining demonic activity that may still lurk in the senses, or in any part of the body. This exorcistic anointing makes more sense in those cases when the candidate is still penitentially kneeling on sackcloth during the rite. (4) Grafting: the one who is to be baptized receives a foretaste of being identified with Christ, the Olive Branch, into which the baptizand is to be grafted. (5) Priesthood (an especially dominant theme in the East Syrian rites): the eastern rites in general focus on the revelation of the divinity of Christ. This theme, which may seem chronologically out of place since the candidate has not yet been baptized, reflects the eastern emphasis on sonship (*huiothesia*).

Apotaxis-Syntaxis: Various forms of renouncing evil, the devil, Satan, his works (*pompae* may also refer to "his followers"), darkness, etc., stand in direct contrast to placing one's allegiance with Christ. This renunciation-adherence took some of the following forms: The candidate would face the West which, nearing dawn, would be the region of darkness. With hands extended, the candidate either responds with an answer to an interrogation by a minister: "Do you renounce Satan. . . ?" or, in some eastern rites, the candidate supplies the entire confession in a statement "I renounce Satan. . . ." Some baptismal liturgies have this *apotaxis* taking place just before the candidate enters the font, and one source records that the candidates are to spit "at the devil" before turning toward the East (the region of light) and descending into the water. The *syntaxis*, "adhesion" or adherence to Christ, takes place in some rites before entering the font, in the form of a statement of allegiance, "I enter your service, O Christ," or it is supplied by the recitation of a variation of the Apostle's creed with its trinitarian formula once having entered the font.

Immersion: The ministries of bishop, presbyter, and deacon are seen at work in the baptismal process from beginning to end, but immersion in the larger churches had all three orders represented at the font. The deacon or deaconess led the candidate into the font, where stood the presbyter(s) and the bishop. In the West, the presbyters assisted the candidate in the triple confession which was creedal in structure: "Do you believe in the Father. . . ?" The mode of immersion depended on the constraints of the font itself, and the pouring of fresh water over the candidate makes a few appearances in the iconography of this period. Perhaps the presbyters submersed the candidate into the water, but it is more common in the source material that the presbyters assisted the candidate in self-immersion with the bishop's hand resting on the top of the candidates' head. There was a triple immersion corresponding to the triple confession in the trinitarian creed, and some postimmersion rites took place while the candidate was still in the font.

Postbaptismal Anointing: In Antioch and in East Syria, the candidates would have *myron* poured over their heads or the sign of the cross would be traced on their foreheads with the scented oil. The pouring of the *myron* corresponded to the priestly and kingly anointings of the Old Testament, while the sign of the cross had several explanations attached to it: marking the candidate as one having joined the ranks of God's hosts; sealing the candidate for eternal life; being a sign of protection, the cross shining so brightly that it blinds the eyes of the devil; having marked the candidate in the manner that circumcision identified the Hebrews, and many other interpretations.

In the West, this postbaptismal anointing was administered by a presbyter, but a *second* postbaptismal anointing with *chrism* was performed by the bishop for the "gift of the Spirit." Here we must bring up a theological point that is not easily answered by the liturgical data of this period: When is the Holy Spirit conferred? The texts of the eastern rites reveal that the Spirit is active throughout all the rites associated with initiation, from the prebaptismal rites to the postbaptismal rites—which include the reception of the eucharist. The same is true, to a lesser degree, in the West where a theology of the Spirit is generally superseded by an emphasis on the theology of Christ. But in both East and West, it is the direct involvement of the bishop (whether in hand-laying or in anointing with oil) with which the giving of the Holy Spirit is primarily associated. As we have seen above, it is the bishop who is the visible sign of unity with the entire Church, and so it is logical that his ministry is especially necessary here. Thus, in the West, the second postbaptismal anointing by the bishop will come to be known as *confirmation* since it is clear that nowhere else in the rite is there such a distinct connection with the impartation of the Spirit. We will jump ahead a few centuries to say that it is this rite of postbaptismal anointing/confirmation that becomes detached from the baptismal liturgy in the Roman Catholic Church during the Middle Ages and often remains so until the present. The reasons for this and an evaluation of its effects will be discussed more fully in chapter 6.

Washing of Feet: In the eastern churches and in Milan, it is recorded that once the candidates had left the baptismal font, their feet would be washed by the bishop. The biblical reference to John 13 here—that service and charity should mark the life of every Christian—is trumped by Ambrose who gives a sacramental explanation: this rite protects the neophyte from the tendency to sin inherited from Adam. Thus, even in the West, the effect of baptism on Original Sin had not been entirely worked out theologically at this point.

The Wearing of a White Garment: Several sources, East and West, indicate the newly baptized wear (or receive) a white garment which, in the West, would have been worn for the entire week following Easter. The symbolism of innocence and purity is unmistakable here, but the white robe is also a metaphor for priestly service; the neophyte has become part of a priestly order: the *order of the baptized.* The neophytes would only look like priests for a week, but it would be a reminder to the entire congregation (the Faithful) of each and every one's ordination to the priesthood by virtue of one's baptism. This, of course, did not mean that simply anyone, baptized or not, would have been able to lead the worshiping assembly without the due process of hierarchical orders, but rather the focus was upon the priestly work of Christ in the reconciliation of the world through all baptized Christians. In fact, the transfiguration of Christ, is a related explanation offered by Ambrose.

A further explanation of the symbolism of the white garment is a eucharistic and eschatological one: this was the marriage garment for the supper of the Lamb. The neophytes were now able to receive communion with the Faithful. They would return, resurrected from the font, with the bishop who had already given them the kiss of peace—to be thus welcomed by all the Faithful.[14]

The Giving of a Lamp or Candle: This was the practice in Constantinople around the fifth century. It was a suitable illustration for all that those who have been "enlightened" should carry a lighted taper into the assembly.

The Eucharist

It is logical that our study of baptism and initiation brings us to a description of the eucharistic celebration in the Byzantine empire. Baptism was not separated from the eucharist at this time and, indeed, initiation was not complete without it. The eucharist was the final rite of initiation and would become the mystical way of continuously reappropriating the baptismal covenant, and the ordination to the common priesthood of all who were initiated. Just as baptism/initiation was not complete without the celebration of the eucharist so, too, the eucharist is never attested to have been celebrated on its own without the preceding liturgy of the Word. It requires some difficult mental gymnastics to think of *two* elements as being *central,* but such was the integrity of Word and eucharist. One was never less important than the other even if, during this period, the delay of baptism to one's more mature years may have resulted in more catechumens present in the liturgy of the Word and fewer communicants remaining for the liturgy of the eucharist.

Let us briefly review the order of service that, with some degree of variation, was common to the Church of the Byzantine Empire:

(1) Greeting by the Celebrant (bishop or presbyter)

(2) 3-5 Readings from OT, Acts, or the Epistles (interspersed with psalmody)

(3) Reading from the Gospel (by deacon)

(4) Preaching (by presbyters, concluding with a sermon by the bishop)

(5) Prayer for and dismissal of catechumens and other noncommunicating groups

(6) The Prayer of the Faithful

*(7) Kiss of Peace (in the East)

(8) The Offertory (primarily of bread and wine)

(9) The Eucharistic Prayer

*(10) Kiss of Peace (in the West: Rome and North Africa)

(11) The Communion Rite

(12) Post-Communion Thanksgiving/Prayer(s)

(13) Dismissal

*The order of the *Peace* among the eastern churches seems to have made more biblical sense following the command of Christ to be reconciled to one's brother/sister before offering one's gift at the altar. On the other hand, if one's gift is to be *left on the altar* while reconciliation is being made, then the position the *Peace* occupied in Rome and North Africa also makes sense. In both cases, the exchange of the Kiss among the faithful took place after the noncommunicating groups had been dismissed and (in the East) the doors would have been shut and guarded. Scholars believe the position of the Kiss among the eastern churches (7, above) is a better reflection of earlier dismissal rites (5, above) whereby the assembly would have been reorganized for the eucharist.

In both East and West it was common for the faithful to bring the gifts of bread and wine that were offered at the eucharist. In the East, deacons received several loaves before the service began and from among them would have determined the number needed for all the Faithful to communicate. In later centuries, a certain amount of ritual preparation was prescribed for the loaves that would be used at the altar. This preparation took place in an anteroom located near the sanctuary of the church called the *skeuophyalkion,* or "sacristy." In some eastern churches it was in this room that bread was baked fresh for the eucharistic liturgy, but in most cases these loaves (called *prosphora,* "offerings") were brought by the Faithful who baked them at home. Newly baptized were not permitted to bring a *prosphora* until the week following Easter.

In the West, it was the Faithful (not deacons) who, after the Prayer of the Faithful, brought the offertory bread and wine from within the nave of the church to a deacon near the sanctuary who received them and took them to the priest at the altar. Such a processional was accompanied by some type of singing, most likely a Psalm, and closed with a prayer called the *super oblata,* or "prayer over the gifts."

The simple model for the eucharistic prayer, which had been in place in the previous century (see chapter 3), had now become a unique prayer text of its own, having gathered complexity, theological substance, and length(!) from developments during the Peace of Constantine. At an introductory level, it is best to look at this prayer in its component parts before examining its variations from one liturgical family to the next. Since there was no singular eucharistic prayer in use during this time, we will use for our study the *anaphora* (eucharistic prayer) and the following communion rites found in *Book 8 of the Apostolic Constitutions.* We cite the text at length so that the beautiful literary quality of the paradoxes can be seen, especially those that occur toward the end of each paragraph in the ANAMNESIS. (Text in ALL CAPS has been added to provide those modern, western categories which describe the individual elements within the prayer):

> OPENING DIALOGUE:
> *Then, after praying privately, the bishop puts on*

a splendid robe and stands at the altar with the priests, makes the sign of the cross on his forehead with his hands, and says,

The grace of almighty God and the love of our Lord Jesus Christ and the fellowship of the Holy Spirit be with you all.

All say together:	And with your spirit.
The bishop:	Up with your mind.
All:	We have it with the Lord.
The bishop:	Let us give thanks to the Lord.
All:	It is fitting and right.

PREFACE:

The bishop: It is truly fitting and right to praise you before all things, essentially existing God, existing before created things, from whom all fatherhood in heaven and on earth is named, alone unbegotten, without beginning, without lord or master, lacking nothing, provider of all good things, greater than every cause and origin, always being in one and the same mode, from whom all things came into being as from a starting-point.

For you are knowledge, without beginning, eternal vision, unbegotten hearing, untaught wisdom, first in nature, alone in existence, too great to be numbered. You brought all things from non-existence into existence through your only-begotten Son; and him you begat without an intermediary before all ages by your will and power and goodness, your only-begotten Son, the Word, God, living wisdom, the firstborn of all creation, the angel of your great purpose, your high-priest . . . king and lord of all rational and sentient nature, who was before all, through whom are all.

For you, eternal God, made all things through him, and through him you vouchsafe a fitting providence over everything. Through him you granted existence, through him also a good existence; O God and Father of your only-begotten Son, through him before all things you made the heavenly powers, the cherubim and the seraphim, the ages and the hosts, virtues and powers, principalities and thrones, archangels and angels; and through him after all these things you made this visible world and all that is in it. [There follows a lengthy, biblical description of the created order, the place of humankind in it, and God's mercy when humankind fell.]

. . . For all things glory be to you, almighty Lord. You are worshiped by every bodiless and holy order, by the Paraclete, and above all by your holy child Jesus the Christ, our Lord and God, your angel and the chief general of your power, and eternal and unending high priest, by unnumbered armies of angels, archangels, thrones, dominions, principalities, powers, virtues, eternal armies. The cherubim and the six-winged seraphim with two wings covering their feet, with two their heads, and with two flying, together with thousands of thousands of archangels and myriads of myriads of angels say unceasingly, never resting their voices:

SANCTUS

All the people say: Holy, holy, holy (is the) Lord of Sabaoth; heaven and earth are full of his glory; blessed (is he) for ever. Amen.

ANAMNESIS

The bishop continues: Truly are you holy and all-holy, most high and exalted above all for ever.

Holy also is your only-begotten Son, our Lord and God Jesus the Christ, who ministered to you, his God and Father, in all things, in the varieties of creation, and in appropriate forethought. He did not despise the race of men as it perished; but after the law of nature and the warnings of the Law and the reproofs of the prophets . . . by your counsel it pleased him who was maker of man to become man, the lawgiver to be under the law, the high-priest to be the sacrifice, the shepherd to be a sheep.

And he propitiated you, his own God and Father, and reconciled you to the world, and freed all men from the impending wrath. He was born of a virgin, God the Word made in the flesh, the beloved Son, the firstborn of all Creation, according to the prophecies spoken beforehand by him concerning himself, from the seed of David and Abraham, of the tribe of Judah. He who fashions all who are begotten was made in a virgin's womb; the fleshless became flesh; he who was begotten outside time was begotten in time.

He lived a holy life and taught according to the law; he drove away every disease and every sickness from men; he did signs and wonders among the people; he who feeds those who need food and fills all things living with plenteousness partook of food and drink and sleep; he made known your name to those who did not know it; he put ignorance to flight; he re-kindled piety; he fulfilled your will; he accomplished the work which you gave him.

And when he had achieved all these things, he was seized by the hands of lawless so-called priests and high-priests and a lawless people, by betrayal through one who was diseased with wickedness. He suffered many things at their hands, endured all kinds of indignity by your permission, and was handed over to Pilate the governor. The Judge was judged and the Savior was condemned; he who cannot suffer was nailed to the cross, he who is immortal by nature died, and the giver of life was buried, that he might free from suffering and rescue from death those for whose sake he came, and break the bonds of the devil, and deliver men from his deceit.

And on the third day he rose from the dead, and after spending forty days with his disciples, he was taken up into heaven and sits at your right hand, his God and Father.

INSTITUTION NARRATIVE

Remembering therefore what he endured for us, we give you thanks, almighty God, not as we ought but as we are able, and we fulfill his command.

For in the night he was betrayed, he took bread in his holy and blameless hands and, looking up to you, his God and Father, he broke it and gave it to his disciples, saying, "This is the mystery of the new covenant: take of it, eat; this is my body which is broken for many for forgiveness of sins."

Likewise also he mixed the cup of wine and water and sanctified it and gave it to them, saying, "Drink from this, all of you; this is my blood which is shed for many for forgiveness of sins. Do this for my remembrance; for as often as you eat this bread and drink this cup, you proclaim my death, until I come."

Remembering then his Passion and death and resurrection from the dead, his return to heaven and his future second coming, in which he comes with glory and power to judge the living and the dead, and to reward each according to his works, we offer you, King and God, according to his commandment, this bread and this cup, giving you thanks through him that you have deemed us worthy to stand before you and to serve you as priests.

EPICLESIS

And we beseech you to look graciously upon these gifts set before you, O God who need nothing, and accept them in honor of your Christ; and to send down your Holy Spirit upon this sacrifice, the witness of the sufferings of the Lord Jesus, that he may make this bread body of your Christ, and this cup blood of your Christ; that those who partake of it may be strengthened to piety, obtain forgiveness of sins, be delivered from the devil and his deceit, be filled with the Holy Spirit, become worthy of your Christ, and obtain eternal life, after reconciliation with you, almighty Master.

INTERCESSIONS/COMMEMORATIONS

Further we pray to you, Lord, for your holy Church from one end of the world to the other, which you redeemed with the precious blood of your Christ, that you would guard it unshaken and sheltered until the consummation of the age; and for all bishops who rightly divide the word of truth.

And we entreat you also for my worthless self who offer to you, and for all the priesthood, for the deacons and all the clergy, that you would instruct them and fill them with [*sic*] holy Spirit.

And we entreat you, Lord, for the Emperor and those in authority and all the army, that they may be peaceable towards us, that we may live the whole of our life in quietness and concord, and glorify you through Jesus Christ our hope.

And we offer to you also for all those holy men who have been well-pleasing to you from everlasting: patriarchs, prophets, righteous men, apostles, martyrs, confessors, bishops, priests, deacons, subdeacons, readers, singers, virgins, widows, laymen, and all whose names you know.

And we offer to you for this people, that you would make them a royal priesthood, a holy nation, to the praise of your Christ; for those in virginity and chastity, for the widows of the Church, for those in holy marriage and child-bearing, for the infants among your people, that you may make none of us a cast-away.

And we ask you on behalf of this city and those who live in it, for those in illnesses, those in bitter slavery, those in exile, those whose goods have been confiscated, for sailors and travelers, that you would become the help of all, their aid and support.

And we entreat you for those that hate and persecute us for the sake of your name, for those who are outside and have gone astray, that you would turn them back to good and soften their hearts.

And we entreat you also for the catechumens of the Church, for those distressed by the Alien, and for those in penitence among our brothers, that you would perfect the first in the faith, and cleanse the second from the works of the devil, and receive the repentance of the third, and forgive them and us our transgressions.

And we offer to you also for a mild climate and an abundant harvest, that we may partake of the good things from you without lack, and unceasingly praise you, who give food to all flesh.

And we entreat you also for those who are absent for good cause, that you would preserve us all in piety, and gather us without change, without blame, without reproach in the kingdom of your Christ, the God of all sentient and rational nature, our King.

DOXOLOGY

For through him is due to you all glory, worship,

and thanksgiving, and through you and after you to him in the Holy Spirit honor and adoration, now and always and to the ages of ages, unfailing and unending.

And all the people say: Amen.

INCLINATION (Litany and Prayer of blessing)

ELEVATION

The bishop says to the people: The holy things for the holy people.

The people answer: One is holy, one is Lord, Jesus Christ, to the glory of God the Father, blessed to the ages. Amen.

Glory to God in the highest, and peace on earth, good will among men.

Hosanna to the Son of David: blessed is he who comes in the name of the Lord.

God is Lord and has appeared to us: hosanna in the highest.

COMMUNION

The bishop gives the offering, saying: The body of Christ.

And he who receives says: Amen.

The deacon takes the cup and gives it, saying: The blood of Christ, the cup of life.

And he who drinks says: Amen.

THANKSGIVING FOR COMMUNION

DISMISSAL (Prayer for protection)[15]

The *opening dialogue* is similar to the one preserved as early as the *Apostolic Tradition.* There is no verb used in the Greek, such as "Lift up your mind," although this has become common in the modern English translations ("Lift up your hearts">Latin: "*sursum corda.*"). The phrase, "Let us give thanks" is central to understanding how the subsequent prayer is functioning: it is, primarily, a prayer of thanksgiving (*eucharistia*).

What we have called the *preface* above varied slightly from East to West. In the East, where the liturgy of the eucharist was more or less reserved to Sunday celebrations, the text of the preface was fixed, and thus the assembly was pastorally instructed each week as to a complete history of creation and salvation. Different eastern churches had their own prefaces, but only two of these would become the most widely used throughout Eastern Orthodoxy: those of Basil and Chrysostom.

The situation was different in the West, where the eucharist was a daily celebration. Here the prefaces were shorter, but varied widely, each corresponding to the liturgical season, or day, or a particular commemoration in the sanctoral cycle. In both East and West, the preface was the textual link between the liturgy of the Word and the eucharist. This is why, in the East, the fixed preface hardly missed a detail of biblical history: it could then fit perfectly with any prior preaching or readings from Scripture. In the West, the multiplicity of prefaces, in spite of their brevity, also made the necessary logical connections to the eucharist and in similar ways, often through the use of an abbreviated salvation history.

It is noteworthy that even though the eucharistic prayer could achieve extensive length; and even though the prayer could contain recognizable forms of thanksgiving, narrative, intercession, commemoration, and praise; it still remains a *prayer,* if we can define prayer as speech addressed to God using the second-person pronouns (*you, your*). The eucharistic prayer (or anaphora) was not a second homily, although its content included proclamation. It was not teaching, although it was a concise lesson in salvation history. It was not a hymn, although it was most likely "sung" and there were congregational "responses." It was not a formal time of praying for those in need, although it contained intercessions and memorials. If anything can be said in general, it is that the eucharistic prayer was a table prayer that had cosmic, epic, and ontic significance and proportion.

The *sanctus*, imported with some alteration from Isaiah 6, was one of the few distinguishable vestiges of the Jewish tradition of prayer. It served, along with its literary segue that typically concluded the *preface*, to locate the action of the assembly's prayer and praise within the larger context of the heavenly worship that was always prior to and concurrent with its own.

The *anamnesis* (memorial) was not a simple remembrance of Christ's passion only, but rather of the whole activity of God, beginning with the Divine attributes; the work of God in creation; the economy of God in establishing a holy people; for the incarnation, ministry, betrayal, voluntary suffering, death, resurrection, and ascension of Christ (the latter being important to make the distinction between the Body and Blood of *Christ* in communion, the Body of *Jesus* who is seated at the right hand of the Father, and the *ecclesial* Body of *Christ* present in the gathered assembly).

The *institution narrative* often was located within the *anamnesis* in its appropriate place along with a variation on the words of Christ at the Last Supper. It is obvious that a direct and accurate rendering of the biblical text is not what is important in these prayers. Additions are often attested: e.g., "looking up to you," "he mixed the cup of wine and water," etc. The integrity of the tripartite action of "taking—blessing—distributing" is preserved, however, along with the words of Christ, "This is my body . . . blood."

In the *epiclesis*, the Holy Spirit is invoked (called upon>*kaleo+epi*) to make the transformation of the natural gifts of bread and wine into the eucharistic food, the Body and Blood of Christ. In the East, the epiclesis often included a request that the Holy Spirit come as well upon the *people* assembled. In the West, there was no epiclesis in the eucharistic prayer which, with the exception of the variable *preface*, remained the only eucharistic prayer of the Roman Catholic Church until the 1960s! In fact, there was very little mention at all of the Holy Spirit in the western rite; the emphasis being centered instead upon the work of God in Christ.

The *intercessions and commemorations* made it clear that the activity of the eucharistic assembly in offering the sacrifice of praise was not for the benefit solely of those gathered in that locality. At the eucharist, earthly time met heavenly eternity, where saints, patriarchs, martyrs, confessors, prophets, apostles were anything but "dead." Here they all were, present in their remembrance and commemoration, having their own place around the Table as if it were the heavenly altar described in the book of Revelation. Special mention is given to Mary, whose title of *theotokos* (literally, "the one who gave birth to God") was formally upheld at the ecumenical council of Chalcedon (451). Even the interior artwork of the church-es depicted this gathered assembly of the departed faithful whose own victory over death was accomplished by the work of Christ.

As the eucharistic liturgy collapsed time, it also collapsed space. Here, intercessions for the absent, the infirm, the imprisoned, the travelers, and the Church throughout the world were collected together in the Great Thanksgiving (another name for the eucharis-tic prayer). The unity of the Church in the liturgy of the eucharist would have been made evident in even more tangible ways in Rome during this era. In a rite known as the *fermentum,* the pope would, by way of acolytes for couriers, distribute fragments of the eucharistic bread from his own liturgy to those of his presbyters who, fulfilling their pastoral duties in other churches throughout the city, were unable to celebrate the eucharist with him. The frag-ments would be used in the weekly liturgies at these "title" church-es. Another rite, performed when the pope himself could not be present, provided that a piece of eucharistic bread consecrated by the pope on a solemnity was placed in the chalice by the priest cel-ebrating in his absence. This rite, called the *immixtio,* still is per-formed in the Roman rite today.

Doxology: At the conclusion of the anaphora, the entire prayer is concluded with praise to God through Christ in the Holy Spirit, to which the assembly adds a crucial *Amen.* It is this congregational response that is a collective assent to the previous prayer, prayed on their behalf by their eucharistic president. The congregational response of *Amen* is by no means a trivial thing. It validates their liturgical function as a legitimate order within the Church that is participating with the clergy in the divine mysteries.

It is from this basic schema that the eucharistic liturgies of both East and West developed. History, however, had profound and lasting effects on the liturgical developments after the fall of Rome and the collapse of the Byzantine Empire, and thus East and West continued along different paths. These developments will be described in greater detail in chapters 5 and 6.

Other Sacraments

Penance

As was mentioned above, the penitential system had a direct effect on who was being baptized, and, subsequently, who was able to receive communion. From the earliest records we can ascertain that for grave sins (i.e., those sins that would have been a public scandal), the protocol was the "one strike" rule. Offenders needed to ask the church for admittance to the penitential system as proof of their remorse and willingness to amend their lives. But the process of amendment was, by modern standards, unbelievably severe. In most cases, penance required abstaining from meat, from public trading in the market, from marital relationship—not just during the time of penance, but until death!—from remarriage in the case of the death of a spouse, and from any other type of worldly gain. In short, the remainder of one's life, even after being readmitted to the communicating fellowship, was to be lived in asceticism; but without the honor of having done this of one's own volition as did the monks! In fact, it was the monks who were most kindly disposed to helping nurture the *penitentes* and it was the monks, particularly those of Ireland, who eventually are credited with reforming the Byzantine penitential system.

In the earliest centuries, the person having committed the scandal came forward asking penance of the bishop who then imposed the penance, marked the penitent with ashes, and gave the individual garb of sackcloth or a shirt of goat's hair. During the duration of the penance, penitents could be "hearers" at the liturgy; i.e., they could stay for the liturgy of the Word but would be summarily dismissed as a group along with the catechumens and demon-possessed who could not yet offer the eucharistic prayer. The Faithful were expected to nurture the penitents who were still considered as part of the Church (and who, indeed, were hearing the Word alongside them), and were to pray on their behalf until their full reconciliation with the assembly. Thus, the penitential process was equally helpful for dissuading the individual Faithful from passing individual judgment. If, after a specified period of penance, the offenders were to be readmitted to communion during the following season of Lent, then this would take place on Holy Thursday. The forgiveness of sins by God was never disputed in all these proceedings. The matter of reconciliation was an ecclesial one and a sacramental one.

It is understandable that such public penance dissuaded both early baptism, since penance was granted only once, and with voluntary admission of guilt. Certainly the postponement of baptism was the easier and more socially acceptable of the two options, and thus the *de facto* separation of the congregation into various groups. By the eighth century, the penitential system had shifted to private penance, and all the faithful participated in the penitential rite of the imposition of ashes at the beginning of the Lenten season: Ash Wednesday.

Matrimony

Even up until the Middle Ages, marriage was under the primary jurisdiction of the households involved and was not performed in the churches. Still, from the fourth century and onward, the involvement of the local clergy in the pronouncing of a blessing on the nuptials was common. Gregory of Nazianzus, writing on occasion regretfully informs of his absence at a significant wedding, and mentions a "crowning" ceremony that still exists in some eastern liturgies today in which the bride and groom are crowned with floral wreaths, and that this was the duty of the patriarch of the family. Gregory mentions that the couple has his blessing *in absentia*, and that blessings are not hindered by distance.

Conclusion

The Church of the Byzantine Empire enjoyed a reasonable amount of time for the early seeds of worship to sprout and flower. There were few novel forms, if any. Most changes were embellishments and enhancements of the traditions that had been established in the previous era. The Jerusalem church, with its holy sites, its stational liturgy, its monastic presence, and its highly symbolic rituals— especially its rites of initiation—greatly influenced the churches throughout the empire who eagerly adopted and adapted these models to fit the local culture. The worship was heavily focused on preaching and teaching due to the large influx of converts who could now freely join in the liturgy of the Word. But the number of baptisms proportionally diminished and, hence, the number of committed worshipers able to participate in the eucharistic liturgy was reserved to the more mature and spiritually committed believers. The eucharistic rite was guarded by closed doors and general secrecy, befitting a truly awesome mystery of which one is not permitted to speak. In a complementary way, church art and architecture and the magnificent ceremonial of the imperial court told volumes about the majesty of God, the victory of Christ, and the holiness and mystery of the Spirit. The ecumenical councils left their imprint on the creeds and the other liturgical acclamations, and a gradual tendency toward a more stabilized worship—without a regulation of uniformity—was beginning to be felt. The remnant of pagan culture, and the increasing secularization of the Church that at first had fueled the monastic movement toward desert asceticism, rebounded with the return of the monks to the city centers. The highly influential monks brought with them their practice of employing the entire Psalter in worship, and the practice became incorporated with small but effective doses into the urban liturgies.

Even as Christendom was nearing its apogee, the Barbarian armies to the North and East were planning their attack on Rome, which was now militarily weakened. A few centuries later, Islam would reduce the once-Herculean Byzantine Empire to the status of small ghettoes in a few important metropolitan centers. It is during this period that churches in the East and West will continue to drift apart and, by the eleventh century, will ultimately make an effective break from each other. Worship in the West will follow a different course than in the East, and so two briefer chapters will follow, each devoted to the worship of one of these two separated siblings.

For Further Reading

Primary Documents

The Apostolic Constitutions: Deiss, Lucien. *Springtime of the Liturgy: Liturgical Texts of the First Four Centuries*, pp. 215-240. Trans. by Matthew J. O'Connell. Collegeville, MN: The Liturgical Press, 1979.

Cyril of Jerusalem: Catecheses: Deiss, Lucien. *Springtime of the Liturgy: Liturgical Texts of the First Four Centuries*, pp. 269-289. Trans. by Matthew J. O'Connell. Collegeville. MN: The Liturgical Press, 1979.

Historical Development of the Liturgy

Bradshaw, Paul F. *The Search for the Origins of Christian Worship: Sources and Methods for the Study of Early Liturgy.* New York: Oxford University Press, 1992.

Cabié, Robert. "Christian Initiation, Article II: The Organization of the Ritual of Initiation until the Spread of Infant Baptism (Mid-second to Sixth Century)." In *The Church at Prayer: An Introduction to the Liturgy.* Vol. 3, The Sacraments, pp. 17-63. Ed. by Aimé Georges Martimort. Trans. by Matthew J. O'Connell. One-volume ed. Collegeville, MN: The Liturgical Press, 1992.

_____. "From House to Basilica." In *The Church at Prayer: An Introduction to the Liturgy.* Vol. 2, The Eucharist, pp. 36-107. Ed. by Aimé Georges Martimort. Trans. by Matthew J. O'Connell. One-volume ed. Collegeville, MN: The Liturgical Press, 1992.

Finn, Thomas M. *From Death to Rebirth: Ritual and Conversion in Antiquity.* Mahwah, NJ: Paulist Press, 1997.

Jasper, R.C.D., and G.J. Cuming. *Prayers of the Eucharist: Early and Reformed.* 3rd ed. Collegeville, MN: The Liturgical Press, 1990.

Johnson, Maxwell E. *The Rites of Christian Initiation: Their Evolution and Interpretation.* Collegeville, MN: The Liturgical Press, 1999.

Jones, Cheslyn, et al. *The Study of Liturgy.* Rev. ed. New York: Oxford, 1992.

Metzger, Marcel. *History of the Liturgy: The Major Stages.* Trans. by Madeleine Beaumont. Collegeville, MN: The Liturgical Press, 1997.

Wegman, Herman. *Christian Worship in East and West: A Study Guide to Liturgical History.* Trans. by Gordon W. Lathrop, 1985. Collegeville, MN: The Liturgical Press, 1990.

⊰ —— ⊱

[1] The great challenge to western Christians who have studied World History from the European perspective is to remain aware that there exist other histories that do not begin and end with "us." At the same time, our objective here is to provide an introduction to the origin and development of those forms of worship that are somewhat more recognizable in the Christian world today.

[2] Most of the sources mentioned here are available at the website: http://www.newadvent.org/fathers/ (accessed July 3, 2005).

[3] A few words about music are in order. The largest selection of early musical documents come to us rather late; in the eleventh century. It is generally safe to assume that sung music was perhaps closer to vocal chant, or "sung speech," or what may still be part of the tradition of singing in the Middle East, or that style of singing that can be heard in the oldest Byzantine chants of the

eastern churches today. It was certainly text-oriented with an inner rhythm that would have been nothing akin to western metrical music. Only if we understand singing from this perspective can we account for the large number of sung texts that would have been incorporated into the typical worship service. If Orthodox churches have faithfully preserved the tradition, there was no instrumental music in Byzantine churches. The tradition of unaccompanied singing continues in the Eastern Orthodox churches today, although it is not uncommon (at least in the United States) to see a small organ hidden in the choir loft of an Orthodox church to keep the singers in tune!

[4]Our word "Lent" comes from the *lengthening* daylight hours from Winter to Spring. Historically, this period of time was known as *The Great Fast.*

[5]Collects survive in modern *sacramentaries*—i.e., books that preserve the prayer texts for specific celebrations—and in the Book of Common Prayer used in the worship celebrations of the Anglican and Episcopal churches. The collects are a rich source to understand the theology of a particular celebration, day, or season of the church. This demonstrates the modern understanding that liturgy is a primary source of theology: it is theology prayed and experienced directly, not "studied" *per se.* In other words, liturgy instructs the believer. Roman collects and prayers, written in a consistent structure in Latin, are characterized by their brevity, balance, and theological play on words. The traditional collects in the *Book of Common Prayer* are noted for their poetic style.

[6]If 14 Nisan was on March 25, as some sources record it, then the incarnation of Christ (never separated theologically and liturgically from Easter) would have been celebrated "9 months" later on December 25. January 6 would have been the case if 14 Nisan would have occurred on April 6.

[7]"Montanism," in *The Oxford Dictionary of the Christian Church,* ed. by F.L. Cross; 3rd edition ed. by E.A. Livingstone (New York: Oxford University Press, 1997) 1107-1108.

[8]Deiss, *Springtime,* 127-128.

[9]Jones, et al., *Study of Liturgy,* 360.

[10]It should be noted that in Roman Catholicism, and in Protestant churches that distinguish between bishop, presbyter, and deacon, the modern presbyter/priest regularly does preside over the eucharist as well as preaches. This is a difficult phenomenon that is not easily explained in historical perspective. One reason proffered is usually that the size of the modern diocese is too large for a bishop to preside over the eucharist of every assembly. Another is that, given the size of the modern Church, the idea of one-bishop-per-assembly would be nothing other than a logistical nightmare, institutionally speaking, when it comes to convening councils. In the Roman Catholic Church, the preaching responsibility is often shared these days among religious (monks and

nuns) who have this ability. Still there are monks who are also ordained as priests and these, given the present shortage of priests, are often required to celebrate the eucharist as well.

[11]Namely, the case of the *lapsi*—those Christians who were persecuted for the faith and renounced Christianity under pain of torture or death. Rigorists refused to admit these to communion since the sin of denial of one's Lord could only be absolved by a lifetime of remorse as one of the *penitentes*.

[12]In Metzger, *History of the Liturgy*, 93.

[13]Such bathing practices offend our modern perceptions, but how might one reckon what attire might be appropriate for baptism by immersion today? Most evangelical churches clothe the candidate with a robe (commonly white), but such clothing had a symbolically important place *after* the water bath (see the main text which follows). When a person is immersed in street clothes, a new problem presents itself that is unique to the last few decades: How is one to symbolically process baptismal "transformation" when the now thoroughly wet candidate is still a human advertisement for the currently popular athletic gear, or is sporting the logo/status symbol of some clothing manufacturer, or is wearing clothing with a slogan lettered on it? No matter how benign all of the above might be, or how trivial such "minutiae" might seem to the worship leadership of contemporary churches, the argument for symbolic detail is much stronger in the period of the Church Fathers and Mothers and preaches better, nakedness notwithstanding!

[14]As catechumens or *electi*, the neophytes would not have exchanged the kiss of peace with any of the faithful or clergy "since their kiss was not yet pure." Now, it is with the bishop that they first exchange this greeting. It is not a difficult leap, liturgically speaking, to see their equal standing with the bishop in this initial exchange of the kiss. However, once assembled with the rest of the congregation, they will only continue to exchange the kiss of peace with the other Faithful; men with the men, and women with the women. This is a clear distinction that all Christians, as baptized members of the Body of Christ, are a type of priesthood; however, within the worshiping assembly, different gifts and roles obtain.

[15]Jasper and Cuming, *Prayers of the Eucharist*, 104-112.

CHAPTER FIVE

Worship
in the
Eastern Churches

*T*o walk into a modern Eastern Ortho-
dox church on any Sunday morning for the celebration of the
Divine Liturgy is to take a step into another world, one in which
the distinctions between time and space, heaven and earth
appear to blur. This impression is the result of a complicated synthesis of art, architecture, liturgical vestments, music, and a liturgy that has changed little since the ninth century. Orthodox
Christian worship is the pinnacle of the traditional, historical
worship that sprang from the Jerusalem church of the fourth
century, stabilized in the eighth century, and crystallized in the
fourteenth. Yet it is far from being passé and outdated to those
who participate in it with the eyes of faith or with even a small
amount of prior historical knowledge. Those who worship God—
an eternal God made accessible through the eternal person of
God's Son, through the eternal working of God's Holy Spirit—
must admit the inadequacy and limitations of a simple chronological conception of time. For it is in the appropriation of all the
symbols, sounds, and smells of the Divine Liturgy that worshipers
experience God in transcendent and mystical ways, quite unlike
most western worship which is often chronologically conscious,
terse, and temporally frugal by comparison. Modern western
worshipers value brevity and lucidity in liturgical prayers and
congregational responses. In contrast, Eastern Orthodox worship
is florid, poetic, ambiguous, and not infrequently redundant.

Westerns tend to scrub worship practices that are not culturally relevant in a contemporary context. Orthodoxy not only preserves these archaisms, but continues to assign to them updated interpretations. Western decoration of the worship space, at least on this side of the Baroque period, tends to be streamlined and straightforward, punctuating only those things that practically demand attention: the altar, the font, the pulpit, a particular window, mosaic, etc. In the eastern churches, every inch of architectural space is occupied with art that situates the worshiper within the entirety of creation, both earthly and heavenly.

A first visit to an Orthodox Divine Liturgy immediately creates the sensation of walking into the middle of a dialogue between the earthly realm and the heavenly that began long before one stepped through the front door. There is, in fact, a simplistic explanation for this. If one arrives at ten in the morning because the marquee reads: "Divine Liturgy at 10:00" it will be difficult to know exactly when the "worship" began, since on Sundays, the Divine Liturgy is preceded by Orthros—Morning Prayer—which can last up to an additional hour. Even when the deacon begins the Great Litany, signaling the beginning of the Divine Liturgy proper, it is commonplace to see latecomers walk into the nave, seemingly disregarding the diaconal instructions and choral responses, and approach an icon on the periphery, light a candle, make the sign of the cross, and pray in that location for a short while. In fact, it is curious to see the congregation hardly respond in any visibly negative way to any of this clerical activity and congregational "commotion," all of which is happening simultaneously: the deacon leading the prayers, the choir continuously singing, the priests moving about the front of the church behind a half-wall, and other pious worshipers traipsing over to an icon with candle in hand. But all of this activity is, in fact, orderly to the Orthodox worshiper who is very much at home in the overflow of movement, symbols, and sounds. One reason for this is the commendable ability eastern Christians have inherited from one generation to another: to let the Spirit speak through the symbols. This exceptional theological and liturgical conditioning has been a part of the Orthodox Liturgy ever since the days of Cyril of Jerusalem (mid-fourth century). Perhaps this is why when one asks an Orthodox Christian to describe Orthodox worship the answer is always, "Come and see."

Context

In the previous chapter we saw the flourishing of Byzantine culture and liturgy that stood until approximately the year 610 under the reign of the emperor Heraclius. We consider now the period from 610 until the present. As it concerns the history of Byzantium as an empire in the East, we note that from the seventh century until the fall of Constantine XI at the hands of the Turks in 1453, the Byzantine Empire provided something of a protection to the church in the West but not without considerable losses in territory due to the spread of Islam. But the eastern churches, operating under a somewhat tolerant Islamic policy that permitted Christianity its coexistence, imported little if any from the surrounding culture of Islam— an entirely different trajectory from that of the Western Church of medieval Europe that borrowed heavily from the non-Christian religious traditions of its neighbors. Instead, the contentedness and maturity of the eastern churches provided the stability that enabled the various liturgical families to hold to their own distinctiveness in worship amidst a culture that was thoroughly non-Christian.

A brief overview of the eastern liturgical families will serve as an introduction to the modern Divine Liturgy: the renown order of worship that emanated from the Great Church, also called *Hagia Sophia* (Holy Wisdom), in Constantinople (Istanbul).[1] It was this liturgy of Hagia Sophia that served as a model for all Orthodox churches—even those few who would later entrust themselves to the papal leadership of the Roman Church! The liturgy of Hagia Sophia is now synonymous with Orthodoxy itself and has, in the majority of liturgical histories, eclipsed all the other eastern liturgical families. We think it important to mention these other liturgical families here since their presence, albeit a modest one in the United States, nevertheless continues to thrive in the native soil in which they first took root. We will proceed counterclockwise around the compass, beginning our tour in Alexandria, Egypt.

1. Alexandria (Egypt)

The Egyptian Church suffered a division in the fifth century due to major theological disagreements concerning the doctrine of Christ. The ecumenical council of Chalcedon in 451 established that orthodox teaching would defend two distinct natures in Christ. The so-called *monophysite* position, which emphasized the singular nature of Christ and was championed by the Egyptian Copts and the churches of Ethiopia, was rejected. The origins of two separate liturgical families can be traced to these early christological controversies of the fifth century. Those Egyptian churches that aligned themselves with the Orthodox position of Chalcedon also adopted the liturgy of Constantinople: the *Byzantine Rite*—the "official" rite of the Church of the Empire. The monophysite liturgy, on the other hand, developed into what is now known as the *Coptic* and *Ethiopic* rites. The former better preserves the old Alexandrian tradition although it later adopted liturgical elements from the West Syrian family (see below).

2. Antioch/Syria (West and East)

Onward, now, to the ancient city of Antioch in Syria. With Alexandria, Jerusalem, Byzantium (Constantinople), and Rome, Antioch was one of the five predominant ecclesiastical centers; a member of the original *pentarchy,* or five historical *patriarchates.* It, too, divided into two separate liturgical families because of the christological controversies surrounding the decision of Chalcedon, but it also divided—quite understandably—on geographical terms because Syria was a vast geographic region of the Byzantine Empire, stretching as far as the eastern borders of the former Persian Empire. In the literature, Antioch and Syria are often used interchangeably to describe the same liturgical family.

(1) *The West-Syrian Family:* The *Melkites,* i.e., followers of the emperor, accepted the Chalcedonian doctrine and adopted the liturgy of Byzantium (Constantinople). In this case, however, Antioch as a liturgical center itself had long influenced the worship of Constantinople, and thus the West-Antioch/West-Syrian rites and the Byzantine Rite had enjoyed something of a mutual influence for quite some time. We should remember that the liturgy of Jerusalem, for which development Cyril is largely credited, influenced much of the Christian liturgy throughout the whole Empire as early as the fifth century. A few centuries later, when Jerusalem fell to Islamic control, the Antiochene church absorbed and continued the Palestinian liturgical traditions of the Holy City. Furthermore, the preaching of John Chrysostom in Antioch left such an impression on the West-Antiochene liturgy that when this liturgy evolved into the *Byzantine Rite* (Constantinople), it would bear the popular title of "The Divine Liturgy of St. John Chrysostom."

Other rites associated with the West-Syrian family are important to note since these can still be found in churches across the world today. The *Jacobite* Church (the name comes from bishop Jacob Baradai), like the Coptic church in Egypt, took the monophysite position after 451 and broke with Constantinople after the council of Chalcedon. It is in the Jacobite Church that the old West-Syrian rite has been preserved. Later, in the seventeenth century, the Church in India (which, according to tradition, the Apostle Thomas established in a first-century missionary venture) officially adopted this Jacobite liturgy to some extent. Traces of it can be seen there in the *Malabar Rite.*

In Lebanon, a third rite developed that was deep-seated in the further christological controversies prior to 681 concerning whether Christ had two "wills" (that were in competition with each other as seen by his agony in the garden of Gethsemane) or only one will. The "one-will" faction (*monothelite*) developed its own liturgy, a sibling of the West-Antioch liturgical family. Known today as the *Maronite Rite,* it has become infused with latinisms—the result of a later merger with the Roman Catholic Church—but it still maintains a distinct connection to the Antiochene tradition.

(2) *The East-Syrian Family:* Ancient Persia and Mesopotamia, the hinterlands of the Byzantine Empire, is where some of the best examples of Jewish influence on the Christian liturgy can be found. Separated by a vast desert wilderness and free from the gravitational pull of Constantinople, it was here that were preserved some of the oldest layers of East Syrian worship; an especially rich field for the modern comparative study of liturgy. Considering the present military, political, economic, and media interests in Iraq and Iran, Americans would do well to remember that this region boasts an ancient Christian heritage that is still a vibrant presence in modern times. Having had Syriac for a primary language, Nestorian influence for theology, and having been completely engulfed by the Moslem world since the Arab conquests of the seventh and eighth centuries, the East-Syrians were considered unmatched rivals to the Greek language, orthodox doctrine, and imperial culture of Byzantium. As a result, much of the East-Syrian identity and liturgy has been eclipsed in the historical record by the liturgy of Constantinople whose survival is credited largely to its obstinacy in the face of overwhelming odds. Rites that scholars are still examining are the *Nestorian* (Georgia-Persia-Mesopotamia), the *Chaldeen,* and the aforementioned *Malabarese* which, like the Chaldeen rite, had been the subject of latinization over the years.

3. Cappadocia and Constantinople

Along with the liturgical family of Alexandria and Antioch, two more important stops remain on our compass route as sources for Orthodox liturgy: *Cappadocia* and *Constantinople*. Cappadocia (Asia, Pontus, and Thrace) is especially important since a triumvirate of pastor-theologians—Gregory of Nazianzus, Basil the Great, and Gregory of Nyssa—would directly influence the doctrine of the ecumenical Church and profoundly affect the worship of the church in Constantinople. We will treat the two liturgical families together in this section, since the original Cappadocian influences survive today only in the *Armenian Rite* which, in all of the Middle East, is best represented in the city of Jerusalem (in the Armenian Quarter).[2]

The liturgy of Constantinople, as the worship of the capital city of the Byzantine Empire, began to eclipse all the other liturgical families so that one can now speak of this liturgy as being the quintessential rite from which all the Orthodox Churches of the present day, whether Greek, Slavic, Romanian, Georgian, Italo-Greek, Bulgarian, Serbian, or Russian, derive their worship. It is this liturgy that is the topic of this chapter, although we should note a profound respect for all the believers represented by those other liturgical families who, remaining on the fringes of liturgical history, have tenaciously cultivated their worship of God in the face of doctrinal controversy, isolation, persecution, and tendencies toward compromise.

Following the position of Alexander Schmemann, one of the foremost Orthodox fathers of modern liturgical theology, Herman Wegman observes: "One can truly assert that what is today called the eastern liturgy is principally the Byzantine liturgy. In Alexandria, in Antioch, in eastern Europe, even in the Syrian, Coptic, and Armenian traditions, Byzantine influence is felt. There is a clear parallel with the influence of the Roman liturgy in the west. By the reception and assimilation of many traditions, the Byzantine tradition became the expression of eastern Christianity, 'the Byzantine synthesis' (Schmemann)."[3]

Sources

It has always been the missionary tradition of the eastern churches to translate the liturgy into the language of the people, the vernacular. However, local languages can and do change substantially over the course of centuries. In this respect Orthodoxy has not always been eager to subject itself to constant revision/translation of the liturgy within a particular ethnicity. For instance, the liturgical language of the Russian Orthodox Church is not modern Russian, but Old Church Slavonic. It is possible to attend a modern

Greek Orthodox church in the United States and hear an occasional liturgy in English, but the practice is not heartily supported among the church hierarchy. Furthermore, it is difficult for musicians to compose and rehearse an entirely new choral setting of a two-hour, translated liturgy with all due attention given to the musical and stylistic demands of the original. Unfortunately, the ethnic divisions of the Orthodox churches have contributed greatly to the mutual suspicion that is characteristic among them. This demonstrates to a small degree that even though their liturgy is essentially the same, achieving practical unity has never been easy among the ethnically divided Orthodox.

If one wishes to go to a liturgical source in the Western Church, a knowledge of Latin will usually suffice. Not so as regards Orthodoxy. While Greek is by far the most common original language, one must often consider those sources originally written in Syriac, Coptic, Bahairitic, Ethiopic, Arabic, and Slavonic, to name a few. Fortunately, many of these have been translated into English and have been the focus of recent study, especially by Catholics and Protestants.

The texts of many eucharistic prayers (*anaphorae*) have survived: the *Anaphora of the apostles Addai and Mari*, the *Anaphora of the apostle Peter*, the *Anaphora of Theodore of Mopsuestia*, the *Anaphora of Nestorius*, the *Anaphora of the Twelve Apostles*, the *Anaphora of St. John Chrysostom*, the *Anaphora of St. Basil*, the *Anaphora of St. James of Jerusalem*, the *Anaphora of Gregory of Nazianzus*, the *Anaphora of the papyrus Dêr-Balyzeh*, and the *Anaphora of Serapion*. The oldest extant manuscript of the Byzantine Liturgy is the *Barberini Euchologion* that reflects the shape of the rite as it existed shortly before the eighth century. Unlike the Western Church of the High Middle Ages, there is no single book like a sacramentary or a missal to consult to see how a worship service fit together. Various books existed for use by particular ministers. What the Barberini manuscript lacks in detail must then be supplied by books like the *Typicon* (the order for the eucharist and for the liturgy of the hours); the *Apostolos, Evangelion, Triodion, Pentecostarion, and Menaia*—all lectionaries; the Psalter; and the *Octoechos*—a hymnbook. An especially fruitful (and often complicated) category of resources is the historical commentaries on the Divine Liturgy. Names with whom the student of eastern liturgy should be familiar are: Theodore of Mopsuestia, Maximus the Confessor, St. Germanos, Nicholas of Andida, Nicholas Cabasilas, and Symeon of Thessalonike. Each commentary contributes to the larger picture—showing how the particular elements of Byzantine worship have been variously interpreted throughout the centuries. The above represent the major names in the "Who's Who" among the historical source material (see "For Further Reading" for modern references and commentaries). English translations of the commentaries are especially accessible to the curious nonspecialist and often make for the most interesting reading.

Space and Setting

Originally a hall for the civil government, the architecture of the basilica had been conquered in the fourth century by Christendom and its Cross. The result was a cruciform division of the square or rectangular interior space. Even up to the present, the basilica has continued to be the identifying architectural style that has long characterized Orthodox churches. In fact, it is difficult now to imagine that Orthodox theology might ever find a more fitting environment for its worship than the basilica. For over seventeen centuries the building and the worship emanating from within it influenced each other in such profound ways that it is almost impossible to speak of one without the other.

The raised sanctuary against the eastern wall, under the half-dome of the apse, continues to enshrine the altar in most basilicas, past and present. If the floor plan is viewed from a bird's-eye perspective, the altar is located precisely at the top of the cross. In the churches of the Byzantine period this sanctuary was opened to the view of the worshipers in the nave (the central gathering space where the laity assembled). Although the sanctuary itself was reserved to the clergy alone, early sources mention that even in the largest churches it was only a low railing—a few feet at the most—that separated the sanctuary from the nave.

By the fourteenth century, however, this low railing had developed into a much taller screen called the *iconostasis* that virtually blocked the sanctuary from the view of the laity. On the iconostasis were magnificent images of Christ, of the *Theotokos* (Mother of God, Virgin Mary), of John the Baptist, the archangel Gabriel, in addition to other significant persons or feasts of the Church, all hierarchically arranged. In the center of the iconostasis was a small gap that in some churches was spanned by a curtain. In other churches it could be closed by doors (called *Royal Doors*). Thus, the vision of the liturgical activity of the clergy around the altar in the sanctuary (which, at certain points in the liturgy, symbolized heaven) could be opened at times to the view of the laity and hidden from them at others. Over the course of history we see in this sanctuary-space an evolution from its *humble, functional,* and *presidential* location at the altar-table of the primitive house-church; to a *raised* area that was visually and acoustically *necessary* in the larger buildings; to a *consecrated* space that symbolized the specialized role of the clergy in the Byzantine Empire; now to a *mysterious* and *heavenly* space that was hidden to all but a few who were assigned to handle the sacred *mysteries* (i.e., the eucharist). The sanctuary had now achieved the theological equivalence of the Holy of Holies in the Hebrew Bible, but with the important New Testament distinction that it was Christ, the High Priest, that had both entered into it and emerged from it in the procession of the Gospel Book and in the sacramental actions surrounding the eucharistic rite.

To the left of the altar in the northern corner of the basilica can still be found the *prothesis* of the ninth century. It was here, in the prothesis, where the bread that would later be consecrated for the eucharist was received by the deacons and prepared for the communion rite before the eucharistic liturgy. In most modern

church buildings the prothesis is a separate room, but in plainer settings it might also be as simple as a specified area within the sanctuary that can accommodate at least a table for preparing the bread
and vessels that will be used during the eucharist. In the oldest surviving structures as well as in modern Orthodox churches, the
prothesis was accessible from both the sanctuary to its right and
from the nave by way of doors within the iconostasis (icon screen).
In the southern corner of the basilica, to the right of the altar, a second room served as a space where the clergy could vest.

In the Byzantine period, the prothesis (called the *skeuophylakion*) was often a structural appendage to the *exterior* of the
basilica. It was here that the deacons received the offerings of
bread (called *prosphora*) from the laity who brought them from
their homes. There was then a subsequent procession of the prepared prosphora into the church. This procession, which at one time
was a practical necessity, remained a part of the liturgy even after
the exterior *skeuophylakion* had been relocated to an interior anteroom next to the sanctuary. To demonstrate how some liturgical
components refuse to go away: even though the starting place for
the procession had changed to within only a few yards of the altar
(at which location a deacon could have, using very few steps, easily transferred the bread) the earlier procession of the bread into the
church building remained intact. In fact, an entire catena of clergy
in procession now carried the prosphora from the prothesis (in a
direction now opposite of the sanctuary!), paraded it throughout a
goodly portion of the nave, and finally entered the sanctuary again
through the Royal Doors of the iconostasis. The whole procession
was accompanied by candles and incense, the laity bowing before
the symbols and making the sign of the cross.

It was not difficult for medieval commentators on the liturgy to
see represented in all of this and other liturgical movement within
the worship space an illustration of the life of Christ. The prothesis
now became associated with, among other things, Bethlehem—the
House of Bread. The image of Christ's incarnation was made com-

plete by the procession of the Gospel book into the nave of the church (the *Little Entrance* as it is now called)—the true Light having come into the world. The second procession, that of the prosphora-bread from the prothesis, through the nave, and into the sanctuary was consequently called the *Great Entrance* and represented Christ in his triumphal entry through the Royal Doors into the heavenly Jerusalem. The rest of the eucharistic ceremony would complete the analogy: Christ's sacrificial death, burial, and resurrection would take place within the sanctuary (the "holy of holies"). The communion rite in the nave would then appropriate all of these mysteries to the faithful communicants still here on earth.

The nave was still free of fixed seating for the assembled laity who then were able to stand, kneel, bow, or move about somewhat at will. The absence of pews still holds true in many traditional Orthodox churches today, especially in the Russian Orthodox churches, and contributes to what contemporary Westerners often find intriguing about Orthodox worship: that the pious laity will respond rather impulsively with a spontaneous act of devotion at various points during the liturgy. They may make the sign of the cross at multiple points during worship—whenever they feel the desire to do so—but especially whenever they hear the trinitarian formulae which conclude the many prayers of the priest. They may also move from the place where they are standing and go over to an icon somewhere else in the nave and pray in that location, or may light a candle in front of an icon as a visual and symbolic accompaniment to their prayers. All of this happens with no order apparent to the Western mind, and yet it is fully appropriate worship behavior to the pious Orthodox. One must bear in mind that with a great part of the Divine Liturgy being prayed by the priests behind the closed doors of the iconostasis, the laity often have no choice but to interiorize the liturgy for which they have been assembled.[4] Hence, great significance became attached to the interior decorations of the nave, of the iconostasis, of the semidome of the apse, and of the large central dome of the nave.

Truly, worship for the Orthodox is a multisensory, experiential way of encountering the Divine. While in many western churches incense is optional or reserved for special occasions, this is not the case in Orthodox churches. Throughout the course of each liturgy the sanctuary and altar are incensed, as is the Book of the Gospels, the priests themselves, the laity, the gifts of bread and wine, the icons of Christ and the Theotokos—in short, everything animate and inanimate that prays or gives praise to God does so in an odiferous way. It is a picture of the heavenly worship described in the book of Revelation.

Furthermore, the entire Divine Liturgy, with the exception of the homily and the congregation's recitation of the creed, is musical. Older Byzantine forms of chant still survive in the modern celebration of the eastern liturgy, although newer choral settings often overlay the ancient melodic structures with a harmonic quality that even Westerners can appreciate. Of course, to participate fully in the singing of the liturgy, whether in the 12th century or in the 21st, an individual had no recourse but to join the choir and attend rehearsals. Apart from this, worshipers may still participate as lay persons in the nave of the church but do so in a more contemplative mode, allowing the sights, sounds, and smells to transport them mystically into the heavenly realm. This realm is made present visually by iconography, and intelligibly by the sensible order in which this iconography is arranged within the church building.

Two-dimensional art (and *only* two-dimensional art), attested since the early days of the house-churches and still extant on some sarcophagi, has been ever-present in the decorations of the Eastern Churches despite the ravages of the iconoclasts in the eighth and ninth centuries who all but obliterated the earliest images.[5] Ever since the victory of the icons at the Ecumenical Council of Nicea in 787, the specific arrangement of iconography within the basilica has become something of a permanent situation. The result is an amalgam of art and architecture that is liturgically and theologically interconnected:

Worshipers passing through the outer vestibule (narthex) look up to the large central dome to see a picture or mosaic of Christ Pantokrator (the Almighty). On small pillars supporting the dome are prophets and apostles. On the four vaults extending downward to the central pillars are representations of the four evangelists along with cherubim and seraphim. On lower strata, and closer to the gathered laity, are depictions of scenes from the life of Christ, feasts of the Church, monks, martyrs, ascetics, bishops, and teachers, who have all joined together in this holy space and are mystically present for the Divine Liturgy. Over the icon screen, just above the Royal Doors, is a reproduction of the Last Supper under which are ranks of apostles turned toward Christ in prayer. John the Baptist and the Theotokos are on either side of Christ since they are, traditionally, the chief intercessors for humanity. On the walls within the apse and surrounding the altar are representations of bishops vested for the liturgy and a depiction of Christ serving communion to the apostles from an altar. Over all of this the Theotokos looks outward toward the center of the nave, directing the attention of all worshipers to the Child she holds, a child that has the proportions of a fully grown man—an artistic convention describing the paradox of Christ's fully divine and fully human natures. As Orthodox historian Hugh Wybrew notes:

> Far more than a utilitarian shelter for the congregation, it is an image of heaven on earth. For while the lower portion of the nave signifies the visible world, the dome, and still more the sanctuary, are images of heaven, where the triune God is worshiped by angels and archangels and the whole company of heaven. There Christ offers himself to the Father in an eternal sacrifice of love and self-giving: and into that sacrifice the worshiper is drawn by participating in the Liturgy which celebrates in spiritual reality what the church building proclaims in sacramental image.[6]

Time

1. Daily Prayer

In chapter four we learned that the daily practice of praying in community at regular intervals—six or seven times in a 24-hour period—began as a monastic innovation to the worship life of the Jerusalem church of the Byzantine period. The *horologion* (prayer book) of the ninth century confirms that by that time the daily office in the east had already been fixed in Palestine to include these *Little Hours*, but even as late as the tenth century the practice had not yet been taken up in Constantinople. There, the *Cathedral Office*, which focused only on morning and evening prayer (and sometimes prayer at night) was much stronger. It is the cathedral office that has remained the more prevalent today among nonmonastic communities, and so our study here will focus on morning prayer (*orthros*) and evening prayer (*hesperinos* or *vespers*). It is uncommon among nonmonastic Orthodox communities (i.e., common parish churches) in the United States to gather daily for orthros and vespers. Nevertheless, it is quite common for both times of prayer to be celebrated in churches on a *weekly* basis and whenever any of the numerous feasts are celebrated. Orthros is always celebrated on Sunday mornings immediately prior to the Divine Liturgy, the principal worship service of the Word and Eucharist, with vespers celebrated on Saturday evenings. As we are about to see, there will be a heavy emphasis on Psalmody in both prayer services, not a small vestige from the earlier monastic influences.

Morning Prayer: Orthros is a combined tradition of both "prayer at night" and the traditional morning prayer that was performed at sunrise. The present structure of Orthros is so complex that if a non-Orthodox Christian attended even a vernacular version of it, most of the inner logic of bygone centuries would be lost. A brief description of it will need at least six artificial divisions:

(1) Orthros begins with an introductory acclamation followed by a set of six invariable Psalms, the *hexapsalmos:* 3, 38, 63, 88, 103, and 143. The deacon then leads the *Great Litany,* a prayer sequence

based on Psalm 118:26, 27, 29. This is followed by the *troparion* of the day: an extended poetic response in a simple musical setting that thematically corresponds to the liturgical year.

(2) The variable psalmody follows. To the *psaltes* (trained singers) is usually assigned the responsibility of singing three appointed portions (*kathismata*) of the Psalter verse by verse. One kathisma may contain as many as eight Psalms! At the beginning and ending of each psalm, a brief troparion introduces the theme of the Psalm and sets the musical key for the chant. Three of these troparia for Sunday focus respectively on the refrain for Psalm 136 (called the *polyeleos* for the frequent repetition of the biblical phrase, "for his *steadfast love* endures forever"), on the myrrh-bearing women that came to the tomb of Christ (called the *troparion Myrophoroi gynaikes*), and on Psalm 119 (called the *eulogitarion*) which is a panegyric on the *Torah*. The content of these three troparia suggests that they may have been used at one time as entrance songs.

(3) After the lamps in the church have been lighted, one of eleven Gospel pericopes of the resurrection is read. Traditionally, when Orthros is preceded immediately by night prayer (as is typical for feast days), there would be something of an intermission at this point. Noneucharistic bread would have been distributed to the psalm-weary faithful, most likely to keep them from exhaustion—recall, traditional Orthodox worship requires standing for a very long time! At the same time, the Gospel book would have been presented to the faithful for veneration by a kiss. Psalm 51 with its troparia would have been sung while the faithful were venerating the Gospel book.

(4) Psalm 51 is followed by a lengthy prayer of supplication.

(5) What takes place at this point is a terribly confusing and lengthy singing of the *canon* or *the canon of the nine odes*. The nine odes, written and used in the monasteries before the tenth century, consist of biblical songs (canticles), each with their corresponding troparia (usually in groups of three: one to set the musical "key,"

another praising the cross and resurrection, and a third in honor of the Theotokos). It can be assumed that these odes replaced the singing of the respective pericopes from Scripture which would have been the more ancient practice. Besides the nine odes, each with three troparia, more psalmodic chanting abounds. Following the third ode, an additional variable set of psalms is chanted (similar to the *kathisma* above). After the sixth ode, the *kontakion* of the day is sung—a type of poetic song in verse form, usually didactic in quality, possibly with a congregational refrain easy enough for all to sing. At the conclusion of the ninth ode, a troparion corresponding to the day's resurrection pericope completes this section of orthros.

(6) Finally comes the most primitive stratum of morning prayer: the singing of Psalms 148, 149, and 150. This is followed by the singing of the *Doxa* (Gloria in Excelsis), more supplicatory prayers, a blessing, and a dismissal.

First-time visitors to an Orthodox Easter Vigil, which preserves much of this ancient structure, often have similar impressions upon experiencing the sheer volume of all these scriptural texts and the accompanying poetry and prayers. They are often surprised to find the whole of biblical salvation history from Exodus to Luke presented in the nine odes; something that few Protestant churches (even the so-called "Bible Believing" churches) are inclined to execute today. Furthermore, and in spite of the technicality that it is not a historical book, the book of Psalms wonderfully comes alive in this elaborate setting. Seen in this broader context, the specific feast day is refracted in a multitude of biblical ways. This is especially true when the feast occurs on a Sunday, since each Lord's Day is a festal celebration of the "Day of Resurrection."

On the other hand, a non-Orthodox enquirer may wonder, thanks to a solid training in a western culture biased toward streamlining and efficiency, "Why all the fuss?" We would like to remind the reader (who now may be exhausted after simply reading about Orthodox worship) that any written description is terribly inadequate to the experience itself. Orthros is no more "tedious" than a very generous dose of Scripture and Psalmody. A second look at orthros, seen now in the light of the Orthodox genius, may be a good way for westerners to remind themselves that sometimes salvation history defies a conversion into convenient "microwave" minutes. To the Orthodox, the worship of God need not be quick and painless!

Evening Prayer: Vespers (*hesperinos*) is a reflection of the Jewish observance of the true day's beginning at sundown. Thus, vespers on Saturday evening is actually considered the first prayer service of Sunday. The structure of the service is parallel to orthros, but with a dual focus on light and incense. In vespers, Christ—the Light that enlightens all nations—is praised as having eclipsed all celestial lights which now grow dim by comparison. The time of the liturgy at the setting of the sun is an unambiguous reference that Christ, the Lamb, reigns over a kingdom that needs neither sun nor moon for light. A secondary symbol in vespers is that of incense as representative of the prayers of the people of God. The order of worship is not as complex as orthros:

(1) An entrance psalm (104) is sung while the celebrant prays eight prayers in silence. These are called the lamp-lighting prayers even though the modern celebration does not call for a wholesale lighting of the church's lamps until (4) below. A litany follows the entrance psalm and prayers, taking as its form Psalms 68, 86, and/or 93, sung responsorially (verse by verse), and may be occasionally punctuated by a congregational refrain. Sources vary as to how many prayers follow after the litany: some mention only one, others mention three.

(2) One *kathisma* is the norm for vespers on Saturdays. Usually it is Psalms 1–8.

(3) Psalm 141, the archetypal evening/incense psalm then follows, along with two or three troparia. At least one of these troparia is in praise of God. Another is in honor of the Theotokos.

(4) All of the lights in the church are now lit. The *phos hilaron* (gracious light) is sung by the congregation or choir and, in its

singing, the "plot" of the evening worship service is revealed: The gracious light, the pure, ever-living brightness of the Father in heaven is, unequivocally, Jesus Christ, holy and blessed. The True Light is not the sun which presently is setting. It is not even the beauty of the vesper (evening) light of moon or stars which is beginning to shine. It is Christ only, who, as one of the holy Trinity, is worthy to be praised and glorified throughout the world. Along with this powerful imagery of the interior lamps being lit, the celebrant picks up the theme of Psalm 141 and begins to incense the entire church and all those gathered in it. Symbolically then, not only will the Church as the assembled members of Christ's Body receive enlightenment and enlighten their world, but their intercessory prayers on behalf of the world will also ascend to God as a sweet-smelling savor.

(5) A reading from the Old Testament, along with a responsorial Psalm (*prokeimenon*) historically occurred here. It is usually omitted in modern practice.

(6) The Litany of Fervent Supplication (the *ektene*), which will be seen later in the eucharistic liturgy (the Divine Liturgy), makes an appearance here. It is especially appropriate, considering the missional mandate for the assembly's gathering: to intercede for the world.

(7) The singing of the Song of Simeon (Luke 2:29-32) comes next with its poignant declaration: "Now you are letting your servant depart in peace, for these eyes of mine have seen your salvation that you have ordained for all the world to see: a *light* to enlighten the nations, and the glory of your people, Israel." At this point, one cannot help mentioning Rachmaninoff's choral setting of Vespers—a staple in the repertoire of Russian cathedral choirs—in which a lyric tenor sings the words of the Saint while the choir provides an accompaniment that is imitative of the rocking of a cradled baby. The musical setting begins fairly subdued until the word *light*, at which mention the chorus positively explodes in a chord that saturates the room before floating downward and out of earshot. It remains one of the best musical paintings of any liturgical text, and

it is little wonder that Rachmaninoff requested it be sung at his own funeral.

(8) As vespers is about to end, the Thrice-Holy Hymn (*trisagion*) is sung (text on page 182), followed by two troparia: one peculiar to the day, and the other in honor of the Theotokos. A blessing and dismissal, as expected, bring the service to its conclusion.

2. The Liturgical Year

The modern Byzantine calendar is organized into three cycles: The Paschal Cycle, the Octoechoes, and the Cycle of Fixed Feasts. In the Paschal cycle, Easter is fixed on a date according to the Julian Calendar and, therefore, it may or may not fall on the same date that it does in the west. Ten weeks of fasting (Lent) precede Easter, and eight weeks of joy follow it until Pentecost.

The Octoechoes is a cycle of offices for each day of the week, corresponding to the eight church tones used for chanting. This cycle begins on the second Sunday of Easter and renews every eight weeks until the next Lent.

The Cycle of Fixed Feasts begins on September 1—the traditional beginning of the civil calendar—and contains immovable dates for all the non-Paschal feasts of the Church. The themes of these feasts are either of Christ, of the Holy Family, or of the Apostles and other Saints. Here are a few to be noted:

> September 8: The Nativity of the Theotokos
>
> September 14: The Exaltation of the Cross
>
> November 21: The Presentation of the Theotokos
>
> December 25: The Nativity of the Lord
>
> January 6: The Theophany of the Lord
>
> February 2: The Meeting of the Lord
>
> March 25: The Annunciation of the Theotokos
>
> August 6: The Transfiguration of the Lord
>
> August 15: The Dormition of the Theotokos

Ministerial Orders and The Eucharist

The Divine Liturgy of St. John Chrysostom (Orthodox Eucharistic Liturgy)

The beauty of the Byzantine prayers and the profound theology with which they are saturated demand that the student secure a modern text of the Divine Liturgy to read firsthand what cannot be duplicated here. Space will only permit an overview of the liturgical framework and some brief insights as to each element's practical and theological function within the worship service. Most libraries have modern translations of the Byzantine Divine Liturgy, and one can purchase a personal-size edition from most booksellers quite inexpensively.

The Divine Liturgy of St. John Chrysostom is the one most commonly celebrated in Orthodox churches, even if other liturgies exist. At first this may have been the weekday liturgy in Constantinople, but it soon began to substitute for the longer and more elaborate liturgy of St. Basil that was used on Sundays. The liturgy of St. Basil continues to be used today on the five Sundays of Lent; at the vigil services of Easter, Christmas, and Epiphany; on Holy Thursday, and on Basil's own feast day (January 1). There are three other liturgies: of St. James, of St. Mark, and of St. Gregory Nazianzen. They are used now only on the feast days of the saint for whom the liturgy is named.

The following description is of the Liturgy of St. John Chrysostom as it is presently celebrated.[7] References to important historical developments will include an approximate century. The Divine Liturgy is rather complex compared to the worship of most other Christian liturgical traditions, so we will begin with a general outline.

   A. Introductory and Entrance Rites
      (1) Liturgy of Preparation (*Proskomidia*)—in Prothesis
      (2) The Great Litany (*Synapte*)
      (3) The 3 Antiphons
   B. Reading of Scripture and Supplications

(4) The Little Entrance (Procession of the Book of the
Gospels) with Trisagion Hymn

(5) The Epistle Reading

(6) The Gospel Reading preceded by Threefold Alleluia

(7) Homily

(8) Litany and Dismissal of the Catechumens

(9) Prayer of the Faithful

C. The Procession to the Altar

(10) The Great Entrance with Cherubic Hymn

(11) Litany of Fervent Supplication and Prayer of
Preparation (*Ektene* and *Proskomide*)

(12) Kiss of Peace

(13) Nicene-Constantinopolitan Creed

D. The Eucharistic Prayer and Communion

(14) Eucharistic Prayer (*Anaphora*)

(15) The Lord's Prayer

(16) Communion Invitation, Communion, Communion
Hymn

E. Concluding Rites

(17) Post Communion Hymn(s) and Prayer of
Thanksgiving

(18) Various liturgical additions (Homily, Memorial
Service for the departed, etc.)

(19) Dismissal Rites: Blessing, Distribution of Antidoron

(1) Prothesis (*Proskomidia*): Introductory/Preparatory Rites:
Originally a practical necessity, the collecting and preparing of the
bread (*prosphora*), it became a liturgical element of its own in the
ninth century. We recall that it was originally the role of the deacons to see to this preparation at the very beginning of the liturgy.
But according to the *Ecclesiastical History and Mystical Contem-
plation* of Germanos I, Patriarch of Constantinople (715–730), this
ritual of preparing the prosphora began to take on such a weighty
symbolic meaning that soon it required a priest to perform it with
the assistance of a deacon. The symbolism, which focused primari-

ly on the birth and passion of Christ, was reflected in the icono-graphic decor of the prothesis as well as in the prayers that accompanied every minute liturgical action. At the Table of the Prothesis, a priest takes a prosphora and cuts out a square from its center. This piece is called the Lamb (*amnos*) and will be consecrated later at the altar for the communion of the clergy and the people. To the accompaniment of the relevant crucifixion texts the priest pierces the side of the Lamb with a ceremonial "spear," arranging it, along with other pieces from additional prosphorae commemorating the living and the dead, on a ceremonial plate (*diskos*). The diskos is then covered with the *Star* (*asteriskos*)—a star-shaped metal frame high enough to cover the bread—while the priest recites: "And the star came to rest over the place where the child lay." Here we see juxtaposed both birth and passion narratives. The star is then covered with a veil and censed. The prepared prosphora remains in the prothesis awaiting the Great Entrance (10) later in the Divine Liturgy.

It is worth noting that an element in some prayers of this Liturgy of Preparation is curiously akin to the epiclesis of some early eucharistic prayers (recall that "epiclesis" is used to identify a prayer in which the Holy Spirit is called upon to sanctify/consecrate a person or thing). It was historically attested that this liturgy of preparation was a point of confusion for many of the faithful who often considered the bread that left the prothesis during the Great Entrance to have already been consecrated and thus worthy of veneration. In this way, the Orthodox church was several centuries ahead of the medieval Church of Rome in pious veneration of the bread used for the eucharist—even before it had been blessed at the altar!

(2) The Great Litany (*Synapte*): The celebrant directs the congregation to pray. A deacon calls out (chants) specific categories for prayer: for the peace of God, for salvation of souls, for peace throughout the world, for the welfare of all the churches of God, for the unity of the churches, for the specific local church and its congre-

gation, for the nation and its leaders, for the local people, for favorable weather, for travelers, for the sick and suffering, for captives and their salvation, and for deliverance from affliction, wrath, danger, and distress. The congregation prays silently after (or during) each of the deacon's intentions, and the choir responds with "*Kyrie eleison:* Lord, have mercy." The sequence of prayers in the litany concludes with a prayer by the bishop, to which all respond, *Amen.*

This element of the Divine Liturgy appears to have moved to its present location from its origins in seventh-century Constantinople as a preparatory ritual for the clergy and people when the liturgy used to begin with everyone assembled *outside* the church. At that time, the entire assembly would gather outside the Great Church for the litany and several antiphons (entrance Psalms). During the singing of the antiphons, the nearly 100 doorkeepers of the Great Church of Hagia Sophia would have been at their respective posts, helping the worshipers to pour through every available door into the nave of the church. The deacon, in procession with the clergy (and, perhaps, Byzantine courtiers), would have carried the Gospel book into the church and "enthroned" it upon the altar.

The Liturgy of the Preparation (*Proskomidia*) and its development in the ninth century is largely responsible for the change in the arrangement of all the introductory rites that resulted in the present order. We will see additional effects of this century on other elements of the Byzantine Rite.

(3) The Antiphons (Psalms): As mentioned above, the antiphons once served a functional and practical purpose: to get people into the church building in something of an orderly way. Since their original purpose was no longer applicable, these antiphons and other hymns (troparia) found their way into other places in the modern Divine Liturgy.

The antiphons we see now at this point of the Divine Liturgy originally served as musical accompaniments to the Scripture readings when, in the seventh century, there was still a reading from the Old Testament. While the Old Testament reading has been discontinued in the modern liturgy, its original antiphon still remains. In fact, it is only the congregational response verse that now substitutes for what would have been the entire Psalm with a congregational refrain. It is called the *prokeimenon*.

(4) The Little Entrance: While a troparion is sung (called the *apolytikion*), the priest carrying the holy Gospel Book comes in procession before the Royal Doors of the icon screen. He blesses the entrance, raises the Gospel Book and proclaims, "Wisdom. Let us be attentive." (In Greek: *Sophia! Orthri!*) In the church of Holy Wisdom—*Hagia Sophia*—in Constantinople this acclamation had a *double entendre*. Perhaps, too, the command to "Straighten up and listen" was no mere formality in such a large worship space! During the Little Entrance the Trisagion Hymn is sung:

> Holy God,
> Holy Mighty,
> Holy Immortal,
>> have mercy on us.
>> (*the above is repeated three times*)
> Glory to the Father and to the Son
>> and the Holy Spirit,
>> now and forever and to the ages of ages. Amen.
> Holy Immortal,
>> have mercy on us.[8]

The Little Entrance now reflects what originally might have been the entrance procession of the entire congregation (clergy and laity) into the Great Church in Constantinople, the trisagion hymn most likely being a congregational refrain to one of the earlier entrance psalms. In any event, the procession of the Gospel Book retains something of the ancient Byzantine practice of beginning the liturgy with the same ritual.

At this point, as elsewhere throughout the Divine Liturgy, several things are happening concurrently. In fact, it seems as if there are almost two liturgies being celebrated at once: one by the clergy in the sanctuary and the other by the laity in the nave. Only at certain points do both converge. For much of the time, the clergy are moving in and about the iconostasis and the sanctuary, the choir is singing, the laity are prayerfully observing, and the priest is uttering prayers in a low voice that only he (and God) can hear. There appears to be a well-ordered choreography that can explain almost all of this, with the exception of the inaudible prayers. Moderns who criticize the practice of inaudible priestly prayers are by no means the first to have done so; the emperor Justinian in 565 flatly prohibited it: "Moreover we order all bishops and priests to say the prayers . . . not inaudibly, but in a voice that can be heard by the faithful people, that the minds of those who listen may be excited to greater compunction."[9] But the East Syrian sentiment for ancient Hebrew hierarchical worship prevailed upon Constantinople, and the prayers of the priest have remained inaudible until only very recently due to the advent of microphones for the clergy and print-ed prayer books for everyone.

(5) The Epistle Reading is traditionally chanted rather than spoken. At the beginning of the readings, the deacon cries: "Let us be attentive!" One can be certain that there was nothing ceremoni-ous about this command, since Chrysostom often complained in his sermons about excessive noise and general commotion while he was trying to preach!

(6) The Gospel Reading is introduced by a liturgical greeting:

Priest: Peace be with all.

People: And with your spirit.

Priest: The reading is from the holy Gospel according to (*N.*). Let us be attentive.

People: Glory to you, O Lord, glory to you.

When the pericope has been read, the people once again sing, "Glory to you, O Lord, glory to you." This special praise of Christ sets this particular reading apart from all the others.

(7) A homily is prescribed in the modern worship books at this point, although modern pastoral practice is to move the homily to the very end of the liturgy, almost as an addendum (see 18 above).

The decline of preaching by the seventh century is obvious, since the Council in Trullo (692) found it necessary to enforce the standard that clergy prepare a sermon every day, and especially for Sundays. After the golden days of preaching by John Chrysostom himself (386–398), it appears that not a few preachers had forgotten Emperor Theodosius's dictum that it was a sacrilege for a priest either to preach inaccurately or not at all!

(8) The modern prayer book in the Greek Orthodox church no longer contains the Litany of the Catechumens and the Dismissal of the Catechumens, since there is no longer anything equivalent to an adult catechumenate. The Russian Orthodox Church in America, however, has printed it in their English translation of the Divine Liturgy.

(9) The Prayer of the Faithful that occurs in this position is not to be confused with the General Intercessions that one finds in western liturgical churches today. This is, again, one of those inaudible prayers spoken by the priest, and is more akin to western medieval prayers known as the "private preparation of the priest." The text is brief:

> Again, we bow before you and pray to you, O good and loving God. Hear our supplication: cleanse our souls and bodies from every defilement of flesh and spirit, and grant that we may stand before your holy altar without blame or condemnation. Grant also, O God, progress in life, faith, and spiritual discernment to the faithful who pray with us, so that they may always worship your Holy Mysteries without blame or condemnation, and become worthy of your heavenly kingdom. And grant that always guarded by Your power we may give glory to You, the Father and the Son and the Holy Spirit, now and forever and to the ages of ages. Amen.

(10) The Great Entrance: In our description of the basilica above we mentioned the procession of the prepared prosphora to the sanctuary, accompanied by incense and the singing of the Cherubic Hymn (*Cherubikon*). We should note that with the decline in lay communion, this procession became a high moment for those

who were especially pious. Efforts were made to get as close to the procession of the gifts as possible. Today, pietistic fervor has subsided, but the Great Entrance remains one of the great liturgical elements for interpretation. Theodore of Mopsuestia and Germanos compared it to Christ being led away to his Passion. Nicholas of Andida and Nicholas Cabasilas preferred the analogy of the triumphal entry of Christ on Palm Sunday; while Symeon of Thessalonike, like Maximus the Confessor before him, interpreted the Great Entrance as nothing less than the revelation of salvation mystery hidden in God and the final coming of Christ.[10]

Musical treatments of the Cherubikon throughout the centuries have been no less grandiose. Here is the text of the hymn:

> We who mystically represent (*ikonizontes*) the Cherubim
> sing the thrice holy hymn to the life-giving Trinity.
> Let us set aside all the cares of life
> that we may receive the King of all,
> invisibly escorted by the angelic hosts.
> Alleluia. Alleluia. Alleluia.[11]

(11) The Litany of Fervent Supplication follows in a form similar to that of the Great Litany, the deacon leading the various intentions. If there were any catechumens in earlier centuries, they would have already been dismissed and would not have participated in this litany. In this sense, it is this litany that most closely corresponds with the "General Intercessions" before the eucharistic prayer in the west.

The priest alone prays the Prayer of the Proskomide, another example in the category of private preparatory prayers for offering the anaphora:

> Lord, God Almighty, You alone are holy.
> You accept a sacrifice of praise from those
>   who call upon You with their whole heart.
> Receive also the prayer of us sinners
>   and let it reach Your holy altar.
> Enable us to bring before You gifts

and spiritual sacrifices for our sins
and for the transgressions of the people.
Make us worthy to find grace in your presence
so that our sacrifice may be pleasing to You
and that Your good and gracious Spirit
may abide with us, with the gifts here presented,
and with all Your people. . . .

(12) The priest says, "Let us love one another that with one mind we may confess:" *People:* "Father, Son, and Holy Spirit, Trinity one in essence and inseparable."

These words are, in fact, the theological explanation for the exchange of the kiss. A pure exchange of peace is only possible when, in a spirit of love, a community is one in essence and inseparable. After the peace has been symbolically exchanged, the deacon cries: "The Doors! The Doors! In wisdom, let us be attentive!" This instruction to guard the doors originally functioned to keep all noncommunicants from taking part in the remainder of the liturgy in those days when the eucharistic mystery was guarded by secrecy. Its present place has changed and no longer reflects that function. In fact, in the tenth century, some interpreters mistakenly believed *"tas thuras"* to refer to the Royal Doors of the iconostasis, whereas the original meaning was certainly for the doorkeepers to guard the exterior doors of the nave from uninitiated intruders. In either case, the ancient admonition has remained as a liturgical element even though its original purpose is no longer necessary. In modern practice, non-Orthodox are permitted to remain for the entire liturgy, and the archaic dismissal of the catechumens may often be omitted.

(13) The Creed is always spoken, never chanted. It is one of the few times when clergy and people perform the same liturgical action in unity. The practice among modern parishes is to say the Creed first in the original Greek, then again in the vernacular.

(14) The anaphora (eucharistic prayer) resembles the anaphorae of the church of the Byzantine empire (see chapter 4) with (a) an opening dialogue between celebrant and people; followed by

(b) a preface, which is always a fixed text in the eastern eucharistic prayers; (c) the singing of the "Holy, holy, holy . . ."; (d) an institution narrative; (e) an anamnesis ("remembering, therefore . . ."); (f) an epiclesis, the moment when the Holy Spirit effects the change of bread and wine to Body and Blood; (g) commemorations of the saints, the Theotokos, all the churches with their hierarchy, and those whose names are remembered by the assembled faithful.

There are a few points to be highlighted: An epiclesis of the Holy Spirit (f) has always been a part of eastern eucharistic prayers. This was not the case in the Roman Canon used by the western church until the latter decades of the twentieth century when additional eucharistic prayers were composed. Cyril of Jerusalem is the first witness to a developed epiclesis in the fourth century. The first ecumenical councils advanced a theology of the Holy Spirit as "Sanctifier" that the churches in the east implemented more precisely than the church of Rome. However, the epiclesis has not always been interpreted (even by the Church Fathers) to good results. For instance: Cyril maintained that the mysterious sacrifice of the eucharist was accomplished as soon as the epiclesis was spoken. With such a definitive assertion it was little wonder, then, that the act of eating and drinking in the communion rite came to be viewed as nonessential. Later interpreters of the liturgy would even appeal to the symbol of the showbread in Hebrew worship as something only to be eaten by those who were holy!

Here is an excerpt of the anaphora of St. John Chrysostom with the epiclesis in italics (toward the end):

Priest (*inaudibly*):

It is proper and right to sing to You, bless You, praise You,
thank You and worship You in all places of Your dominion;
for You are God ineffable, beyond comprehension, invisible,
beyond understanding, existing forever and always the
same;
You and Your only begotten Son and Your Holy Spirit.
You brought us into being out of nothing,

and when we fell, You raised us up again.

You did not cease doing everything until You led us to heaven
and granted us Your kingdom to come.

For all these things we thank You and Your only begotten
Son
and Your Holy Spirit;
for all things that we know and do not know,
for blessings seen and unseen that you have bestowed
upon us.

We also thank You for this liturgy
which You are pleased to accept from our hands,
even though You are surrounded by thousands of
Archangels
and tens of thousands of Angels, by the Cherubim and
Seraphim, six-winged, many-eyed, soaring with their
wings,
singing the victory hymn, proclaiming, crying out, and
saying:

People:

Holy, holy, holy, Lord Sabaoth,
heaven and earth are filled with Your glory.
Hosanna in the highest.
Blessed is He who comes in the name of the Lord.
Hosanna to God in the highest.

Priest (*inaudibly*):

Together with these blessed powers, merciful Master,
we also proclaim and say: You are holy and most holy,
You and Your only begotten Son and Your Holy Spirit.

You so loved Your world that You gave Your only begotten
Son
so that whoever believes in Him should not perish,
but have eternal life.

He came and fulfilled the divine plan for us.

On the night when He was betrayed,
>   or rather when He gave Himself up for the life of the
>>   world,
He took bread in His holy, pure, and blameless hands,
>   gave thanks, blessed, sanctified, broke,
>   and gave it to His holy disciples and apostles saying:

(*audibly*): Take, eat, this is my Body which is broken for you
>   for the forgiveness of sins.

(*inaudibly*): Likewise, after supper, He took the cup, saying:

(*audibly*): Drink of it all of you;
>   this is my Blood of the new Covenant which is shed for you
>   and for many for the forgiveness of sins.

People: Amen.

Priest (*inaudibly*):
Remembering, therefore, this command of the Savior,
>   and all that came to pass for our sake, the cross, the
>>   tomb,
>   the resurrection on the third day, the ascension into heav-
>>   en,
>   the enthronement at the right hand of the Father,
>   and the second, glorious coming . . .

(*audibly*): . . . we offer to You these gifts from Your own
>>   gifts
in all and for all.

People: We praise You, we bless You, we give thanks to You,
and we pray to You, Lord our God.

Priest (*inaudibly*):
Once again we offer to You this spiritual worship
>   without the shedding of blood,
and we ask, pray, and entreat You:
send down Your Holy Spirit upon us
>   *and upon these gifts here presented.*

And make this bread the precious Body of Your Christ.
Amen.
And that which is in this cup the precious Blood of Your
Christ. Amen.
Changing them by Your Holy Spirit. Amen. Amen. Amen.
So that they may be to those who partake of them for vigi-
lance of soul,
forgiveness of sins, communion of Your Holy Spirit,
fulfillment of the kingdom of heaven, confidence before
You,
and not in judgment or condemnation. . . .

(15) The Lord's Prayer, along with the communion rite (below)
is another moment when the liturgical activity of clergy and laity
converge into a unison.

(16) The following invitation by the priest sets the communion
rite apart:

Priest: The holy Gifts for the holy people of God.

People: One is Holy, one is Lord, Jesus Christ,
to the glory of God the Father. Amen.

Then follows the Communion Hymn, which may change
according to the feast day. The ordinary text is: "Praise the Lord
from the heavens; praise Him in the highest. Alleluia." The bread is
now broken, to the words of the priest,

The Lamb of God is broken and distributed; broken but not divided. He is forever eaten yet is never consumed, but He sanctifies
those who partake of Him.

A portion of the sanctified bread is placed in the cup as the priest
says, "The fullness of the Holy Spirit. Amen." At this point, a ritual
was added at the beginning of the seventh century called the *zeon*.
The priest blesses a vessel of warm water saying, "Blessed is the
fervor of Your saints, now and forever and to the ages of ages,
Amen." He pours the warm water into the chalice in the form of a
cross, saying, "The warmth of the Holy Spirit." This ritual—which

was not accepted ubiquitously in the east—was interpreted as the coming of the Holy Spirit that brought resurrection life to the crucified body of Christ (Cabasilas).

The priest then places the remaining pieces of consecrated bread into the chalice and, taking it to the Royal Doors, elevates it and says, "Approach with the fear of God, faith, and love." Communion, consecrated bread dipped into the consecrated wine in the chalice, is administered to the faithful by means of a spoon. The obvious illustration here is that of a father—in the person of the priest—spoon feeding his children the bread of heaven.

(17) Post Communion Hymn:

People:

We have seen the true light;
we have received the heavenly Spirit;
we have found the true faith,
worshiping the undivided Trinity,
for the Trinity has saved us. . . .

Let our mouths be filled with Your praise, Lord,
   that we may sing of Your glory.
You have made us worthy to partake of Your holy mysteries.
Keep us in Your holiness,
   that all the day long we may meditate upon Your righteousness.
Alleluia. Alleluia. Alleluia.

Prayer of Thanksgiving

Priest (*inaudibly*):

We thank You, loving Master, benefactor of our souls,
that on this day You have made us worthy once again
of Your heavenly and immortal Mysteries.
Direct our ways in the right path,
establish us firmly in Your fear,
guard our lives, and make our endeavors safe,

through the prayers and supplications
of the glorious Theotokos and ever virgin Mary and of all
Your saints.
(*audibly*):
For You are our sanctification and to You we give glory,
to the Father and the Son and the Holy Spirit,
now and forever and to the ages of ages. Amen.

(18) The homily, if there is one, often occurs here at this point in the modern celebration of the Divine Liturgy. There may also be a brief memorial service if it is an anniversary of the death of a departed parishioner. Frequently, there may be a procession to the cemetery where the departed has been interred for this brief service.

(19) The deacon gives the dismissal, and the priest pronounces a blessing on the assembly in full voice. The people return the blessing with the words, "Lord, grant long life to him who blesses and sanctifies us." Now comes a ritual which was added in the 11th century, perhaps as a means of disposing of extra prosphorae that were not used in the eucharistic liturgy, as well as a means of "breakingfast" for those who had observed the prescribed fast since the evening before communion. Additional pieces of blessed bread (but not that which was consecrated at the altar) are distributed to all the worshipers who come forward to receive it from the hand of the priest. The name for this bread, *antidoron*, means literally, "instead of the gift" which distinguishes it from communion proper. In many ways, the antidoron provides the way for every noncommunicating worshiper, even non-Orthodox visitors, to share in at least some kind of ritual meal.

The symbol of the antidoron is a confusing one. The Orthodox do not see the sharing of the eucharist with non-Orthodox as a means to future unity since, for them, the eucharist is a sign of *active* unity—the unity of those who confess the faith as it has been preserved by the Orthodox Church. And yet, the antidoron is a gesture of hospitality that provides all believers with a sense of fellowship, since community is best manifested when food is shared.

Initiation: Baptism

The baptismal rites in the Orthodox church have hardly changed at all since the ninth century. There are two orders which date back to as early as the eighth century as preserved in the Barberini *Euchologion* : (I) The order for the making of a catechumen, and (II) The order for baptism. The modern rite for making a catechumen follows this order:

(1) Hands are laid on the candidate in the Name of the Trinity

(2) Triple exsufflation (breathing) and triple signing of the cross on the forehead and breast with prayer.

(3) Three exorcisms, and a fourth accompanied by exsufflation upon the forehead, mouth, and breast of the catechumen.

(4) (*Apotaxis*) The catechumen turns to the west, arms upraised, and thrice renounces Satan, his angels, his worship, and his pomp. The renunciation is completed when the catechumen blows and spits in a symbolic act of severance.

(5) (Syntaxis) The candidate professes the faith by reciting the Nicene-Constantinopolitan Creed.

(6) A prayer for baptismal renewal and enlightenment concludes the rite.

The modern rite of baptism is basically this:

(1) The blessing of the baptismal water. This begins with a prayer-sequence (litany) led by the deacon, while the priest prays inaudibly a prayer similar to the anaphora in the eucharistic liturgy (see above). The prayer gives thanks for creation and redemption, invokes the Holy Spirit to descend upon the water (accompanied by a triple breathing upon the water in the form of a cross), requests that the regeneration may be truly fruitful, and concludes with a doxology.

(2) The blessing of the "oil of gladness." The water is signed three times with the oil.

(3) The anointing of the forehead, breast, and back of the candidate.

(4) Baptism proper: The candidate stands (or sits) upright in the

font and is then immersed three times, once for each person of the Trinity. If the candidate is an infant, the infant is triple-immersed. The formula used is: "The servant of God, *N.,* is baptized in the name of the Father, Amen; and of the Son, Amen; and of the Holy Spirit, Amen."

(5) Psalm 31 is read, and the neophyte is clothed with a white garment.

(6) The priest signs the neophyte with chrism (scented oil) that has been earlier consecrated by the bishop or patriarch. A prayer, petitioning the gifts and seal of the Holy Spirit is repeated as the celebrant signs the candidate's forehead, eyes, nostrils, mouth, ears, breast, hands, and feet with the chrism.

(7) A full-length Divine Liturgy does not ordinarily or immediately follow baptism. There may, however, be a brief form of the Liturgy of the Word at which the appropriate epistle and Gospel readings may be proclaimed.

Conclusion

In one visit to an Orthodox worship service it is possible to experience much of Christian worship as it looked and sounded more than eleven centuries ago in the Byzantine empire. Many elements are worthy of acclaim and preservation: the rich theological language of the prayers and hymns; the care with which much of the Bible has been incorporated into the structure and substance of the liturgy; the ceremonial that communicates how worship of God is not to be approached haphazardly; the sense of awe and transcendence which pervades the music, decor, and ritual action; and the list may continue.

Yet there are other peculiarities in this arguably mysterious worship world that provoke serious questions: Is an ancient world empire the best model for the organization of church hierarchy? Is courtly ceremony the best way to express the public worship due God? Is opulence and affluence (even for aesthetic purposes) an authentic portrait of the worship of the first-century Church? Are the all-too-pronounced ethnic and national divisions in liturgical rites and church governance consistent with the teachings of Christ and the apostles?

It might seem easy for modern western Protestants and Roman Catholics to require answers of the Orthodox church as regards its worship. Perhaps this is due to acute myopia—our intimate familiarity with our own local churches and ways of worship. Could it be that it is more difficult to see those ways in which our own traditions have taken the contemporary culture for their models? If the Orthodox church has preserved a hierarchical structure based on Byzantine civil government, how are those churches to be judged who look to the representative-democratic system of government (like that of this nation) for their model of ministry? Is the modern entertainment industry reflected as proportionately in modern churches as the ceremonial of the Byzantine court is reflected in the Divine Liturgy? What kind of worship do modern western churches feel is worthy of their worship budget? And what about our own sad divisions? The searchlight works both ways.

Perhaps an understanding of the Church and her worship as a *Mystery* is the best thing to be learned from Orthodox Christians. Mystery, according to the eastern tradition, is not so much a hopeless puzzle as it is a never-ending font for inquiry. Mystery promises hope for a better understanding at some future point. Perhaps this is especially important for all those who worship a transcendent, invisible, eternal God whom even the heaven of heavens cannot contain.

For Further Reading:

The Divine Liturgy of Saint John Chrysostom: A New Translation by Members of the Faculty of Hellenic College/Holy Cross Greek Orthodox School of Theology. 3rd ed. Brookline, MA: Holy Cross Orthodox Press, 1973. The introduction to this edition is recommended.

Foley, Edward, ed. *Worship Music: A Concise Dictionary.* Collegeville, MN: The Liturgical Press, 2000. Various entries for all Byzantine musical genres.

Norris, Frederick. *Christianity: A Short Global History*. Oxford: Oneworld Publications, 2002.

Wegman, Herman. *Christian Worship in East and West: A Study Guide to Liturgical History*. Collegeville, MN: The Liturgical Press, 1990.

Wybrew, Hugh. *The Orthodox Liturgy: The Development of the Eucharistic Liturgy in the Byzantine Rite*. Crestwood, NY: St. Vladimir's Seminary Press, 1996.

⊰ —·— ⊱

[1]See the drawings and photos of Hagia Sophia on the website.

[2]In case, at this point, the reader is beginning to feel that all of this information is hardly relevant to any worshiping church in North America today, I should say that there is a thriving Maronite congregation less than a few miles north of my family's home in suburban Detroit, Michigan. A few miles to the west one passes (in order) Greek Orthodox, Romanian Orthodox, and Chaldeen (Antiochene) Orthodox churches—and a good majority of these worshiping Christians enjoy lunch at the same restaurant on Van Dyke Ave. During doctoral studies I served a Disciples of Christ church in Arlington, Virginia, who had a choir director from the Malabarese tradition. Less than a block away from the hospital where I was born is a Serbian Orthodox Church, and the Russian Orthodox Church has recently moved about five miles to the east. Aside from some obvious language barriers, I have enjoyed being able to worship with several of these communities, especially now that I have learned a little about the beauty and sometimes sorrow of their individual histories.

[3]Herman Wegman, *Christian Worship in East and West: A Study Guide to Liturgical History* (Collegeville, MN: The Liturgical Press, 1990) 239.

[4]The modern exception being that Orthodox churches now provide prayer books of the Divine Liturgy in which are printed all the prayers, even those spoken in secret by the priest.

[5]Unlike the Western Church, the Eastern Church has always prohibited three-dimensional art in the worship space (statuary, sculpture, and the like), but finds that two-dimensional representations richly communicate what is at the theological heart of the Incarnation of Christ: God, in Christ, took on material substance, being divinized by the power of the Holy Spirit. Therefore, material substance is elevated to something which can participate in the

Divine Nature to the extent that it is imbued with the Holy Spirit. Two-dimensional art (such as icons, mosaics, frescoes, etc.) require the active participation of the onlooker in order for it to become three-dimensional. Thus the Christian, filled with the Holy Spirit, is integral to the process by which religious art, such as icons, come to represent (literally, *make present again*) what they symbolize. This distinction is important, lest the representations become something divine *in and of themselves*—the very definition of idolatry the iconoclasts had attacked.

[6]Hugh Wybrew, *The Orthodox Liturgy: The Development of the Eucharistic Liturgy in the Byzantine Rite* (Crestwood, NY: St. Vladimir's Seminary Press, 1996) 4.

[7]Subsequent references to this liturgy come from the commonly used Greek-English 1973 pew edition of *The Divine Liturgy of Saint John Chrysostom: A New Translation by Members of the Faculty of Hellenic College/Holy Cross Greek Orthodox School of Theology*, third ed. (Brookline, MA: Holy Cross Orthodox Press, 1973).

[8]See especially the modern musical setting by Tchaikovsky.

[9]Wybrew, *Orthodox Liturgy,* 86.

[10]Ibid., 182-183.

[11]See especially the several musical settings by the Russian composer Dmitri Bortnyansky.

CHAPTER SIX

The Western Church in the Middle Ages

$\mathcal{M}$odern worshipers who are unaware of the history of their Church often take it for granted that they are directly connected to some primitive and immutable form of Christian worship that can be found somewhere in the New Testament. Others have learned of Christian worship's deeper footings in the Jewish tradition and these can, at the very least, appreciate the ways in which the older forms achieved a radically new significance by the saving mystery of Christ as proclaimed by the New Testament authors. But our closer examination of this topic reveals that we are hard pressed to find any singular, original, biblical pattern of Christian worship that once existed or exists in its pristine form today—even among those churches who make such claims.

A naïve and schismatic assumption often made is that somewhere down the line, some unfaithful person or group disrupted this primitive, "original" form of worship that was known to Jesus and his disciples. Having made this assumption, the next course of action typically attempted is to establish who messed it all up, how, and when. Intelligent students of worship history will see that this quest, so narrowly framed, is doomed to fail. Without a *thorough* knowledge of the historical development and the cultural contextualization of Christian worship *from "then" until "now,"* the questions of faithfulness and authenticity in modern worship can only be incorrectly answered by what liturgical historian Robert Taft has referred to as the "pick-a-century" game. In other words, to ask, "Is there a golden age of authentic worship?" is to be consistently frustrated.[1]

Unfortunately, the "pick-a-century" game has been a popular one among factious types who, without any serious study, blame the western Church of the Middle Ages for all of Christianity's problems, great and small. Protestant Christians of our time who do not know what their forebears "protested against" run the risk of being blindly prejudiced especially against Roman Catholic Christians— who were, indeed, the entire western expression of Christianity— and their *unique* worship context.[2] It is true that many of the more problematic worship forms of the Roman Catholic Church can indeed be traced to medieval innovations, but not *all* of these innovations were problematic, at least at their inception. Nevertheless, even the monumental reforms of the western liturgy by the Second Vatican Council (1962–1965) could only and with great difficulty revisit, rationalize, repair, restrain, or redefine some of the approaches to worship that had their roots in Western Europe during this period.

More important, to throw out these medieval changes in worship without comprehending their unique story is to run the risk of not looking at other (non-Catholic) contemporary worship practices with the same critical eye. In fact, it can be argued that contemporary "innovations" to worship among mainline Protestant churches and Pentecostal/Charismatic churches of the last century broadly reflect the medieval western Church more than that of any other historical period. Note how this becomes rather obvious given the following characteristics of medieval Roman Catholic and modern Evangelical worship: (1) interiorized, i.e., *personal*; (2) expert-driven; (3) popular by the local culture's standards; (4) focused on validated "methods" and "moments"; (5) attempted explanations are either systematic (tightly logical) or allegorical (highly representational of "something else"). Whether it is admitted or not, for most western Christians, this church of the Middle Ages is our common taproot.

Context

It is not as easy for scholars to decide on the exact beginnings of the Middle Ages in the West. The earliest proposals cite the fifth century, which marks the first of several waves of barbarian invasions in present-day France, Spain, and Italy. The military and cultural influence of Rome had continued to rapidly diminish since the fourth century, with the exception of brief flowerings in nearby Ravenna and Milan, whereas the moral and ecclesiastical authority of the papacy continued to prevail. We can now speak of a "Roman Catholic Church" that is beginning to exert its supremacy *vis a vis* the Byzantine Church in the East.

Latin had continued as the official language of the Roman Church, but its place in the culture of the commoner as a *lingua franca* was beginning to disappear. Forms of Old French and German were beginning to replace Latin in the European marketplace while the latter became the privileged property of the wealthy and the religious clerics who institutionalized it in monastic schools. Language is power, and since that power was no longer accessible to the multitudes of the faithful who attended worship services, their participation began to take different forms. The entire speech of the western worship service remained in Latin with two exceptions: in the preaching—which would ordinarily be in the common tongue— and in the small amount of Greek that refused to go away quietly, such as the penitential response *Kyrie eleison* (Lord, have mercy).

There was, essentially, one primary liturgical rite (order of worship, liturgical family) in the West—the Roman Rite—even though other regions of Europe had modifications of their own that are, technically speaking, also called *rites.* Among these, the *Gallican* (Gaul), the *Mozarabic* (Spain), the *Old Sarum* (Britain), and the *Milanese* (North Italy) appear often in more in-depth presentations of western liturgical history. This Roman Rite can now be spoken of as the *Mass,* its Latin name being derived from the final words of the dismissal: *Ita missa est.* The Mass still reflected the dual stress of Word and Sacrament, but the "Word" was now in a hieratic (priestly) language that was foreign to most of the hearers. Consequently, in this period, the Sacrament also became foreign for the same reason. The separation of the clergy from the laity was now a simple matter of fact. The latter could no longer understand what the former were saying and thus had no real "share" as coparticipants in the community's worship. Their role as observers and objects of priestly ministry would necessarily be heightened during this time.

Politically, the ancient system of local governmental divisions that were centralized in Rome was a shadow of bygone days. With the barbarian invasions of the fifth centuries came the emergence of a new kind of political map in Europe, characterized by smaller kingdoms. Each nation-state was ruled by landowners who had their own subjects (serfs), their own armies, and even their own clergy. It would not be until the reign of Charles the Great (c. 742–814) that these small nation-states would become a unified Holy Roman Empire. This Frankish emperor, Charlemagne, would further take it upon himself to unify the worship of all of his churches by means of that liturgy which was being used in the Papal court in Rome. Thus, the bonds between Church and State constricted in ways not altogether dissimilar to what had happened in the East four centuries earlier under Constantine.

As far as relations between the Orthodox Church in the East, and the Roman Catholic Church in the West; the estrangement that initially began as a result of different languages, cultures, and considerable geographic distance grew until it became mutual isolation. The earlier excommunication of the Patriarch of Constantinople by Pope Leo IX's legate, Cardinal Humbert, in 1054 which, in turn, resulted in the Patriarch's excommunication of Humbert, seemed to mark the "official" beginnings of the Great Schism. There was now clearly a Greek Church and a Latin Church. With the rise of Islam in the early seventh century, the vast territories formerly occupied by the eastern Church gradually fell under Moslem control until the once-thriving Orthodox patriarchates/centers were reduced to mere ghettoes in the Middle East and Africa—islands of Christianity that continued to survive, but were largely cut off from each other and from the West. The violent bloodbaths of the ill-conceived crusades, originally intended to allow western Christian pilgrims unrestricted access to the holy sites in Moslem-controlled Palestine, would forever mar the historical relationship of the Church with Islam, and put a rift between eastern and western Christians that continues to this day. In the third crusade (c. 1204), the Venetian armies sacked the city of Constantinople as repayment for a host of earlier grievances. The Roman Catholics imposed their Latin liturgy on the Orthodox who had, ever since Constantine, celebrated their own liturgy in Greek. Even the leavened communion bread that was the traditional eucharistic symbol in the East was replaced by the unleavened variety of the West.

Especially worth noting, the West also witnessed the rise of the various mendicant orders of monks in this period. The missionary efforts of these monastic orders, especially the preaching orders of the Dominicans (c. 1220) and the Franciscans (1209) resulted in the evangelization of much of the known world. From the early Benedictine and Irish monastic influence in Great Britain, to the Franciscan outreach ministry to the Moslem world, and to the later forays of the Jesuits into the far East; the monks not only carried the gospel message in word and deed, but with them came western liturgy as well. In their efforts to introduce "pagans" to the new culture of a liturgy that still was thoroughly Roman, and to revitalize the worship of a disenfranchised peasant class, the monks either developed or promoted worship "enhancements" that came most notably in the form of devotional practices. The creative vernacular hymnody during this period, along with the "Passion plays" and other liturgical drama, the appearance of the nativity scene at Christmas, and many more innovations can largely be credited to the monastic orders. The monks made a valiant effort to reconnect a laity who had been summarily denied its full, active, participation in the liturgy, by supplying them with more interior means of worshiping God.

This is a crude but functional backdrop against which we will set our subtopics for worship during the Middle Ages. Space will not permit to speak of the immense variety of innovations, but we can still make a few dangerous generalizations about this period. First of all, we should note that the Roman Rite, the Mass, is on a journey from stability toward rigidity, and from relative local variety to uniformity. Second, innovations that began as enhancements to a communal celebration of the Mass are on their way to becoming liturgically detached from it and will, in some respects, eventually eclipse the Mass in popularity. Third, all the changes in the worship of this period can be read through a variety of lenses. There were political motivations, both secular and ecclesial,[3] to secure and consolidate power. There were also religious motivations to conserve/ preserve liturgical forms and to explain them academically or theologically. There were evangelical/missional motivations to address the needs of the common people by preaching in their own language, and to nurturing them with devotional aids. These are only a few ways of understanding the reasons for many of the changes in the worship of this period. Fourth and perhaps the most important for our study: the laity are gradually not participating (or, rather, essentially being denied participation) in the Mass. This resulted in a priestly class who became focused on the ritual performance of worship, and a spectator class of the faithful who were necessarily resorting to interior experiences.

For practical purposes, we can speak of two divisions within this lengthy period which we are now roughly considering to be between the sixth and fifteenth centuries. Charlemagne wanted to unify the worship of the empire by means of the liturgy of Rome, a colorful process that will be discussed in the next section with greater detail. We will use those initiatives of Charlemagne that affected the Roman Mass to provide a middle point of reference, thus dividing our discussion of the Middle Ages into *pre-Carolingian* and *post-Carolingian*.

Sources

The Book of Readings

In earlier chapters we saw how the Church in the earliest centuries needed only a few written sources for use within the course of a worship service. The Bible, at its various stages of compilation, contained the primary written material that, along with freely composed prayers and ritual action, would have been proclaimed verbatim. With the exception of some extrabiblical material that would have been read in specific contexts (martyrologies, letters, etc.) we know of no other liturgical texts as such, at least before the third century. But even at this early date there were different books in use throughout the course of a worship service: there existed no Bible that was bound into one "complete" edition. Such a manuscript, handwritten, would have been terribly cumbersome at best. Its various components, then, were bound separately for facility of use by their particular liturgical functionaries. The Psalter was often a separate volume, as would have also been the case with the book of the Epistles and the book of the Gospel (in some cases, each of the four Gospels were separately bound).

During the Byzantine period, the books themselves became icons of what was written in them. The Gospel book especially began to take on more liturgical importance, its durable covers having begun to be constructed with more artistic detail and the use of precious metals and gems. In this we see at work the outward liturgical expression of an underlying theology: the supremacy of the gospel itself. It was through the lens of the gospel, the Good News (*evangelion*) that the early Christians interpreted the totality of Scripture. Not surprisingly then, the book itself consequently became the object of liturgical action: it was placed reverently on the altar of the church, carried in procession, elevated, and incensed. The symbolism at work in the prominence of the Book of the Gospels can be seen in a variety of liturgical rites, such as those we have already seen in the variety of Byzantine ordination rites of presbyter and bishop. Other books also make an appearance in these early ordination rites: the Epistle Book that was ceremonially handed to the Reader, and the Psalter that was presented to the cantor.

The Sacramentary: The Celebrant's Book

In the Byzantine period we also saw the rising interest in the collection and compilation of the individual prayer texts into *libelli* (i.e., the "little books"). These collections of prayers, when organized into specific celebrations, would give rise to a new genre of worship book: the *sacramentary*. The historical development of the earliest sacramentaries is complex, but it is from around the seventh century that the oldest books have survived. The sacramentary typically contained a calendar that highlighted the year's liturgical feasts and fasts. The *formularies*—i.e., groupings of prayers for use within a specific liturgical celebration—would have followed the calendar. Near the middle of the sacramentary, perhaps to preserve it considering the book's frequent use, would have been the *Canon of the Mass* (the *Canon* was another name for the eucharistic prayer in the Roman Church). The sacramentaries would have contained a multitude of other texts: the *ordo missae*, the "order of the Mass" which was, in effect, everything that would have preceded the *Canon of the Mass*; ritual *ordines* (the plural form of *ordo*) for the administration of baptism, penance, funerals, ordinations, etc.; thematically specific masses, e.g., for the dedication of a baptistery, for the consecration of a virgin, for the feast day of a saint, etc.; and miscellaneous blessings.

The Antiphonal: The Cantor's Book

The oral tradition of chanting the Psalms cannot be overstated. This was a highly developed and nuanced art form reserved for specialists who passed it down from one generation to another. The practice achieved some degree of unity in the worship of the Jewish synagogue, and was further cultivated by the Christian monks who refined its forms and melodies. As the status of the Church increased in the Byzantine period, so did its musical worship. Cantors as soloists had existed early on, but several singers would have been needed to lead the singing of the larger assemblies. We can safely assume that the many congregational responses were chanted rather than spoken, and so our picture of congregational worship is one of a vocal symphony of praise in which everyone had a part. Soon the complexity of the melodies and incorporation of the lengthy texts of 150 Psalms required the expertise of a select group of singers. In the West, this group was called the *schola cantorum*. A special system of notation developed, perhaps as early as the 9th century, that looked nothing like our modern musical staff (the continuous lines on which notes could be positioned). Rather, certain ornamental marks, having the appearance of phonetic accents, appeared over the individual words of the text. These did not result in a one-to-one relationship as in modern musical notation, but served instead as memory aids, mapping out the general "direction" of the melodic line. Later books of the tenth and eleventh centuries show a musical notation that would be more comparable to the modern musical staff.

The Pontifical: The Bishop's Book

Gradually, those parts of the sacramentary that pertained only to the bishop were collected and gathered into one slim volume. The bishop could celebrate Mass using the sacramentary; or could simply consult his own book which provided everything necessary for him to perform his particular duties. As the pontifical became larger and larger we can see the liturgical function of the bishop increasing. This was, no doubt, a reflection on his cultural status, which is difficult to understate during the medieval period.

The Breviary: The Daily Office/Liturgy of the Hours

Having originated in the deserts near Palestine, then having spread via monastic influence to Rome, the celebration of prayer throughout the day began to require its own book. Later called the *breviary*, a book developed that contained everything that one would need to pray the daily Liturgy of the Hours whether in common (the normal practice) or alone. In its final stage, the contents of the breviary included the following:

—Readings: tailored selections from the Bible, from patristic

literature (the writings of the Church fathers/mothers),
and from hagiographic works (the lives of the saints)

—The Psalter

—Antiphons and Responsories (short chants to be sung
along with the Psalms)

—Prayers

—Chapters (the "rule" of the specific monastic community,
e.g., *The Benedictine Rule*)

—Order of the Office (the "order of service" for celebrating matins, vespers, lauds, terce, sext, none)

—Order of the Mass (the Mass should not be confused with
the Office)

—Hymns

—Collectar (a compilation of *collects;* see chapter 3)

As can be imagined, this book would have been enormous.
Thus it was often shortened in a number of ways: the readings
were often truncated, the Psalter itself might have appeared in a
separate volume, the entire breviary might have appeared in two or
more volumes that would have been used during specific liturgical
seasons (Lent-Easter, "Ordinary Time," etc.).

Section Summary: The History of the Sacramentary and Its Effect on the Mass

The list above represents a very small subset of the multitude
of liturgical books that were produced in the Middle Ages, but we
will refer to many of these later in this chapter. We direct the reader to the definitive works on the historical development of these
sources and others. For the time being, it is important to note the
important role that books were beginning to play in medieval worship. Much like a dramatic presentation, each "actor" in the worship
service had a corresponding "script," whether bishop, priest, cantor,
deacon, master of ceremonies, or reader. It is interesting to note that
the laity did not have their own book as yet, but this would hardly
have mattered since the majority were illiterate in either Latin or
their own vernacular. Because the printing press had yet to be

invented, these books were of necessity copied by hand—the work of many a monk or nun in many a monastery's scriptorium. The use of color and gold paint in the beautiful illuminations of these manuscripts indicate the value given to artistic detail; these were no mere carbon copies of letters on a page. The Book of Kells (c. 800) is perhaps the most famous of all illuminated manuscripts.

On the one hand, the books provided the means for the cross-fertilization of European liturgy. Books from Rome could "travel" across the Alps or the Pyrenees or the English channel; and Irish and Gallican books could travel back to Rome. Thus, an exchange of ideas could take place based on the printed page and, as can be expected, new books could be written. On the other hand, the books necessarily made any liturgical celebration much more consistent. The script was primarily "there to be followed." This being the case, it is not surprising that great attention to the details of words and *rubrics* (the instructions accompanying the spoken texts) became a fixation in this and later periods. Words and rubrics, a locus of power within themselves, could also be politically controlled by ecclesial authorities and by those who moved their hands.

This is why Charlemagne in the latter half of the eighth century asked Pope Hadrian (772–795) for a strictly Roman sacramentary in order to impose it on all the churches of his empire. The objective here was to press all the churches into *uniformity*—a political move to be sure, since such a requirement was never explicitly such a high priority of any church in earlier centuries. (Orthodoxy, apostolicity, and historic continuity were indeed important in earlier centuries, but never before had the imposition of a liturgical book been attempted on this scale, or by a monarch no less!) The sacramentary as *the book* of the Mass held a place of importance higher than any other liturgical book and, therefore, became the logical vehicle for Charlemagne's designs. Since the history of this "Roman" sacramentary (the so-called *Hadrianum*) has had such far-reaching implications, its story is worth retelling here.

Charlemagne *asked* for a genuinely "Roman" liturgy. What

Charlemagne *got* was *not* the book for the Mass that was being regularly used by the churches in Rome. Instead, what had been sent back to him was the sacramentary that the *Pope* used when he celebrated Mass—in his private chapel (the *Curia* in the Vatican) and those Masses in the *stational* liturgies at which he officiated "on location" at the other churches in Rome. Thus, the *Hadrianum* had to be reedited. The new edition was completed by the labors of Benedict of Aniane, and his supplement is known as the *Hucusque* (addendum). The emperor's order that this new sacramentary (the "Hadrianum with Supplement") be used in every church put an official end to the era of oral tradition and improvisation within the liturgy. But beloved local traditions die hard, and over the next three hundred years local bishops in France and Germany continued to add their own worship practices to those rites prescribed in the Hadrianum. By the time of the reforms of Gregory VII (1073–1085), these Gallican and Germanic rites had made their way back across the Alps to Rome where the new (and more interesting?) rituals were adopted. Thus the "Roman" liturgy of 1085 was, in actuality, a hybrid of Roman *and Franco-Germanic* worship forms! The earlier simplicity of the Roman rite had mixed with colorful local traditions, which in turn were readopted at their points of origin, and the final form was claimed by Rome as its own! A significant amount of addition, repetition, and excess in the Mass resulted from this journey, but the liturgy of this period (from the so-called *Gregorian* sacramentaries) was to remain unchanged in the Roman Catholic Church until a little less than fifty years ago!

Space

The architectural advancement in the West, specifically that structure known as the flying buttress, allowed a central worship space to be constructed whose ceiling could be much higher than the ones built in the earlier Romanesque style. The Gothic style, with its more visually delicate arches, became the model of choice for the more impressive buildings of this period, the cathedral at

Chartres holding the undisputed title of the most magnificent example as it was centuries in the making. The interior walls could now allow for tall and slender windows further functioning to direct the gaze of the worshiper upwards—but not toward a mosaic of a Christ Pantokrator in the vault of the ceiling. Since the building itself was the chief work of art, all other iconography would have to come from the artistry in the stained glass windows or, after the fourteenth century, in statuary. The theologically pregnant notion of light entering the church through the images of Christ, of the Blessed Virgin Mary, of the apostles, and the saints especially dominates the Gothic period.

In contrast, interior light provided by candles continued to provide an equally rich image, and took on increasingly anthropological dimensions by means of the Franco-Germanic rites. For instance, at the beginning of the Easter Vigil, the Paschal Candle would have been lit from the "new fire" which would have been burning outside the church building.[4] Five grains of incense were then pressed into it, symbolizing the five wounds of Christ. The celebrant would have then carved the year near the base of the candle with a stylus, and it would have been carried into the church, the clergy and the rest of the congregation following in train. The candle would come to rest near the baptismal font where, as part of the baptismal liturgy of the Vigil, it would have been dipped into the water; a clearly phallic representation of impregnating the waters of "new birth."

Thus we take note of the newer location of the baptistery within the *interior* of the church building itself. Infant baptism having become the norm during this period, the location of the font could have been in any number of places: in an anteroom near the gathering space (*narthex*) of the church, in the narthex itself, or offset at the front of the nave near the sanctuary to one side. The Paschal Candle would have been situated on an elaborate stand near the font and would have burned each of the fifty days throughout the Easter season and, thereafter, whenever baptism was administered throughout the remainder of the year.

The oblong shape of the nave where the laity would have gathered seemed to grow longer and narrower in the new Gothic style. While in many church buildings this may simply be an optical illusion (the distance to the ceiling being considerably higher), it was, nevertheless, an indication that the laity had become much more distanced from what was going on in the priestly domain at the front in the sanctuary. Long rows of tiered choir stalls, each facing the other, commonly flanked the raised area between the nave and the sanctuary. This seems to have been an incorporation from the monastic tradition of chanting the Psalms in two "choirs" and would have been of a proportionate length to have accommodated the glut of clerics and monastics during this period. The area gradually became their exclusive space with the bishop's chair often being incorporated into the choir itself. In the most extreme cases, a rood screen separated the sanctuary from the nave, blocking all but a very narrow view from the nave to the high altar at the sanctuary's farthest end. In some churches, the screen was an appendage to the intricate woodwork or stonework that had evolved architecturally from the pulpit-lectern arrangement on either side of the choir. Eventually, the screen became more akin to a wall, leaving only a doorway in the center through which a few of the laity might be able to see the movements of the clergy. When a second altar/table for the laity was positioned in front of the rood screen (in the nave) the result was that *two liturgies*, in effect, were being celebrated. This made the segregation of the clergy from the rest of the people unmistakable.

The *tabernacle*, a newer addition near to the high altar, began to make a visible appearance. It had always been common for uneaten eucharistic bread to be reserved in various ways and places from as early as the third century. However, in the Middle Ages, forms of eucharistic worship *outside* the liturgy of the Mass began to develop in which the *Blessed Sacrament* had itself become the object of personal devotion. More will be said of the tabernacle and the worship of the Blessed Sacrament later in this chapter under the heading of The Eucharist.

On the right and left sides of the church, the construction of smaller *side altars* in small apses (*apsioles*) also became normative. The number of Masses during any particular day had grown exponentially, to the point where it was typical for several of these so-called *private Masses* to have been celebrated simultaneously in any one church! The multiplication of relics also called for the construction of *reliquaries* within the side altars or *reredoses* behind them. A larger medieval church might have twenty or more such side altars or chapels where either the Mass or the Office would have been celebrated, often without a congregation present. The complexity of the buildings' architecture itself resembled the medieval town marketplace; and its daily, disconnected liturgies—interrupted by the commotion of noisy loiterers in the nave (*and even a few dogs!*)—appears terribly incoherent with the communal worship of earlier centuries.

Several factors, distinct to the worship of the western medieval Church, were responsible for the multiplication of Masses as architecturally evidenced by the increase of the side altars. (1) *Penance:* In the preceding chapters we saw how the penitential system of public confession and public penance for grave sins was problematic for the Church. If, on the one hand, the punishment were too severe, people would have been less inclined to be baptized for fear of sinning afterwards and having to endure the rigors of the subsequent penance. If, on the other hand, the punishment were too lenient, it might appear that grave sins were not taken seriously, and scandal would have multiplied. When, due to the influence of the Irish monks, penance became privatized, penitential systems of *tariffs* started to appear in liturgical books. Sins of all sorts were listed, along with a proposed penance that in some cases had to be fulfilled before the sinner could be granted absolution; i.e., receive communion. In other cases, the sinner was granted immediate absolution with the understanding that the penance still had to be carried out. The local parish priest could consult the current list of tariffs in use so that penance could be fairly administered. (Attending

Mass was a commonly assigned penance—and it certainly would have made sense if only the sinner could have benefited fully by hearing the Gospel, prayers, and eucharist in the common tongue!) Later developments, however, proved to be harmful. Penitents could also supply money to a priest to have Mass prayed on their behalf. The resulting system of *indulgences,* which necessitated a huge task force of numerous priests, escalated in the later Middle Ages and opened the way to the abuse of the system (a major target that was attacked by the Protestant Reformers). (2) *Requiem Masses:* Masses prayed on behalf of the departed were equally validated as having spiritual benefits for the deceased who, as still part of the Church, could be the subject of intercessory prayer. In both the requiem Mass and the Mass celebrated on behalf of a penitent, the larger sacramental theology of Christ's all-surpassing and all-encompassing sacrifice, made present in the eucharist, was pushed to the fore—and with a reasonable logic: How could the fervent prayers to Christ by the faithful on earth (at Mass) not be ubiquitously efficacious in light of the supremacy of Christ's sacrifice? In other words, can the death of a person place that one out of the saving reach of Christ and the prayers of the Church? But while the sacramental theology of the eucharist remained as high and steadfast as ever, the institutional framework controlling it invited abuse, fueling the fires for the Reformers. (3) The nature of the *"private"* Mass: Technically speaking, even in the Middle Ages there was no official encouragement for a priest to celebrate the Mass alone. The sacramentaries contain the formularies for, specifically, a *Missa sine populo*: a Mass without a congregation. True, there may not be a gathering—even a small one—of people for this Mass; however, there would have indeed been at least one server present with the priest who would make the perfunctory responses at the given times (thus fulfilling the words of Christ, "wherever *two or three* are gathered in my name"). Nevertheless, this could all be done at a side altar, or in an *oratory* of a monastery without a congregation present.[5] It goes without saying that the Liturgy of the

Word, now bereft of its hearer-participants, began to dwindle in its significance.

Time

1. The Daily Office

The diversity that was characteristic of the daily office in the West from the fifth until the twelfth century is too complicated for anything but a brief overview in this volume. We can, however, offer a few generalities. The daily singing of psalms; interspersed with the short, biblically based compositions known as *antiphons*; prayers, a hymn, and a brief reading from Scripture or another devotional text developed along three separate traditions. (1) *Churches that celebrated only morning and evening prayer:* In Rome, these were normally associated with the "cathedral" churches in comparison with the "basilica" churches that were served by monks. (2) *Churches that celebrated the full course* (cursus) *of prayer throughout the day:* The basilicas in Rome were generally the larger churches where various assemblages of monastics were present to say the regular hours of prayer. (3) *Monastic communities who adopted the Benedictine rule for daily prayer:* Benedict of Nursia (c.480–550), who was familiar with the basilica style of daily prayer in Rome, organized the daily office into a reasonable system that monks, clergy, and even lay persons could follow and still maintain a lifestyle that included other kinds of work.

Historians admit it is difficult to know how much the Benedictine Office borrowed from the structure of the Basilica Office in Rome. In any event, it was a combination of these that spread across Europe beginning in the eighth century and remained in place until the Office was reformed in 1912. One thing is certain: it is to the Benedictine model that is credited the *community* aspect of daily prayer that went beyond the cloister walls of convents, and the chapels of monastic houses. Soon nonmonastic clergy began to commit themselves to praying the office together. Eventually Charlemagne would impose this Office as an *obligation* on all his clerics.

The form of the Office as it appeared in the twelfth century looked something like this:

Daily Vigils—later called '**Matins**' to differentiate between vigils before feasts
(said before dawn)

6 Psalms
6 Antiphons sung between each Psalm verse
3 Readings with 3 sung *Responsories* (short antiphonal responses)
Hymn: *Te Deum*

Lauds
(said at dawn)

4 Psalms
Canticle of Zechariah (Blessed be the Lord, the God of Israel)
Psalms 148–150 (the *laudes*)
Short Reading and Collect
Benedictus
Closing Prayer

Prime
(said before work)

Kyries (Lord, Have Mercy)
Psalm 50
Creed
Lord's Prayer
Fixed Collect

The "Little" Hours:
Terce (9:00 A.M.**), Sext (noon), and None (3:00** P.M.**)**

Hymn
3 Psalms
Concluding Prayer

Vespers
(said in the evening)

Kyries
5 Psalms
Canticle of Mary (My Soul Magnifies the Lord)
Creed
The Lord's Prayer
Concluding Prayer

Compline
(said before retiring to sleep)

4 Psalms
Canticle of Simeon (Now Let Your Servant Depart in Peace)

In the course of a week, according to the model of daily prayer that emerged in the twelfth century, the entire Psalter would have been sung. Benedict chose the placement of specific Psalms during the corresponding time of the day so that Psalms that mention morning were said at Lauds, Prime, or Terce; Psalms that mention the evening or night were said at Vespers, Compline, and Vigils/Matins. We have seen this type of reordering the biblical Psalter earlier during our study in the daily prayer services in fifth-century Jerusalem.

2. The Church Year

With the exception of the additional season of Advent, we see in the Middle Ages the familiar celebrations from the Byzantine calendar dressed up, so to speak, in medieval costume. For instance, to the Palm Sunday celebration was added the singing of the *Hosanna to the Son of David* as the entrance antiphon, and in Germany the *Palmesel*—a wooden donkey with a figure of the Savior that could be wheeled into the church—became part of the entrance procession.

The nature and theological emphasis of Lent changed more dramatically, however. Because adult baptisms had declined, the focus of earlier centuries on the catechumenate during Lent became irrelevant. The catechumenate was logically replaced by the more penitential aspects of this season in which everyone could participate. Thus, after the tenth century, it became increasingly common for all to receive ashes on Ash Wednesday and not just those who were doing public penance.

Originally stemming from the fasts during the month of December called *Ember Days*, the season of Advent marked the four weeks prior to the Feast of the Nativity on December 25. This season is not found in the eastern Churches but only in the western Church of the Middle Ages. Originally, its especially penitential character was attributed to Gallican influences which had prescribed the fast to be six weeks in length. A competing tradition (from Rome?) is also attested as late as the twelfth century that was more festal in character in which the priest wore white vestments rather than purple. (Purple was a penitential color that was used throughout Lent, while white was worn for all the solemn feasts such as Christmas, Easter, and Pentecost.) Irish influences eventually won the day, and the theological emphasis on the preparation for the *Second Coming of Christ* brought the season back into the penitential disposition that remains to this day.

It is especially remarkable during the later Middle Ages that the readings and prayers for saints' days began to trump the ordinary readings and prayers that were already in place on any given Sunday in the church year. The festal celebration of the saints (the *sanctoral cycle*) had now filled up such a large portion of the calendar that they were unquestionably considered to be more important than the earlier readings and prayers which had been chosen to provide a broad introduction to biblical salvation history. It wasn't until 1911 that Pius X reversed this trend of almost one thousand years.

Ministry

Most notable in the Middle Ages is the shift from a liturgical celebration in which all participated according to a variety of clearly defined roles to a celebration that was reserved primarily for the clergy. Bishops, priests, deacons, and monks had now become the worship professionals, leaving the laity with no other course than to watch the ceremony. The obligation of saying the Daily Office, the multiplication of private Masses, and the creation of *Canon Laws* that legalized the liturgy as the domain of a consecrated priesthood, all took their toll on the communal aspects of worship that had once thrived—even among the hierarchically organized congregations of the Byzantine Empire. We should be reminded that this expression of hyperclericalism did not occur in the Orthodox East. Its origins stem from the unique situation in medieval Europe.

The mostly illiterate laity could not pray the Psalms with the literate monks (even though the latter, in turn, had memorized the entire Psalter, anyway). In a somewhat uneven substitution, the monks provided the formally uneducated laity various devotional tools to assist them in prayer. The Rosary, a string of beads in several *decades* of ten beads, each representing a *Hail Mary,* could be said in various combinations of *chapters* (punctuated by the *Our Father* and the *Gloria Patri*) that allowed the pious to meditatively reflect on the *15 Mysteries of Christ.* The mysteries were a chronological sequence of the life and ministry of Christ from his conception to his glorious reign in heaven. Ten times fifteen equals one hundred fifty; the exact number of Psalms in the Bible. The Rosary and other devotional aids were the gifts of the monks to a disenfranchised laity who could still pray even if they could not participate at Mass. The focus of many of these devotions on the Blessed Virgin Mary, however, was out of balance, since even earlier patristic prescriptions recommended that the illiterate pray the *Our Father* if they could not pray the Psalms.

The laity now came to Mass, not to be nourished by either the liturgy of the Word or the Holy Sacrament of the Eucharist, but to *see* a priestly class perform sacerdotal duties. The gestures in the Mass changed during this period primarily so that the people could indeed benefit by *seeing*, but, ironically, not even this was well achieved due to the long and narrow naves common to Gothic architectural structure. Thus in the eucharist, at the point where the bread and wine, having been blessed, were elevated, a bell would be rung so that the people would know it was time to genuflect. It is even recorded that this genuflection "interrupted" that growing majority of lay people who were saying their own private devotions (the Rosary, perhaps)—and even a few monks who were praying the Office from their breviaries—while the Mass was in progress!

The priest was also now assuming the liturgical functions of the deacon in most parishes. Eventually, Masses would bear the name of *Three Priest Masses* because of this number of priests that would have substituted for the roles formerly assigned to deacon and a*colyte* (server). The bishop, too, having become a powerful political character, could also perform those ministries typically assigned to the priest-presbyter in earlier centuries; that is, when he was not busy with the affairs of the State. The Byzantine picture of a ship and crew, or a sheepfold, had now given way to a monarchi-cal priesthood with subjects.

In spite of what we might consider to be terrible declines, we must remember the monastic orders who, in spite of carrying a peculiarly Roman liturgy to the four corners of the world, were largely responsible for evangelizing the multitudes and incarnating the message of the gospel across the trade routes to the far East, to Scandinavia, and into the Moslem world. For the European com-moner, the model of worship was embodied in the work, preaching, and devotional practices of the monks. The rise of the medieval mystics, the most notable among whom were women, turned the thoughts of those who were not receiving communion at Mass to more spiritual and sometimes pietistically excessive levels. Worship became interiorized. Whether one knew the text of the Mass or not, one could have a personal experience with Christ through con-templation, through *desiring to see* the consecrated Host at the Mass, and through other spiritual means that were more individual-istically oriented than they were communal.

Initiation

1. Baptism

Easter and Pentecost were, in theory, the preferred days for baptism to be celebrated, this custom having survived from the earlier Byzantine period. The common practice of baptism in the Middle Ages, however, yielded to the pragmatism that was seemingly required of situations: (1) the conversions of entire peoples, and (2) the rising infant mortality rate.

In the first case, pagan baptisms were essentially a civic event: as the prince, so the people. Once the ruler accepted Christianity, it naturally followed that all the subjects of his domain would follow suit. Baptism was thus associated in the mind of the Carolingian princes with participation in the Holy Roman Empire. The symbolic association of baptism as participation in the Pascal mystery of Christ may have been completely lost if baptism had not been administered on Easter and the Latin rites had not been explained at some point. Of an organized adult catechumenate for these large groups of pagan converts we know very little, but historical trends suggest there was little theological education prior to baptism as regarded the masses of newly converted peoples.

As for the rising infant mortality rate, it had long been the practice of the Church to baptize those who were near to physical death, and infants were no exception. But by the eighth century, baptismal theology became less centered on a symbolic identification with Christ in his dying and rising as it had become a primarily instrumental means by which original sin was washed away. Baptism as the instrumental means for the remission of sins was never singled out as an exclusive topic in the baptismal treatises of the Patristic Era: it was almost always a part of a larger picture that included identification with Christ and the People of God; passing over from Egypt to Sinai and from the Wilderness into Canaan, circumcision of heart, verbal renunciation of a former life and its environment, *huiothesia* (adoption/"son"-ship), and priestly ordination/anointing, among others. Even Augustine, in speaking of baptism for the remission of original sin, did not see infant baptism as the preferred mode, but rather as a fortunate accommodation. A few centuries later, however, it was considered a practical imperative that baptism be administered as soon as possible after birth if a baby was not expected to live. We can safely posit infant baptism as the exception to the norm, since there existed, at least in the western Church, no specific rite for the baptism of infants.

The same rites that were originally disposed towards adults were utilized with only minor (but awkward) changes. During the weeks of the scrutinies in Lent, the infants were given blessed salt on their tongues, a practice that might have mixed with a more ancient tradition of giving salt to newborns. As with the adult cate-chumenate, the Lord's Prayer and Creed were recited to the infants in theory that they would learn them before baptism. Immediately before baptism proper, the *effata* rite (opening of the ears and nos-trils) was performed by the priest along with the anointing of the infant's breast and back, followed by the renunciation of Satan—this time, by the godparents!—and the recitation of the creed, again by proxy (the infants having learned it, theoretically). At all times, the priest addressed the infant(!) while the godparents made the appropriate responses, an indication that the exact adherence to rit-ual word and gesture superseded any practical concessions! The infants were then immersed three times by the trinitarian formula, anointed by the priest, clothed with a white garment, and handed over to the bishop for chrismation. It is at this point that a very important shift in western initiation took place. This uniquely Roman structure of two postbaptismal anointings (one by the priest/presbyter, and the second by the bishop) was difficult to per-form if the bishop was not present at the celebration, and this was simply the case most of the time.

2. Confirmation

No matter how easy it would have made the bishop's job, preg-nant mothers in the Middle Ages simply could not agree on a unified date for their babies to be born and, subsequently, baptized. The threat that the infant might die made the postponement of baptism until Easter parentally, and even pastorally, unacceptable. Thus, all of the rites of baptism would be administered by the priest as soon as it was convenient with the exception of the episcopal anointing. The infant would have to wait until the bishop's travels brought him to the town or church to perform the final rite of initiation. While it would be reasonable to conclude that parents might not have had to wait longer than a year for this episcopal visit, sources tell us that it was often longer. Some bishops were apparently not very good at paying visits. Some were no doubt busy in the affairs of state. There is even evidence that suggests some parents did not consider the second postbaptismal anointing to be all that important, since they were specifically admonished not to neglect this rite.

Eventually, the episcopal anointing that was once originally situated within the larger ritual of initiation became commonly postponed so that, writing in c. 1265, Thomas Aquinas knows *Confirmation* to be a separate sacrament![6] The eucharist too, which would have ordinarily been administered by the bishop immediately after baptism, would also have to wait until confirmation. Thus, a child's Confirmation and First Communion (at age seven, according to the Fourth Lateran Council of 1215) proceeded something like this:

Opening Prayer
  Collective Laying on of Hands
  Anointing with Chrism (with the accompanying words:)
    I sign you with the sign of the cross
    and confirm you with the chrism of salvation
    in the name of the Father, and of the Son, and of the
      Holy Spirit
    that you might be filled with that same Holy Spirit
    and may have eternal life. Amen.
Sign of Peace

The sign of peace indicated here could have been a "tap" on the cheek but, more than likely, it was a "slap!"[7] Several explanations for this strange ritual exist, and perhaps the least inadequate is that such a gesture was common in the dubbing of knights. One can only wonder what happened to the more gentle *Kiss* of Peace from bygone rituals!

Eucharist

It is important to consider the entire context of the medieval Mass as we begin a discussion about the eucharist. Whether or not the Pope prepared a homily as he celebrated daily Mass in Rome is unknown. However, that Roman liturgy that became mixed with the content of the Franco-Germanic books attests clearly to a service of both Word and Eucharist. Due to the large amount of variants from place to place, we will conflate the sources to provide something of a skeleton for the medieval Mass:

Introductory Rites:

Introit Antiphon (Psalm or other sentence from Scripture used as an entrance)

Kyrie (Lord, have mercy; Christ, have mercy; Lord, have mercy.)

Gloria (Glory to God in the highest and peace to God's people on earth, etc.)

Dominus vobiscum (Greeting: "The Lord be with you.")

Oratio (Prayer)

Service of Readings:

Two selections from the New Testament

Reading from the Gospel (ceremonial ritual accompanies this reading)

Service of the Altar:

Procession of the gifts of bread and wine

Oratio super oblata (Prayer over the Gifts)

Roman Canon (Eucharistic Prayer—described below)

The Lord's Prayer

Breaking of the bread and Comingling Rite

Communion procession

Oratio post communio (Prayer after Communion)

The above represents the Mass as celebrated in the papal chapel in Rome. While it was performed with much of that pomp and ceremony that had carried over from the Byzantine period, it nevertheless was austere and straightforward. What became added to it, when the liturgical books went north of the Alps, were several prayers that are known to specialists as *apologies*. These prayers precede the entrance rites, frame the eucharistic prayer (the Roman Canon), and the communion rite. They generally speak of the personal unworthiness of the priest to perform his ministry and return often to the themes of admission/confession of sin. These were most likely prayers spoken "in private," perhaps in an audible voice but one so soft that no one but the priest (and God) could hear. Already one can see how these *private prayers of the priest* have begun to reflect the medieval practice of a *Private Mass*. Traces of these prayers can be identified in the modern Canon of the Mass.

The following is from the *Mass of the Roman Rite* as compiled/translated by R.C.D. Jasper and G.J. Cuming. We reprint it here at length so that its component parts may be compared with that of the Apostolic Constitutions in Chapter 4.

OFFERTORY PRAYERS: [One of the following would be spoken softly.]

Receive, holy Father, almighty eternal God, this unblemished offering which I, your unworthy servant, offer to you, my living and true God, for my innumerable sins, offences, and negligences; for all who stand round, and for all faithful Christians, alive and dead; that it may avail for my salvation and theirs to eternal life.

O God, who in a wonderful way created human nature in its dignity, and more wonderfully restored it; grant us through the mystery of this water and wine, to share his divinity who vouchsafed to share our humanity, Jesus Christ, your Son, our Lord; who is alive and reigns with you as God in the unity of the Holy Spirit through all the ages of ages.

We offer you, Lord, the cup of salvation, and pray that of your kindness it may ascend in the sight of your divine majesty for our salvation and that of the whole world, in a sweet smelling savor.

Receive, Lord, our humble spirits and contrite hearts; and may our sacrifice be performed today in your sight so as to please you, Lord God.

Come, Sanctifier, almighty, eternal God, and bless this sacrifice prepared for your holy name.

Through the intercession of blessed Michael the archangel, who stands at the right of the altar of incense, and of all the elect, may the Lord vouchsafe to bless this incense and receive it as a sweet smelling savor; through Christ our Lord.

(Psalm 142:2-4; Psalm 25:6-12.)

. . . Pray, brothers, that my sacrifice and yours may be acceptable to God, the almighty Father.

People: May God receive the sacrifice from your hands to the praise and glory of his name, and to our benefit, and that of all his holy Church, through the ages of ages. Amen.

THE CANON

Priest: The Lord be with you.

People: And with your spirit.

Priest: Up with your hearts.

People: We have them with the Lord.

Priest: Let us give thanks to the Lord our God.

People: It is fitting and right.

Priest: It is truly fitting and right, our duty and our salvation, that we should always and everywhere give you thanks, O Lord, holy Father, almighty eternal God, through Christ our Lord;

through whom angels praise your majesty, dominions adore, powers fear, the heavens and the heavenly hosts and the blessed seraphim, joining together in exultant celebration. We pray you, bid our voices also to be admitted with theirs, beseeching you, confessing, and saying:

People: Holy, holy, holy, Lord God of Sabaoth. Heaven and earth are full of your glory. Hosanna in the highest. Blessed is he who comes in the name of the Lord. Hosanna in the highest.

Priest: We therefore pray and beseech you, most merciful Father, through your Son Jesus Christ our Lord, to accept and bless these gifts, these offerings, these holy and unblemished sacrifices; above all, those which we offer to you for your holy catholic Church; vouchsafe to grant it peace, protection, unity, and guidance throughout the world, together with your servant N. our pope, and N. our bishop, and all ortho-dox upholders of the catholic and apostolic faith.

Remember, Lord, your servants, men and women, and all who stand around, whose faith and devotion are known to you, for whom we offer to you, or who offer to you this sacrifice of praise for themselves and for all their own, for the redemption of their souls, for the hope of their salvation and safety, and pay their vows to you, the living, true, and eternal God.

In fellowship with (*here a seasonal clause may follow*) and venerating above all the memory of the glorious ever-Virgin Mary, mother of God and our Lord Jesus Christ, and also of your blessed apostles and martyrs Peter, Paul, Andrew, James, John, Thomas, Philip, Bartholomew, Matthew, Simon and Thaddaeus, Linus, Cletus, Clement, Xystus, Cornelius, Cyprian, Laurence, Chrysogonus, John and Paul, Cosmas and Damian, and all your saints; by their mer-its and prayers grant us to be defended in all things by the help of your protection; through Christ our Lord.

Therefore, Lord, we pray you graciously to accept this offering made by us your servants, and also by your whole family; and to order our days in peace; and to command that we are snatched from eternal damnation and numbered among the flock of your elect; through Christ our Lord.

Vouchsafe, we beseech you, O God, to make this offering wholly blessed, approved, ratified, reasonable, and acceptable; that it may become to us the body and blood of your dearly beloved Son Jesus Christ our Lord;

who, on the day before he suffered, took bread in his holy and reverend hands, lifted up his eyes to heaven to you, O God, his Almighty Father, gave thanks to you, blessed, broke, and gave it to his disciples, saying, "Take and eat from this, all of you; for this is my body." Likewise after supper, taking also this glorious cup in his holy and reverend hands, again he gave thanks to you, blessed and gave it to his disciples, saying, "Take and drink from it, all of you; for this is the cup of my blood, of the new and eternal covenant, the mystery of faith, which will be shed for you and for many for forgiveness of sins. As often as you do this, you will do it for my remembrance."

Therefore also, Lord, we your servants, and also your holy people, having in remembrance the blessed Passion of your Son Christ our Lord, likewise his resurrection from the dead, and also his glorious ascension into heaven, do offer to your excellent majesty from your gifts and bounty a pure victim, a holy victim, an unspotted victim, the holy bread of eternal life and the cup of everlasting salvation.

Vouchsafe to look upon them with a favorable and kindly countenance, and accept them as you vouchsafed to accept the gifts of your righteous servant Abel, and the sacrifice of our patriarch Abraham, and that which your high priest Melchizedek offered to you, a holy sacrifice, an unblemished victim.

We humbly beseech you, almighty God, bid these things be borne by the hands of your angel to your altar on high, in the sight of your divine majesty, that all of us who have received the most holy body and blood of your Son by partaking at this altar may be filled with all heavenly blessing and grace; through Christ our Lord.

Remember also, Lord, the names of those who have gone before us with the sign of faith, and sleep in the sleep of peace. We beseech you to grant to them and to all who rest in Christ a place of restoration, light, and peace; through Christ our Lord.

To us sinners your servants also, who trust in the multitude of your mercies, vouchsafe to grant some part and fellowship with your holy Apostles and martyrs, with John, Stephen, Matthias, Barnabas, Ignatius, Alexander, Marcellinus, Peter, Felicity, Perpetua, Agatha, Lucy, Agnes, Cecilia, Anastasia, and all your saints: into whose company we ask that you will admit us, not weighing our merit, but bounteously forgiving; through Christ our Lord.

Through him, Lord, you ever create, sanctify, quicken, bless, and bestow all these good things upon us. Through him and with him and in him all honor and glory is yours, O God the Father almighty, in the unity of the Holy Spirit, through all the ages of ages. Amen.[8]

The reader should remember that the preceding prayer, with all of its rich theological content, was spoken in Latin, a language that the faithful could not understand. Their short responses: "And also with you," "It is fitting and right," "Holy, holy, holy Lord, etc." would have been easily learned and memorized, and perhaps they would have even been translated at some point over a lifetime of saying them. But the people remained generally ignorant of what was being said during the rest of the Mass.

They could, however, participate with their eyes. They could see when the priest raised the consecrated bread and wine above his head (his back was to the people during the Canon). They knew that this *elevation* was an important moment, and they had been taught to genuflect for it. Being present to see the elevation soon became more important than receiving communion.

The exact reason for the decline of the faithful in communicating is unknown, but the possibilities are numerous. Lack of encouragement in local preaching,[9] faulty or nonexistent catechesis, the foreign tongue of the whole liturgy, the focus on personal unworthiness, a plethora of private devotional options at hand (literally)—all of these have some merit. One proposed theory even suggests that the extremely pious, i.e., those who would have wanted to communicate in any case, were wont to run from church to neighboring church simply to see the elevation. When the faithful *did* actually communicate, the earlier practice of the faithful receiving the bread in their hand changed to the priest placing the bread directly on the individual's tongue.

The elevation of the *Host* (the perfectly round eucharistic bread characteristic of the western churches), led to copious theological debates about *how* and *when* the actual consecration took place. The debates had no small impact on the gestures of the celebrant within the eucharistic Canon![10] Consider some of the questions: If the host is consecrated when the priest says the words of Christ, "This is my body," then should he elevate the bread at that moment for the faithful to adore? If the bread is not consecrated until the cup, also, has been consecrated, then must the priest wait to elevate the bread until both are consecrated? Should the faithful be denied the cup, since eating the consecrated host will suffice for both species (this is the theory of *concomitance*)? How is the cup consecrated: by the words of Christ, "This is my blood," or by dropping a piece of the consecrated bread into it (*commixtio*)? What should be done when too many hosts have been consecrated for one Mass? What is the priest to do/say if he runs out of hosts while the faithful are communicating? At what point in the Canon should he begin in order to consecrate more hosts?

These debates, which to some will appear to be "straining at gnats," are actually indicative of an early attempt to talk about the eucharist *outside of the language of symbol*. Such polarized (and we should add, medieval) positions have unfortunately been inherited by the Church in our day. The discussion of *what it is* "that has become the Body of Christ" can be all-important or not important at all, but either way such discussions continue to separate Christians.

In effect, the eucharistic sensibilities of the Middle Ages can be seen in the following paradigmatic shifts: (1) Symbols have become *things*. (2) Verbs have become *nouns*. (3) Subjects have become *objects*. (4) Actions (taking, blessing, breaking, distributing) have become verbal formulae. (5) Reverence has become superstition. (6) A ceremony situated within an actual meal (the *agape*), then having become a ceremonial meal (the *eucharist*), has now become no meal whatsoever (rather, an object of adoration). (7) Communal celebration has become individual devotion. (8) Mysteries, defined as eternally revealing truth, have become *mysticism* as unknowable, unapproachable, unfathomable, though in some special cases, personally mediated reality. (9) The eucharistic *symbols* that once represented a sharing in the meal(s) of Christ with his disciples have become allegorically interpreted as the dramatic reenactment of the body of Jesus at his Passion. (10) The universal Body of Christ has become localized in the eucharistic species. (11) *Ocular communion*— i.e., the desire to *see* the Host—has replaced eating the Body of Christ.

All of this resulted in a *cultus* (worship) of the eucharist outside the context of the Mass that took a variety of shapes: Consecrated bread that, before, was carried from the eucharistic assembly to the sick, or from church to church, had now become an object of worship. Processions thematically centered upon the Blessed Sacrament sprouted and gained immediate popularity, for instance: that of Palm Sunday in which the Blessed Sacrament replaced the Book of the Gospel that was carried in the triumphal procession! or the feast of *Corpus Christi* in which the Host would be paraded through the city streets. A rite known as *Benediction* developed as a conclusion to the Daily Office. Those present would be blessed with the Sacrament, now placed in a *monstrance* (a crosslike ornament in which the Host could be displayed on an altar) and elevated by the celebrant who made the sign of the cross with it over the people. Visits of the pious to the tabernacle in which rested the reserved sacrament (extra hosts that had been consecrated), became allegorically interpreted as visiting Christ "when he was in prison." The roots of all of these devotional practices had their origins within actual liturgical celebrations that had withstood the test of a millennium. However, the "enhancements" quickly became removed from their original context and, in many places today, they still vie for the affections of those who look uncritically at tradition.[11]

Summary

The evolution from Byzantine worship to western medieval practice was largely attributed to those political authorities, within and without the Church, who sought to bring the liturgy under uniform control and impose it on the rest of the Church. The Latinists clearly had the upper hand since, as language specialists, they now controlled the once-common tongue of the Roman Empire. The result was a large class of clerics with its own mysterious language, ritual, and action into whose "professional" hands the commoners could only commit themselves and their worship.

In the years of more or less "free exchange" of liturgical variations on the western rite, a hybrid worship culture was created which fused the ancient Roman papal model with a variety of European accretions. The result was a distinctly western liturgy that would crystallize in the sixteenth century and become the rule for every church in Roman Catholicism. In this medieval style of worship, the clerics had monopolized most of the dominant roles, and the assembly (if there was one at all) was reduced to a band of pious spectators, watching the ceremony and worshiping by means of the private devotional practices given them by the monks.

We moderns see in the Church of the Middle Ages much that we think we can critique. But this Church is common to all churches with roots in both Roman Catholic and Protestant Christianity . . . and not all of its more questionable effects have completely disappeared. While the Protestant Reformers might have chipped away at some of the abuses of the medieval Church, they inherited many of its worship forms and, with this, the frequently unsound interpretation of these forms. Yet for all our critique, we see within the Medieval Church a fecund source of cultural variety. From the simple beauty of plainchant echoing in a monastery's chapel to the rich polyphony of the early Renaissance, from the powerful grandeur of Romanesque basilicas to the elegant strength of Gothic cathedrals, from humble parish priests serving their localities to mendicant monks traveling the silk route to China, from the Papal chapel where the pope and his curia would celebrate the Mass to the "interior castles" of the women mystics who have left for us the stories of their visions, God was being praised. And not all liturgy was uniform. Monastic communities who had had a particular liturgical practice in place for two hundred years were exempted from Charlemagne's reforms. Geographically, Milan would never quite look or sound like Rome. And the Mass in the West was considerably more flexible, both seasonally and daily, than the weekly Divine Liturgy in the East—the variable texts of the Mass (prayers, readings, etc.) continued to paint the fixed texts (eucharistic prayer, creed, Lord's Prayer, etc.) with ever-changing hues. We are fortunate to have inherited some of the beauty of this legacy, while we are equally thankful that the much-needed reforms did not tarry long.

For Further Reading

Cabié, Robert. "The Eucharist." In *The Church at Prayer: An Introduction to the Liturgy*, pp. 125-148. Ed. by Aimé Georges Martimort. Trans. by Matthew J. O'Connell. One-volume ed. Collegeville, MN: The Liturgical Press, 1992.

Cramer, *Baptism and Change in the Early Middle Ages, c. 200–c. 1150*. New York: Cambridge, 1993.

Jasper, R.C.D., and G.J. Cuming. *Prayers of the Eucharist: Early and Reformed*. 3rd ed. Collegeville, MN: The Liturgical Press, 1990.

Johnson, Maxwell E. *The Rites of Christian Initiation: Their Evolution and Interpretation.* Collegeville, MN: The Liturgical Press, 1999.

Jones, Cheslyn, et al. *The Study of Liturgy.* Rev. ed. New York: Oxford, 1992.

Mazza, Enrico. *The Origins of the Eucharistic Prayer.* Trans. by Ronald E. Lane. Collegeville, MN: The Liturgical Press, 1995.

Metzger, Marcel. *History of the Liturgy: The Major Stages.* Trans. by Madeleine Beaumont. Collegeville, MN: The Liturgical Press, 1997.

Mitchell, Nathan. *Cult and Controversy: The Worship of the Eucharist Outside Mass.* Collegeville, MN: The Liturgical Press, 1990.

Norris, Frederick. *Christianity: A Short Global History.* Oxford: One World, 2002.

Palazzo, Eric. *A History of Liturgical Books from the Beginning to the Thirteenth Century.* Trans. by Madeleine Beaumont. Collegeville, MN: The Liturgical Press, 1998.

Power, David N. *The Eucharistic Mystery: Revitalizing the Tradition.* New York: Crossroad, 1992.

Vogel, Cyrille. *Medieval Liturgy: An Introduction to the Sources.* Trans. and rev. by William Storey and Niels Rasmussen. Washington, The Pastoral Press: 1986.

Wegman, Herman. *Christian Worship in East and West: A Study Guide to Liturgical History.* Trans. by Gordon W. Lathrop, 1985. Collegeville, MN: The Liturgical Press, 1990.

⊰ —— ⊱

[1]A similar argument is often made for ecclesiology: Has there ever been a "golden age of the Church"? Not surprising is the recent theological emphasis in the last century on the biblical, sacramental, and ethical relationship between worship and ecclesiology.

[2]Of the Eastern (Orthodox) Church, the average Protestant knows or cares relatively little since the Protestant Reformers were not concerned with

reforming the Church in the East and, thus, bequeathed no remarkable legacy of invective against it. What is surprising, however, is that the liturgy of the Orthodox Church—which, in general, far surpasses the ritual complexity of the Roman Catholic Church—is not usually the subject of Protestant discrimination. Sadly, modern Protestants remain cool to, or unaware of, the worship heritage of their Christian brothers and sisters in the Orthodox churches and continue to understand themselves "over and against" Roman Catholics.

[3]In fact, such strict dichotomies of sacred *versus* secular are hard to apply in this period, the genius of which was the establishment of a thoroughly Christian culture.

[4]The ritual of the new fire exists in the Byzantine period, as does the Paschal Candle, but the two became fused around the twelfth century.

[5]The so called "private Mass" had fallen into such abuse that by the sixteenth century, *ordines* exist which limit the number of Masses a priest could "say" in any given day to thirty! A stipend would also be supplied to the priest for each Mass, so the abuse was not only on the part of the penitent or the one requesting a Requiem Mass.

[6]Aquinas was not responsible for establishing the number of sacraments in the Roman Catholic Church to Seven (Baptism, Eucharist, Orders, Confirmation, Penance, Matrimony, Extreme Unction). In his treatment of the question in his *Summa Theologica:* "How many Sacraments are there?" his response is simply, "There are seven." He took for granted the liturgical practice of his own time. That Confirmation had emerged as its own sacrament, having historically been attached to Baptism as an accompanying rite, was beyond the knowledge of one of the preeminent doctors of the western Church!

[7]Wegman, *Christian Worship,* 228.

[8]Jasper and Cuming, *Prayers of the Eucharist,* 162-166.

[9]By the sixteenth century, it would be required of the faithful to receive communion *at least once* each year!

[10]Detailed historical information on the theoretical development of the eucharistic cult in the Middle Ages can be found in Nathan Mitchell's *Cult and Controversy: The Worship of the Eucharist Outside Mass* (Collegeville, MN: The Liturgical Press, 1990).

[11]We jump ahead to the second half of the twentieth century to make a modern comparison: The music that originated within the context of the worship service (e.g., African-American Spirituals, Gospel/Soul, Contemporary "Praise and Worship") quickly became an "industry" once detached from it. One thinks of the many "Christian concerts" that the marginal church-goer preferred as a substitute to the "ordinary" worship service complete with Word and Sacrament.

CHAPTER SEVEN

Worship Reformations

Context

In late medieval times many reform movements arose in what had until that time been one church in Europe. The Roman church was able to incorporate or suppress the earlier reform movements. The twelfth and thirteenth centuries saw the rise of Franciscan and Dominican movements that became parts of the Roman Catholic Church. The fourteenth century saw the rise of movements led by John Wycliffe, who died in 1384, and John Huss (1373–1415), who was burned to death. Both were condemned by the church. Wycliffe worked to put the Bible in the language of the people, and he reject-ed the doctrine of transubstantiation, teaching that the presence of Christ in the sacrament was a spiritual presence that did not change the substance of bread and wine. Huss's Bohemian Brethren began communing in both kinds, that is, administering both the bread and the cup to lay people. These directions, along with their attacks on the authority of priests and bishops, got the Brethren into trouble with the hierarchy; and the political climate of their time and place could not tolerate or support their reforms, which were carried through with obvious success in the sixteenth century.

The sixteenth century saw the rise of reformers who were able to get enough political clout to escape the fate of Wycliffe and Huss. The Protestant Reformation is usually dated from 1517, when Martin Luther posted his debate theses on the door of the Castle Church in Wittenberg, Germany. He was soon joined by Ulrich Zwingli and others, who although they disagreed in details, attempted to reform the church on the basis of Scripture. We now turn our attention to the reforms in worship resulting from the work of these reformers, along with the more radical Anabaptists, and the response of the Roman church to those reforms. This chapter, as well as those following it, will be organized around the context and acts of worship, so that we can see what impact each movement has made on the space, time, and order of worship, as well as the specific actions of baptism, the Lord's Supper, praise, and preaching.

Space

The churches of the Protestant Reformation inherited the art and architecture of the middle ages. As we have seen, the basilica building was originally used by the Roman government for judges and other officials in their direct dealings with citizens. Some of these buildings were ceded to churches for worship, with the bishop taking the seat of the judge in the apse and the bema being used for the altar-table, pulpit, and reading desk. Beginning in the fourth century, churches began to build their own houses of worship according to the basilica model. Then what we now call the Romanesque style was developed, which did away with the semicircular apse for the bishop's seat and moved the table back against the east wall, thus making it an altar. Multiple altars were then placed along the side walls of the building, and much artistry went into the exterior, which in basilicas is rather plain. Out of this came the Gothic style, with its pointed (as opposed to round in the Romanesque) arches that permitted even higher ceilings and with its exterior flying buttresses that allowed for wider interior space unhampered by rows of columns to hold up the roof. This style made possible the magnificent cathedrals we visit in Europe, with their beautiful stained-glass windows and ribbed vaulted ceilings. The Renaissance saw a return to Greek and Roman architecture, and especially in Italy the churches built during those years display massive columns and huge domes.

So the churches that were reformed were meeting, at least in the cities, in cavernous buildings of one or a mixture of these four styles. In every case the work of the priests at the altar was far removed from the seats or standing places of the people. Since most of the service was in Latin, a language that only the educated understood, this was not a problem. However, one of the projects of the Reformation was getting both sermons and liturgies into the language of the people; so acoustics soon became a concern. Another concern was the presence of works of art in the buildings. In some cases the statuary and portraits of saints were demolished or thrown away, to be salvaged by others. In other cases some of the art was allowed to stay—especially the window art that was so much a part of the architecture. The pulpits were placed closer to the people, sometimes out toward the center of the nave, where people could gather near to hear the word in their language.

The more radical reformers, including the Anabaptists, often rejected the ornate architecture and imagery of medieval church buildings and met in houses or modest structures. This suited their lifestyle, especially as they were chased from place to place, many of them eventually emigrating to the Netherlands, England, and America.

Time

Worship on the first day of the week goes back as far as the apostolic age, but soon the church had added other special days to the calendar. Earliest was likely the celebration of the Lord's resurrection on what we call Easter. Then a period of preparation for that celebration was developed during the forty days before Easter (not counting Sundays), and we now call this Lent. Then special festivals appeared around Pentecost and later Christmas and Advent. Over time, special days of memorializing the heroes of the faith, whom we call saints, were specified. These were usually on the day of the saint's death. The medieval church developed special days to honor Mary as more than just a human saint. By the sixteenth century the church had a full calendar of special days, in addition to weekly observances and hourly acts of worship, especially for monks, nuns, and priests.

The reformers, in their drive to simplify and keep only those things for which they found precedent in the Bible or good reason in Christian theology, were faced with the formidable task of reforming the calendar as well as the weekly and hourly acts of worship. The **Lutheran** reformers were moderate in their approach, maintaining daily prayer routines, the fasting seasons of Advent and Lent, and celebrating the festivals of Christmas, Circumcision, Epiphany, Good Friday, Easter, Ascension, and Pentecost.[1]

The reformers in **southern Germany and Switzerland** were generally a bit more radical. For the most part, they kept the first day of the week as the Christian Sabbath, although some tried to revert to the seventh day. Most also celebrated Easter and Pentecost, but there was much discussion about Christmas since it appeared so late in church history. Saints days they dropped altogether, although they attempted to continue the memory of the martyrdom of the heroes. Among the reformers the use of time took a different tack to make up for centuries of neglect of preaching and teaching. As early as 1525 Luther was holding a 6:00 A.M. Sunday preaching service for household servants, as well as weekday morning and evening services for school children for study of the Gospels and the catechism. Soon after his arrival in Geneva, Calvin began preaching five sermons a week. Such a regimen became quite common, since the reformers all wanted people to be taught the Scriptures.

The **English Reformation** was similar to the Lutheran in this regard, except for the Puritan movement and the Reformation in Scotland that rejected much of the liturgical calendar, while laying heavy emphasis on the keeping of the Christian Sabbath. When Archbishop Thomas Cranmer began leading the English church to reform, he developed daily morning and evening prayer services, as well as the more generally attended Sunday services. Cranmer's work also included many of the saints days of the medieval tradition.

Orders of Worship

Changes in the order of the main Sunday services of worship came gradually, although the use of the new invention of mass printing made the dissemination of orders of worship relatively easy, and the increasing numbers of literate people made prayer books and worship books a desired commodity for the first time in history.

Luther's *Deutsche Messe* (German Mass) of 1523 was little more than a translation of the Latin rite, and in fact Luther kept the service in Latin (his *Formula Missae*) for special occasions, since Wittenberg was populated by many university students and well-educated people, and Latin remained the academic language of Europe. The German Mass kept the basic order of the Papal Mass, as he called it, but did away with the complicated and rather secretive rites of the blessing of the communion elements, referred to as the canon of the Mass, since they were so closely connected to the doctrine of transubstantiation and the concept of the Lord's Supper as a repetition of the sacrificial crucifixion of Christ at the hands of the presiding priest.[2] In its place he put the simple words of institution from the Gospel accounts. In addition, he insisted on a place of prominence for the sermon, which had for many years been deemphasized almost to the point of extinction.

Luther was reticent to push more radical reforms until the people had heard the gospel preached enough to be ready to accept them. Then in 1525 he judged that the people of Wittenberg were ready to receive both the bread and the wine of the Lord's Supper, and so he instituted that change, along with some more simplifying of the general order.[3] He also began composing music for the services and recruiting others to do the same. His *Ein' feste Burg ist unser Gott* ("A Mighty Fortress Is Our God") remains a favorite hymn today in a number of languages. Luther continued to insist that the order of worship in Wittenberg should not be seen as a new law for all reformed churches, and as a result the churches in the regions of northern Germany and Scandinavia followed Wittenberg, while those in Württemberg, Baden, Palatinate, and Alsace adopted yet simpler orders from the Swiss reformers.

The order of Luther's 1526 German Mass:
    Opening Hymn or Psalm in German
    Kyrie (in Greek, chanted to a psalm tone)
    Collect (short introductory prayer)
    Epistle (chanted)
    German Hymn (replacing the Gradual and Alleluia)
    The Gospel (chanted)
    The Creed (in the German hymn, "We All Believe in One True God")
    Sermon
    The Lord's Prayer (in German paraphrase)
    Admonition to Communicants concerning the Lord's Table
    Words of Institution
    Communion, during which the German forms of the *Sanctus* and the *Agnus Dei* or other German hymns might be sung
    The Collect
    The Aaronic Benediction

The primary movers of worship order reform in southern Germany, Alsace, and French-speaking Switzerland were Martin Bucer and John Calvin. Ulrich Zwingli had revised the Latin Mass in 1523 when in his *An Attack Upon the Canon of the Mass* he substituted four of his own Latin prayers for the Catholic prayers that included the words of institution. Then in 1525 he completely revised the order in his *Action or Use of the Lord's Supper*. His new order mandated communion four times a year, the service in German, and preaching at every weekly service. We should note here that the medieval Roman Catholic Church mandated just one communion per year for each individual, so quarterly communion was an improvement.

Meanwhile in Strasbourg Diebold Schwarz, a Lutheran, translated the Latin low mass into Alsace German in 1524. This was the simplified mass used at small chapels and side altars, in contrast to the high mass that Luther translated. Soon Martin Bucer revised Schwarz's translation, emphasizing the place of the sermon and removing references to the work of the priest as sacrifice. In contrast to Zwingli, whose reform separated the Lord's Supper from the sermon by making the communion services special but rare occasions, Bucer's rite reunited pulpit and table in each service. When in 1538 Calvin settled in Strasbourg to lead the French-speaking congregation there, he adopted Bucer's order and the metrical psalms used in praise and translated them into French.

When Calvin returned to Geneva he was determined that the balance of word and table he had enjoyed in Strasbourg should be applied also in Geneva, but the town officials refused to let him serve communion every Sunday, staying with the schedule set by Zwingli. Calvin's Geneva liturgy, however, generally followed the Strasbourg pattern, so that the people would know that they were leaving out the Lord's Supper except on those four special communion Sundays. Here is the order of his Genevan liturgy of 1542:

The Ministry of the Word
Scripture Sentence (Psalm 124:8)
Confession of sins; Prayer for Pardon
Metrical Psalm
Prayer for Illumination
Reading of Scripture and Sermon

The Ministry of the Upper Room
Collection of Alms
Intercessions
Apostles' Creed (sung, while elements are prepared)
Words of Institution
Exhortation
Consecration Prayer
Fraction
Communion (while a psalm is sung or Scripture is read)
Postcommunion Prayer
The (Aaronic) Blessing

The services of the **Anabaptists** were much simpler than those of the other reformation movements, since instead of accepting actions and doctrines not expressly contrary to Scripture or theology, they attempted to return to the New Testament for worship patterns. Their order usually consisted of an opening prayer, Scripture reading, a longer prayer, a sermon, testimonies by other members, closing prayer, and offering.

The **Anglicans**, on the other hand, in their *Book of Common Prayer* developed rather ornate rites both for regular Eucharistic services and morning and evening prayer services without communion. Their reform of worship orders began slowly, as had Luther's. Archbishop Thomas Cranmer was a careful man, who only reluctantly led the church in England away from Rome. He was, of course, pushed in that direction by King Henry VIII, who demanded annulments and divorces from the wives who did not give him a male heir. Cranmer, however, soon came to value the Lutheran reforms, and later those of Bucer and Calvin. In 1543 Cranmer had the daily offices translated into English, and by 1547 (the year Henry VIII died, succeeded by his nine-year-old son, Edward VI) he was working toward a translation of the mass, the communion part of which appeared alone in 1548, and then the fully integrated order of service was included in the 1549 Prayer Book. This revision shows rather clearly Cranmer's migration to the Calvinist understanding of worship. The following year a book of musical notation was published that ensured that every word of the service could be understood by all participants. At this point Cranmer began to accept input from Bucer and other continental reformers, and his 1552 Prayer Book shows the effects of this input. When Edward VI died in 1553, his half sister Mary took the throne and abolished all turns toward reformation, restoring the Roman Catholic Church. Mary's death in 1558 led to the coronation of Elizabeth I, who then encouraged further reforms. In 1559 the next revision of the Prayer Book was published, and its order became the standard for the *Book of Common Prayer* in 1662, as well as succeeding slight revisions.

The order is as follows:

The Liturgy of the Word
   The Lord's Prayer (minister alone)
   Prayer (collect) for purity
   Ten Commandments and *Kyries* in English
   Collects (Prayers)
   Epistle
   Gospel
   Creed (usually Nicene)
   Sermon

The Liturgy of the Upper Room
   Offertory (Scripture sentences, collections, elements prepared)
   Intercessions
   Exhortation and Invitation
   General Confession and Absolution
   Sursum corda ("Lift up your hearts, etc.")
   Consecration Prayer
   Prefaces and Propers, *Sanctus*, "Prayer of Humble Access,"
   Commemoration, Words of Institution
   Communion
   The Lord's Prayer
   Postcommunion prayer of thanksgiving
   Gloria in excelsis Deo
   Peace and Benediction

As we see, the reformation of orders of worship started early and developed slowly, with some concern for their reception by the common people. However, the simplification of the rites and the renewed insistence on the understanding of the worshipers marked, in all cases, these reforms.

Baptism

The Roman church had developed the belief that there were seven sacraments—seven priestly acts through which the grace of God was bestowed on people. These seven means of grace were baptism, confirmation, penance, the Lord's Supper, ordination, marriage, and extreme unction, often called last rites. The reformers soon came to the position that only two of these were mandated by the Lord and practiced universally by the church. They are baptism and the Lord's Supper.

By the dawn of the Reformation the baptismal practice of the church in Europe had developed from the earlier process of preparation for baptism that took up most of Lent, with the baptisms being done on Easter, to a ceremony that was compressed into about thirty minutes. The earlier tradition included catechetical instruction and several exorcisms and anointings during the preparation period and then prayer and fasting in a candlelight vigil the day before Easter. On Easter morning, the candidates were taken to the baptistery (often a small building near the church containing a pool), where they recited the creed, renounced the devil, disrobed, were anointed, immersed, and given white robes. They were then taken into the church for the Easter communion service.[4]

The assumption by the sixteenth century, however, was that the candidates for baptism were infants, there being no longer a rite of adult initiation in use. That and the general lack of interest in education appears to have caused the dropping of the connection between instruction and baptism.[5] Now the ceremony began with a series of three (and later seven) "scrutinies," that took the place of the earlier catechetical practice of learning doctrine to develop faith and also prayer and fasting to develop a spiritual discipline. These times were spent mostly in prayer and exorcism to make sure the infant was not possessed by an evil spirit. The prayers were combined with enrollment in the list of initiates and placing in the infant's mouth some salt appropriately prepared and the recitation to the infant of the creed and the Lord's Prayer. The noses and ears of the children were then touched with saliva and they were anointed with oil on breast and back, as the priest renounced Satan on their behalf. In theory now the infant was a believer and was ready for baptism. This rite began with the bishop's blessing of the bap tismal font (now a small container inside the church), which was to give the baptismal water sacramental power. Then the priest made the sign of the cross over the water, breathed on the child, anointed the child with oil, and dipped a candle in the water. Three questions were then put to each infant, answered by the parents or godparents, after which the child was dipped in the water. Following this the child was again anointed with oil and clothed with a white robe (*chrisom*), and a prayer of blessing was recited by the bishop. Such a sequence of acts was followed in different formats in different dioceses and often condensed into one relatively brief service beginning at the door of the church and continuing to the font at the front. Thus some of the ceremony and even the wording of the briefer rite made much more sense in the extended preparation period than in the single service.

The best-known reformers were careful to make changes in this liturgy slowly, and they kept everything they could justify on scriptural or theological grounds. However, their changes simplified the rite so that people could begin to understand again what was happening to the person being baptized. In addition, their move toward using the common language instead of Latin, clarified much even of what they did not reform. Luther especially was concerned not to rush his reformations to the detriment of the faith of common people.

Martin Luther published a booklet on baptism in 1523, which was comprised of his explanation of the meaning of baptism and its accompanying ceremonies and a rather literal translation into German of the Latin rite of the Catholic church of Saxony.[6] One of his primary changes was to insert what has become known as Luther's "Flood-Prayer":

> Almighty and eternal God, who hast through the Flood, according to thy righteous judgment, condemned the unfaithful world, and, according to thy great mercy, hast saved faithful Noah, even eight persons, and hast drowned hard-hearted Pharaoh with all his in the Red Sea and hast led thy people Israel dry through it,

thereby prefiguring this bath of thy holy Baptism, and through the baptism of thy dear Child, our Lord Jesus Christ, hast sanctified and set apart the Jordan and all water for a saving flood, and an ample washing away of sins: we pray that through thy same infinite mercy, thou wilt graciously look upon this *N.*, and bless him with a right faith in the spirit, so that through this saving flood all that is born in him from Adam and all that he himself has added thereto may be drowned and submerged: and that he may be separated from the unfaithful, and preserved in the holy ark of Christendom dry and safe, and ever fervent in spirit and joyful in hope serve thy name, so that he, with all the faithful may be worthy to inherit thy promise of eternal life, through Christ our Lord. Amen.[7]

Three years later, Luther revised the baptismal rite in his second booklet. Here he deletes such ceremonies as the use of chrisma, salt, clay, and spittle, laying the emphasis on the words of the creed, the Gospel reading about Jesus blessing the children, and the Lord's Prayer. He preferred the form of immersion, even with children, but continued to defend the baptism of infants on the basis of the faith and promises of the family and godparents. He continued the rites of exorcism of evil spirits from the child, believing that everybody is born sinful and thus in need of the forgiveness promised by the Lord in the water of baptism.

Another early German language rite of baptism was done by the church in Strasbourg, where as early as January, 1524, church leaders were using a translation of their former Latin rite. This translation was probably done by Diebold Schwartz and was published in June, 1524. As with Luther's earliest translation, this one differs little from the Latin rite in use earlier in that city. However, when **Martin Bucer** arrived there that year, he began seriously reforming this rite, writing in 1524 that ceremonies would be evaluated on the basis of Scripture and that the inner reality of such rites was primary and the outward sign secondary. In his words, "Therefore, our practice is to baptize children without all this pomp after a short exposition of the nature and significance of baptism and common prayer that Christ will baptize the child with his Spirit and cleanse him from all his sins, and to commend them to their godparents and the other brethren, that they may love them as their fellow members in Christ and lead them to Christ as soon as possible by wholesome doctrine."[8]

Bucer's simplified liturgy must have had some influence on **John Calvin**, who ministered with him in Strasbourg from 1537 to 1540, when Calvin returned to Geneva with the full authority to lead the Reformation in that French-speaking region of Switzerland. He took full credit and responsibility for the baptismal rite he published in 1542 as part of his *Form of Prayers*. Calvin insisted that children should be brought for baptism when the whole church was gathered—either Sunday mornings or at the weekday afternoon times for preaching. Following the sermon the child is brought to the minister at the font. The parents are then instructed about the meaning of baptism, after which they pray the Lord's Prayer. Then the parents are challenged to instruct the child in the faith that is summarized by the creed they recite together. After the promise, the minister baptizes the child in the name of the Father and of the Son and of the Holy Spirit.[9] Calvin insisted that children are appropriately baptized by the church as recipients of the new covenant of grace through the sacrifice of Christ. He writes in his instructions to parents, "as he imparts to us his riches and blessings by his word, so he distributes them to us by his sacraments."[10]

Ulrich Zwingli, on the other hand came to the conclusion that baptism is merely an outward sign of an inward reality. His reform of baptism was introduced in 1525, the year before Luther's second booklet. Zwingli had been priest at the Great Minster in Zurich, Switzerland, since 1518, and when he broke with the Catholic hierarchy in 1523 he moved quickly, with the backing of his town council, to some positions and works radically different from his Roman Catholic background. He also had begun slowly with a translation of the Latin baptismal rite by his colleague Leo Jud in 1523,[11] but by 1525 he had abandoned the belief that baptism conveyed grace in any direct way. Some of his statements sound as though he is moving toward a believer's baptism position, since it is faith that effects salvation and not outward signs, but he soon was defending the baptism of infants on the basis of the faith of their parents. In May 1525 he published his revised rite of baptism, which expunged from the former ceremony all that had no footing in Scripture as he saw it. The rite includes a welcome, prayer, a reading of Mark 10:13, the naming the child, and baptism in the name of Father, Son, and Holy Spirit, bestowal of a white robe, and dismissal blessing.

When **John Knox** moved into the leadership of the reformation in Scotland, after several years of exile in Frankfurt and Geneva, he revised the rite of baptism. In 1556, while still in Geneva, he had used strong words to condemn the Catholic additions to the simple act of baptism in water. After his return to Scotland in 1559 he instituted a simple liturgy that included a full explanation of the rite and its meaning from the standpoint of Reformed covenant theology, a prayer, closed with a congregational praying of the Lord's Prayer, the baptism (with a handful of water) of the child in the name of the Father and of the Son and of the Holy Ghost, and a final prayer. This rite was to be part of a regular service and to follow the sermon, so word and sacrament were kept together.

As with other aspects of the Reformation, the church in England was quite conservative, continuing many of the rites of the Catholic church as before, only translating them into English. After the death of King Henry VIII in 1547, archbishop **Thomas Cranmer** published a prayer book in 1549 that contained a rite of baptism keeping much of the earlier ceremony. This book was never very popular, and a revision was published in 1552 that did away with more of the ancient ceremony.[12] The baptismal liturgy here begins with an introduction at the font followed by a prayer patterned after Luther's "Flood-Prayer." Then comes the reading of Mark 10:13-16 and a brief exposition and another prayer, after which the godparents are addressed about their responsibility and are asked to reply on behalf of the child renouncing the devil, confessing the creed, and requesting baptism. The priest then prays for the efficacy of the rite and immerses the child (or in case of illness pours water on the head) in the name of the Father and of the Son and of the Holy Ghost. The sign of the cross is then made on the forehead of the child as the priest welcomes the child into the congregation. They then pray the Lord's Prayer and the ceremony ends with a prayer and blessing.[13]

Many of the reformed rites we have just surveyed contain rejections of what their authors saw as the heresy of the **Anabaptists**. This movement was what more recently has been called "The Radical Reformation" or "The Left Wing of the Reformation." They wanted to take Luther's ideas of reform to what they saw as their logical conclusion and go back to the Scriptures to restore the practices of the earliest Christians. They found in the New Testament no explicit mention of infants being baptized and decided on that account that baptism was meant only for those who were able to make their own profession of faith. They then decided they had not really been baptized and arranged to be baptized (again, as seen by the others) as believers. From this came the designation *Anabaptists,* or *Wiedertäufer* in German, both of which mean rebaptizers.

As early as 1521 Andreas Karlstadt and the so-called Zwickau Prophets had pushed for more radical reforms during Luther's absence in Wittenberg. When he returned in 1522, Luther effectively ended this rush to reform,[14] and Karlstadt and his friends left town. Not much later Thomas Müntzer began publishing and practicing a more radical reform of church life based on a personal, mature faith and baptism when a person came to that profession of faith. Müntzer became more and more mystical in his approach to faith and began to espouse social reforms that eventually led him to involvement in the Peasants Revolt. Müntzer and others taught that only believers should be baptized, but they did not insist on rebaptism, since for them the inner (in Spirit) baptism is more important than the outer (in water).

Other similar groups seeking radical reform (sometimes termed restitution, what was later called restoration) arose during this time in Strasbourg and Basel. Early in their work of reform both Zwingli and Bucer had questioned the meaning and efficacy of infant baptism, but eventually justified it on the basis of its analogy to circumcision in the older covenant. Luther (and Calvin) held to the medieval doctrine of original sin, which taught that every child is born with the taint of Adam's sin and so should be baptized for forgiveness of those sins and to escape punishment for them. This seemed vital in that time when so many children did not live to adolescence, let alone adulthood. The first obvious break from that position came in Zurich, Switzerland, when Georg Blaurock, Conrad Grebel, and Felix Manz openly disagreed with Zwingli over both infant baptism and the concept of the *Volkskirche* in which all people born in a Christian region were considered Christians. The earliest recorded adult baptism in this period was on January 21, 1525,[15] when Blaurock was baptized by Grebel. By this time Balthasar Hübmaier (1480–1528) was pushing reform in his parish in Waldshut, Switzerland, and many of his parishioners were postponing the baptism of their children. On Easter in 1525, he and sixty others were rebaptized and within a few days, three hundred more. The movement grew fast enough that in 1529 the imperial meeting at Speyer declared that these rebaptizers should be put to death. They were hunted, arrested, tortured, and killed in many parts of Europe.

Their best-known statement of positions on various issues was published in The Schleitheim Confession of Faith, which includes as Article I the following on baptism:

Baptism shall be given to all those who have been taught repentance and the amendment of life and [who] believe truly that their sins are taken away through Christ, and to all those who desire to walk in the resurrection of Jesus Christ and be buried with Him in death, so that they might rise with Him; to all those who with such an understanding themselves desire and request it from us;

hereby is excluded all infant baptism, the greatest and first abomination of the pope. For this you have the reasons and the testimony of the writings and the practice of the apostles (Mt. 28:19; Mk. 16:6; Acts 2:38; Acts 8:36; Acts 16:31-33; 19:4). We wish simply yet resolutely and with assurance to hold to the same.[16]

A large number of these people made their way to the Netherlands, where they were greeted and pastored by Menno Simons and his followers, from whom they get the name Mennonites. The spectrum of beliefs among the radical reformers is broad, but what unites them is their insistence that the true church is comprised of people who have come to a personal belief in the Lord Jesus Christ and have freely chosen to follow him as Lord. For some this was an inner state and had little to do with a physical act like water baptism, but for many baptism in water (at this point the amount was not an issue) was an important act of an individual's free will, initiating the person into the church, the body of believers. This does not sound very radical to us today, but in sixteenth-century Europe, where for over 1,000 years the church had been made up of everybody born in a Christian land, it was revolutionary and therefore was dealt with as a threat to public order in both Catholic and Protestant regions.

So baptismal rites and teachings differed widely among the reformers, with Luther changing little from the Catholic understanding and practice, and the Anabaptists attempting to reinstitute both the understanding and the practice of the early church, while the Reformed wing adopted a middle ground. The most radical position was that of the Quakers (Society of Friends), who declared that outward forms were not meant to continue and that baptism is a work of the Holy Spirit in the heart of the individual and thus water was not needed. The Anabaptist position, of course, removed the need to deal with confirmation. With the ascendancy of infant baptism the Roman church had developed confirmation as a time when the individual baptized in infancy could be admitted to communion on the basis of his/her understanding of and confession of the

Christian faith. The reformers who continued the practice of infant baptism were compelled also to hold to the practice of confirmation or something akin to it. Luther refused to consider confirmation a sacrament, since it had no biblical backing, but he was willing to practice it as a helpful expedient. Zwingli abolished it, while Calvin urged that children be led to confess their faith publicly.[17]

The Lord's Supper

As we have seen, in the development of the eucharistic prayers since roughly the fourth century, sacrifice has been a dominant image of the eucharistic celebration. In both East and West, language of sacrifice in the rites of the Lord's Supper appeared in many forms. The bread of the supper was referred to as "the body of Christ" or "the Lamb of God," although never as the earthly Jesus. The eastern church generally allowed this identification to remain in the realm of mystery; while the church in the West made more systematic attempts to explain it by using philosophical terms like *substance* and *accidents*, terms adapted from Aristotle and based on Plato's understanding of reality. With this system of thought the bread could appear as normal bread (its accidents) while changing on a deeper level to the body of Christ (its substance). The difficulty with this explanation was that only the educated could follow the logic, and quite often the priests simplified it to the extent that the people understood what transpired at the altar in magical terms, as though the priest were once again sacrificing Christ for the sins of the people.

Along with this development, the church had developed a liturgy to correspond with its understanding of the meal, so at the dawn of the Reformation the prayers of consecration (canon of the Mass) were private prayers of the priest and not intended to be heard or understood by the people. In addition, the wine was reserved for the priests alone and only the bread was given to the people. The practice of offering masses as indulgences for the sins of the living and the dead encouraged the multiplication of masses and led also to the practice of private masses, since the sacrifice itself was significant with or without people there to receive the elements.

Against these developments the reformers battled early and directly. **Luther** saw this as representative of all the negative aspects of the papacy. Thus his earliest reforms of worship struck all mention of sacrifice from the prayers. Luther attempted to maintain a conception of the real presence of Christ in the supper by means of the doctrine of consubstantiation, by which he saw Christ present *with* the bread and wine instead of the elements *becoming* Christ's body and blood. In Luther's absence from Wittenberg, Karlstadt and others instituted reforms of the mass in which both bread and wine were offered to all participants, but Luther insisted that they go more slowly with their reforms. He postponed this step for two years while the people were instructed more fully in the biblical backgrounds of the Lord's Supper. Luther in this way laid great emphasis on the preaching and hearing of the word to elicit faith in the congregants, in contrast to the earlier Catholic insistence that the sacraments, when correctly administered, carried their own validity (*opus operatum*). Luther's emphasis on Christ's words of institution as words to be understood by communicants and not as magical ("Hocus Pocus" comes from the Latin, *"Hoc est corpus meum,"* "This is my body") led him to understand those words quite literally. He railed against Zwingli and others who insisted that Christ meant, "This represents my body." He insisted that communicants should honor the blessed bread and wine as the very body and blood, even if not in the sense of a miraculous change as held by Catholic doctrine.

On the other hand, **Zwingli** reacted strongly against the medieval notion that at the elevation of the host by the priest the bread became the actual body of Christ and the wine his blood. He held that bread and wine, far from becoming body and blood, merely represent to the worshiper body and blood. That move, along with his strong emphasis on preaching the word, tended to deemphasize the Lord's Supper. Zwingli scheduled communion every quarter for his congregation, which was in many instances an improvement over the annual communion legislated by the Catholic church, but it also placed the Lord's Supper in the shadows, compared to its central place in every mass.

In many ways it was left to **Calvin** to work out a more comprehensive theology of the Lord's Supper. In his *Institutes*, Book IV, Chapters 14–17 he lays out his understanding of the sacraments, and in 17 especially the Lord's Supper.[18] In Chapter 14, Section 9 he maintains that the sacraments are efficacious only if the Holy Spirit is present in their administration: "this ministry, without the agency of the Spirit, is empty and frivolous, but when he acts within, and exerts his power, it is replete with energy." He also insists that the actions and objects of the sacraments are not efficacious in themselves, but they become so when the faith of the recipient is awakened by the presence of the word. Thus Calvin stands between Zwingli, who emphasizes the word at the expense of the sacraments, and Luther, who tries to keep the real presence of Christ in the material bread and wine. Calvin defends this moderating position first by pointing out the impossibility of Christ's being physically present both in heaven and at the same time in many places on earth and second by arguing that God has always accompanied revelation and grace with physical manifestations, such as the rainbow.

Calvin also holds that what the believer receives in the Lord's Supper is Christ, but not by Christ's being present in the elements; rather by receiving bread and wine the believer is lifted to the heavenly realms where Christ is. His serious understanding of the incarnation, resurrection, and ascension of Christ prohibits any confusion of earthly elements with the real presence of the Christ who is now in heaven, but he sees the power of the Holy Spirit working so mightily with the faith of communicants that those believers are exalted for a time to the spiritual reality of the abode of the ascended Christ. In his words:

> They are greatly mistaken in imagining that there is no presence of the flesh of Christ in the Supper, unless it be placed in the bread. They thus leave nothing for the secret operation of the Spirit,

which unites Christ himself to us. Christ does not seem to them to be present unless he descends to us, as if we did not equally gain his presence when he raises us to himself (*Institutes* IV, 17, 31).

Thus what the communicant receives at the Lord's table is truly and fully the Christ; yet since the Christ is not physically in bread and wine and since one receives him in a Holy Spirit-accompanied experience of heaven, Calvin's conception of the presence of Christ in the sacrament is a spiritual presence, even though, using the words of John 6, he continues to talk about it in terms of bread and wine.

As to just how this is accomplished, Calvin is understandably reticent to detail. He sees it as a great mystery of the faith:

Now, should any one ask me as to the mode, I will not be ashamed to confess that it is too high a mystery either for my mind to comprehend or my words to express; and to speak more plainly I rather feel than understand it. The truth of God, therefore, in which I can safely rest, I here embrace without controversy. He declares that his flesh is the meat, his blood the drink, of my soul (John 6:53f); I give my soul to him to be fed with such food. In his sacred Supper he bids me take, eat, and drink his body and blood under the symbols of bread and wine. I have no doubt that he will truly give and I receive (*Institutes* IV, 17, 32).

So it is, by the work of the Holy Spirit and by the reception of it in faith, the actual body and blood of Christ one receives when partaking of bread and wine. However, this happens not by the power of a priest, nor by the power of ceremony, but rather by divine power energized by faith. "Christ himself is the matter of the Supper, and that the effect follows from this, that by the sacrifice of his death our sins are expiated, by his blood we are washed, and by his resurrection we are raised to the hope of life in heaven. . . . But I deny that it can be eaten without the taste of faith, or, (if it is more agreeable to speak with Augustine,) I deny that men carry away more from the sacrament than they collect in the vessel of faith" (*Institutes* IV, 17, 33).

So without downplaying the importance of the physical elements and ceremony of the Lord's Supper, as Zwingli did, and without trying to defend a presence of Christ in, with, or under bread and wine, as Luther did, Calvin developed a rich understanding of and celebration of the Lord's Supper. One of his greatest disappointments was his failure to convince the Geneva magistrates to institute weekly communion.[19] They opted instead to stay with Zwingli's quarterly celebration.

The **Anglicans**, on the other hand, continued weekly communion as part of the reformed order of worship. The first part of the mass translated into English was the communion service (1548), which was integrated into the whole English service the next year. The revision of 1552 shows Bucer's influence on Thomas Cranmer. All indications of transubstantiation, of elevation and adoration of the elements, and of sacrifice are gone, and the simple words of institution are substituted. Now the emphasis is on the reception of the bread and wine by the people and not, as in the Catholic mass, on the actions and words of the priest.

In contrast to the Anglican high ceremony, **John Knox** led his Scots followers to a simple meal of communion at a long table in the center of the worshiping community—a reminder of the Lord's last supper with his disciples.[20]

Praise

As is true with other reforms, there is great variety among the various reformers in relation to music as praise of God. **Zwingli**, even though he was arguably the best musician of the major reformers, decided that even congregational singing detracted from the reception of the preached word, and so he developed a service with no music. **Luther**, on the other hand, loved music and early in his reforming activities began to write praise words and compose (or borrow) music to which to sing them. He also encouraged others to do the same. **Calvin** followed Luther's lead here, although he preferred to limit congregational singing to the Psalms translated into metrical French. This tendency was adopted by **Knox** for the Scottish reformation, from which we have many metrical psalms in

English. "The King of Love My Shepherd Is" and "The Lord's My Shepherd, I'll Not Want" are both good examples of metrical versions of Psalm 23 in English. The world would wait until the time of Isaac Watts and then the Wesley brothers for the flood of Christian worship music that continues unabated.

Preaching

The reformers were eager to restore preaching to its place of prominence in the early church—a place that had been slowly superseded by the complications introduced into the mass in the early middle ages. Their emphasis on reading the Scripture lessons and praying the prayers at the Lord's Table in the language of the people was naturally carried over to preaching in the common tongue. There were exceptional preachers during the middle ages, but with the added emphasis on preaching among the reformers, great preaching flourished in sixteenth-century Europe. Luther's sermons are available for study in many languages, as are those of Calvin, Knox, and a few from Zwingli, and some from Hugh Latimer in England.

Perhaps the most important development in preaching during this time is the *lectio continua*—the practice of preaching through a biblical book in sequential fashion, as opposed to using a lectionary that listed texts somehow related to saints days or festivals of the church and thus chosen from various parts of the Bible, with no connection from week to week. With the *lectio continua* approach, learned from the fourth-century ministry of John Chrysostom, congregations were fed a solid diet of insight into the books of the Bible in context and sequence.

Counter-Reformation

The Roman Catholic reaction to the Reformation was quick and strong. The Council of Trent was convened in 1545 and its bishops deliberated off and on until 1563. The first statement in the decree on the sacraments reiterates the doctrine that there are seven sacraments:

CANON I.—If any one saith, that the sacraments of the New Law were not all instituted by Jesus Christ, our Lord; or, that they are more, or less, than seven, to wit, Baptism, Confirmation, the Eucharist, Penance, Extreme Unction, Order, and Matrimony; or even that any one of these seven is not truly and properly a sacrament; let him be anathema.[21]

Since nearly all reformers had by this time reduced the number of sacraments to the two biblical ordinances, baptism and the Lord's Supper, this canon is a direct repudiation of the basis of all reformation based on the Bible. Canon IV upholds the position that the sacraments in general are necessary for salvation, another position repudiated by most of the reformers. The reformed position that the sacraments effect grace only through the faith of the recipient is also repudiated:

CANON VI.—If any one saith, that the sacraments of the New Law do not contain the grace which they signify; or, that they do not confer that grace on those who do not place an obstacle thereunto; as though they were merely outward signs of grace or justice received through faith, and certain marks of the Christian profession, whereby believers are distinguished amongst men from unbelievers; let him be anathema.

CANON VII.—If any one saith, that grace, as far as God's part is concerned, is not given through the said sacraments, always, and to all men, even though they receive them rightly, but (only) sometimes, and to some persons; let him be anathema.

CANON VIII.—If any one saith, that by the said sacraments of the New Law grace is not conferred through the act performed, but that faith alone in the divine promise suffices for the obtaining of grace; let him be anathema.

Following this there are fourteen canons concerning baptism upholding the doctrines and practices of the medieval Catholic church and cursing those who disagree, especially those who teach and practice rebaptism.

It was in Session thirteen, convened in October, 1551, that the council got to their "DECREE CONCERNING THE MOST HOLY SACRAMENT OF THE EUCHARIST." Chapter I deals forthrightly with the real presence of Christ in the Eucharist, recognizing how difficult it is to describe this in human language, nevertheless maintaining the literal understanding of the "is" in the Lord's words of institution. This is more explicitly tied to the doctrine of transubstantiation in Chapter IV, which reads:

> And because that Christ, our Redeemer, declared that which He offered under the species of bread to be truly His own body, therefore has it ever been a firm belief in the Church of God, and this holy Synod doth now declare it anew, that, by the consecration of the bread and of the wine, a conversion is made of the whole substance of the bread into the substance of the body of Christ our Lord, and of the whole substance of the wine into the substance of His blood; which conversion is, by the holy Catholic Church, suitably and properly called Transubstantiation.

This chapter is followed by one that therefore upholds the ancient tradition of veneration of the consecrated bread ("host"), including the annual processions of *Corpus Christi*, so beloved by the people. The canons that follow are curses aimed directly against the teaching of the reformers denying transubstantiation. Later sessions also upheld the Eucharist as a sacrifice and the determination to continue offering only the bread to lay persons.

The Council of Trent did institute a number of reforms, especially as touching the morals and education of priests and bishops. There is one concession to the importance of lay people's understanding what happens in the Eucharist—priests are instructed to explain from time to time what is being said or done, but the language of the mass was to remain Latin.

Summary

The Protestant Reformation destroyed any semblance of unity in the church in Europe, not only dividing from the Roman Catholic Church, but also distancing itself from Catholic ritual practices and their supporting teachings. However, as we have seen, there was little agreement among the reformers on the details of worship practices and doctrines. Thus, as we turn our attention to developments following the era of Reformation we can expect to see continuing disagreements and increasing variety of worship practices as Christians try to understand and apply the principles of Christian worship as received from the Scriptures and the history of theological thinking.

For Further Reading

Calvin, John. *Institutes of the Christian Religion.* Trans. by Henry Beveridge, Esq. Available online at **http://www.reformed.org/ books/institutes/**.

The canons and decrees of the sacred and oecumenical Council of Trent. Trans. by J. Waterworth. London: Dolman, 1848. Available online: **http://history.hanover.edu/texts/trent/ct07.html**.

Fisher, J.D.C. *Christian Initiation, the Reformation Period: Some Early Reformed Rites of Baptism and Confirmation and Other Contemporary Documents.* London: S.P.C.K., 1970.

Karant-Nunn, Susan C. *The Reformation of Ritual: An Interpretation of Early Modern Germany.* New York: Routledge, 1997.

Old, Hughes Oliphant. *The Shaping of the Reformed Baptismal Rite in the Sixteenth Century.* Grand Rapids: Eerdmans, 1992.

_____. *Worship Reformed according to Scripture.* Louisville, KY: Westminster John Knox Press, 2002.

Wallace, Ronald S. *Calvin's Doctrine of the Word and Sacrament.* Grand Rapids: Eerdmans, 1957.

White, James F. *A Brief History of Christian Worship.* Nashville: Abingdon Press, 1993.

[1]Hughes Oliphant Old, *Worship Reformed according to Scripture* (Louisville, KY: Westminster John Knox Press, 2002) 28.

[2]Luther had attacked these doctrines in his *The Babylonian Captivity* of 1520.

[3]See B.J. Kidd, ed., *Documents Illustrative of the Continental Reformation* (Oxford: Clarendon Press, 1911) 193-202, or in electronic form at http://www.iclnet.org/pub/resources/text/wittenberg/luther/germnmass-order.txt (accessed May 10, 2005).

[4]Hughes Oliphant Old, *The Shaping of the Reformed Baptism Rite in the Sixteenth Century* (Grand Rapids: Eerdmans, 1992) 1-31.

[5]Ibid., 16-20.

[6]The Latin rite and his *"Taufbüchlein"* are available in parallel columns translated into English in J.D.C. Fisher, *Christian Initiation, the Reformation Period: Some Early Reformed Rites of Baptism and Confirmation and Other Contemporary Documents* (London: S.P.C.K., 1970) 6-16.

[7]Ibid., 11.

[8]Ibid., 34.

[9]Ibid., 112-117.

[10]Ibid., 115.

[11]Old, *Reformed Baptismal Rite*, 40-45.

[12]Williston Walker, *A History of the Christian Church* (New York: Charles Scribner's Sons, 1918) 409-410.

[13]Fisher, *Christian Initiation*, 106-111.

[14]See Neil R. Leroux, *Luther's Rhetoric: Strategies and Style from the Invocavit Sermons* (St. Louis: Concordia Academic Press, 2002).

[15]Walker (*History*, 367) has it February 7, while Old (*Reformed Baptismal Rite*, 93) dates it 1523, but most sources use the date above.

[16]http://www.anabaptistnetwork.com/book/view/34 (accessed May 10, 2005). This site contains much good information about the past and present and hundreds of links to other Anabaptist sites. See also Harry Emerson Fosdick, *Great Voices of the Reformation* (New York: The Modern Library, 1852) 288.

[17]James F. White, *A Brief History of Christian Worship* (Nashville: Abingdon Press, 1993) 112.

[18]Calvin's *Institutes* are available in many translations and editions. Quotations here are from John Calvin, *Institutes of the Christian Religion,*. trans. by Henry Beveridge, Esq., available online at http://www.reformed.org/books/institutes/ (accessed May 10, 2005).

[19]Calvin states his case strongly and in some length in his *Institutes*, Book 4, Chapter 17, Sections 43, 44, and 46. In Section 43 he writes, "All this mass of

ceremonies being abandoned, the sacrament might be celebrated in the most becoming manner, if it were dispensed to the Church very frequently, at least once a week."

[20]Old, *Worship Reformed*, 136-137.

[21]The Council of Trent, The Seventh Session, *The canons and decrees of the sacred and oecumenical Council of Trent*, trans. by J. Waterworth (London: Dolman, 1848) 53-67. Available online: **http://history.hanover.edu/texts/trent/ct07.html** (accessed May 10, 2005).

CHAPTER EIGHT

Post-Reformation Developments: 1600-1800

Context

From the time of the death of the major reformers (around 1580) to the close of the eighteenth century, the familiar European world of what we now call the middle ages was changing rapidly. Rene Descartes was born in 1596. King James I of England and Scotland commissioned a new translation of the Bible, which was published first in 1611. Several British excursions to North America culminated in the Mayflower's arrival in New England in 1620. Inventions and scientific discoveries began to multiply: the slide rule in 1622, circulation of blood in 1628, the adding machine in 1645, the work of Kepler and Galileo in astronomy, and Newton's theory of gravitation presented in 1687. The philosopher John Locke began to get the attention of academics in 1690, followed by Leibniz, Hume, and Kant. Add to these the literary figures of Cervantes, Shakespeare, John Milton, Daniel Defoe, Jonathan Swift, and Johann von Goethe (1749–1832), as well as artists such as Rubens, Rembrandt, Handel, Bach, Hayden, and Mozart, and one gets the impression of a time of extreme change in European manners as well as understandings of reality. And of course this period covers the settlement of North America by Europeans and eventually the American revolution and the constitutional government it produced, as well as the French revolution and the coming to power of Napoleon in 1799.

During this same time period the main concern of the Lutheran and Reformed churches appears to have been solidifying their gains by defining in great detail the doctrines and practices they had fought so hard for. Therefore, the period 1580 to 1800 is often characterized as the age of Protestant Orthodoxy, which spawned the reactions of both pietism and enlightenment rationalism. During this time the churches in various regions wrote and published confessions of faith, catechisms, and books of worship. It was also during this time that the European church traditions were transplanted to the colonies in the Americas. The year 1583 saw Sir Walter Raleigh's expeditions to Virginia. Jamestown, Virginia, was founded in 1607. The Mayflower's landing at Plymouth meant that the proliferation of traditions that had been regional in Europe were now being established side-by-side in North America.

Space

The Reformers had reacted strongly in many instances against ornamentation and artistic grandeur, and thus during the sixteenth century church construction ceased for the most part, and in many places painting, sculpture, and ornamental windows were destroyed. By the seventeenth century the most extreme of these excesses had disappeared, and it was now time for building again.

Church architecture changed with the prevailing artistic traditions during the post-Reformation period. The dominant European style from the mid-seventeenth through the eighteenth century was the Baroque. The Roman Catholic Church emerged from its Counter-Reformation with a determination to build new houses of worship that would strike awe in the hearts of worshipers and would contrast with the more rational art of the Renaissance. A leader in this movement was Lorenzo Bernini(1598–1680), who designed much of St. Peter's Basilica in Rome. The French builders were soon using the methods favored in Italy, and beginning with the Church of the Sorbonne (begun in 1629) in Paris, they erected great domed buildings with classical entries. The best known of these is the Hôtel des Invalides, later the burial place of Napoleon.

The best known builder in England used the Baroque style to good advantage also. After the great fire of London in 1666, Sir

Christopher Wren (1632–1723), at the time a professor of astronomy, became the primary architect in the rebuilding of the city. His masterpiece, St. Paul's Cathedral, was completed in 1710.[1] It was the first English cathedral built in 150 years.

The Baroque style was also put to good use in eastern Europe by the Orthodox churches and others. With its multiple rounded towers and its proliferation of sculpture and gold and white colors, it adapted well in the East, where the reigning, cosmic Christ figure looks down from the central dome on the Christ-centered prayers and actions of the worship of the Orthodox believers. The interior of Orthodox churches continues in the liturgical space traditions of the East, with the people gathered around a bema from which they receive the word and later the sacrament. The altar is on the far side of a screen (*iconostasis*), which, since it bears icons of the holy family and other saints, is understood as a bridge between the mundane world of everyday life and the mysteries of the Spirit of God.

In those lands where the Europeans took the gospel, there were even more radical changes. In Asia, where Francis Xavier (1506–1552) effectively evangelized for the Roman Catholic Church, church buildings took on a distinctively oriental look. In South and Central America and parts of southern North America, where the Catholic traditions were brought from Spain and Portugal, buildings were made of adobe and other native materials, thus looking quite different from the stone structures of western Europe. As the Protestant forces spread the gospel in North America, rural meeting houses were erected that looked like the log houses of frontier people, and buildings in the cities and towns took on the flavor of the buildings that were their neighbors. Thus what is called colonial or Georgian architecture, with its red brick or clapboard exterior walls and large front porch with its roof supported by white pillars, became the standard.

Time

Time was a different matter. Where the Roman Catholic church remained dominant, the daily masses and the tolling of church bells divided the day and week for the population. Priests, nuns, and monks were, of course, able to maintain the rigorous schedule of the daily office, while most others attended mass weekly at best. European Protestantism was for the most part able to continue its Sunday services and preaching and teaching multiple times during the week, especially in the cities. However, in places where people lived far apart from one another and great distances from cities, the luxury was rare that allowed people to be in church even once a week, let alone daily. In many instances on the American frontier baptisms, weddings, and even funerals had to be postponed until a minister could visit the area. In such a survival economy the church calendar or Christian year was rarely thought about.

One interesting exception to this is the development in Scotland of sacramental seasons in late summer or early fall. These "Holy Fairs" appear to have filled a void left when the radical Geneva-influenced reforms did away with the Roman Catholic liturgical calendar and its heavy focus on the sacramental bread (the "host"). These seasons lasted usually four days or more and consisted of time for serious preparation for receiving the sacrament. The days were filled with preaching, teaching, prayer, and fasting and led many participants into ecstatic experiences credited to the work of the Holy Spirit. As we shall see in the next chapter, such practices were brought to America and appear to be the basis of both revivalism and the camp meeting movement.[2]

Orders of Worship

Since the Reformation had little effect on the churches of the East, the liturgical traditions that were set in the fourteenth century for the Eastern Orthodox churches continued through the Reformation and Post-Reformation eras as they had before and for the most part do to the present. The most used and best known of these liturgies is one credited to St. John Chrysostom. It consists of introductory rites, during which the presiding priest and his aids prepare the round loaf of bread for its consecration and the people recite several litanies of prayer. The Liturgy of the Word follows, in which the Gospel book is carried in the "Little Entrance," while the people sing praise to Christ. Hymns, Scripture readings, and a prayer of intercession are then followed by the dismissal of catechumens. The eucharist proper begins with a pre-anaphora, consisting of prayers and the "Great Entrance," with which the bread and wine are transferred from the table of preparation to the altar. The anaphora itself begins with a greeting of peace and the creed, followed by the eucharistic prayer, consecration, preparation for communion, and the reception of the bread and wine by intinction. The service ends with a set of concluding prayers and a blessing. This brief outline is misleadingly simple, representing a liturgy normally lasting two hours or more. (For more detail see Chapter Four.)

The churches on the European continent were now locked into their Reformation and Counter-Reformation patterns of worship. As late as 1750 the Reformed churches around Zurich had changed Zwingli's service pattern very little. The one obvious change was the introduction of hymn singing, which Zwingli had ruled out. A hymn began the service, followed by an invocation and the Lord's Prayer. Then came the sermon text and sermon. The service closed with the offering, a benediction, and a final hymn.[3] Lutheran services, as we saw in the last chapter, were much more formal than this, highlighting both the preaching of the word and the Lord's Supper.

Even continental pietists, led by Philipp Jakob Spener (1635–1705) and later those called the Moravians, guided by Count Nikolaus von Zinzendorf (1700–1792) continued their main weekly service of worship with the Lutheran congregations of which they were part. They resisted separating from the established churches and instead developed small group meetings for prayer and Bible study. Here they emphasized the personal, heartwarming application of Scripture and close fellowship with other believers. The pietistic societies were precursors to the more recent small group movement within the local congregation. It was only as they emigrated to North

America that they found themselves so distant from a familiar service of worship that they established separate congregations.

A good example of an attempt to unify worship practices in a region is the *Westminster Directory for the Publick Worship of God*, approved by the British Parliament under the leadership of Oliver Cromwell, in 1645. This was at the same time a reaction against the *Book of Common Prayer* of the Anglican Church and a means to control and unify the worship of the churches of Great Britain according to patterns of the Reformed family of churches. Its opening sentence begins, "WHEREAS an happy unity, and uniformity in religion amongst the kirks of Christ, in these three kingdoms, united under one Sovereign, having been long and earnestly wished for by the godly and well-affected amongst us. . . ." Because of the changing political situation in Britain its enforcement was never fully realized, and its impact was not felt for another generation, when it became the standard for Presbyterian congregations in Great Britain. This order of worship is as follows:

> Call to Worship
> Prayer of Approach
> Psalm Reading
> Old Testament Chapter
> New Testament Chapter
> Psalm (sung)
> Prayer before the Sermon
> Sermon
> General Prayer
> Lord's Prayer
> Psalm (sung)
> Blessing
> Exhortation before the Lord's Supper
> Warning (Fencing of the Table)
> Invitation to the Table
> Words of Institution
> Prayer/Blessing of the Bread and Wine

Fraction and Delivery
Exhortation
Solemn Thanksgiving
Collection for the Poor

The original document was accompanied by extensive commentary and explanation to aid worship planners and leaders.[4] Even though the power to enforce Reformed worship was in the hands of Cromwell's followers for only fifteen years, this pattern continued among the Presbyterian and Congregationalist congregations in Britain for many years.

Meanwhile, in the colonies, John Cotton (1584–1652) left us with a description of worship in Puritan New England that appears to have been much simpler than its Old World counterpart. It consisted of these acts:

Prayers of Thanksgiving and Intercession
Singing of Psalms
Reading, Expounding, and Preaching the Word
Exhorting and Questioning by the Laity
Celebrating the Lord's Supper (monthly)

Cotton also wrote extensive descriptions and commentary.[5] There he shows how the basic liturgical acts were ordered with great flexibility. The general order was:

Psalms sung as people gather
Invocation
Scripture Reading with Exposition
Pastoral Prayer (sometimes called "the long prayer")
Singing of a Psalm
Sermon
Baptism and/or Communion, when called for
Offering of Alms
Benediction

As can be seen, there was considerable congregational participation among the New England Puritans, especially in a period of open discussion of the sermon, as lay people were urged to ask questions or to exhort one another. The expounding of the word was a lesson explaining and applying the text read. The sermon that followed would seem to us a second sermon. It might have been based on a different text and was usually preached by a different minister from the one who read the word and expounded. The two then often switched roles in the evening service. With or without the sacraments each service lasted at least two hours. Monthly communion was an improvement over the European model of quarterly observance, but even on communion Sundays the service was quite simple, well suited to a frontier situation.

Baptists in both England and North America developed orders of worship similar to the simple order of the American Puritans, with the emphasis on the reading and preaching of the word and prayers.

On the other hand, something radically different was developed in England by George Fox (1624–1691) and his followers, the Society of Friends, commonly called Quakers. Fox was so repelled by the hypocrisy he saw in his nominally Christian acquaintances that he sought a deeper way, finding it in silence and waiting on the movement of God's Spirit. The Quakers did not develop a clergy system, but rather met as equals in silent expectation that the Spirit would move in someone to speak a word to the group. The meeting would close when an elder stood and shook hands with another worshiper. This order of silence broken only by the instigation of the Spirit remains the pattern for most Friends Meetings, although some have recently developed a worship tradition more like general American evangelical services. The Quaker movement was brought to America by William Penn, who established Pennsylvania (Penn's woods) as a refuge open to people of all religions. The following poem by the Quaker poet, John Greenleaf Whittier (1807–1892) describes nicely the Quaker worship experience:

First-Day Thoughts
In calm and cool and silence, once again

I find my old accustomed place among
My brethren, here, perchance, no human tongue
Shall utter words; where never hymn is sung,
Nor deep-toned organ blown, nor censer swung
Nor dim light falling through the pictured pane!

There, syllabled by silence, let me hear
The still small voice which reached the prophets ear;
Read in my heart a still diviner law
Than Israel's leader on his tables saw!
Here let me strive with each besetting sin,
Recall my wandering fancies, and restrain
the sore disquiet of a restless brain;
And, as the path of duty is made plain,
May grace be given that I may walk therein,
Not like the hireling, for his selfish gain,
With backward glance and reluctant tread,
Making a merit of his coward dread,
But, Cheerful, in the light around me thrown,
Walking as one to pleasant service led;
Doing God's will as if it were my own,
Yet trusting not in mine, but in His strength alone![6]

The later rise of the Methodist movement is an interesting study of worship developments in England and the American colonies. During their university years John (1703–1791) and Charles (1707–1788) Wesley had been part of a Christian movement that developed a discipline of regular, systematic Bible study and prayer. These Anglican clergymen became deeply committed to the spread of the gospel, and so the two brothers came to America as missionaries. Their success at that venture was minimal, but the sea voyage put them in touch with some Moravians, in whose meeting house on Aldersgate Street, London, John later had his well-known heartwarming experience. He became a traveling preacher, often preaching to great crowds in fields and open ground in towns, while Charles preached and wrote hymns, the number totaling at least 6,500. The resulting Methodist movement maintained its ties with the Anglican church in England, but as it spread to the colonies it began to develop its own practices and governance. Wesley's preferred order of service for the primary assembly of the week was strongly dependent on the 1662 edition of the Anglican *Book of Common Prayer.*[7] However, as the movement expanded into the frontier areas of the United States, following the revolution, the difficulty of getting an ordained minister to administer the Lord's Supper, caused a veering away from the Anglican eucharistic service and the development of a less formal, more lay-led worship assembly of prayers, hymns, Scripture readings, and when possible a sermon.

Frontier pressures caused a loosening of liturgical traditions among other European heirs of the Reformation in America as well. This prepared the way for the revivalistic worship that was born in the nineteenth century, as we shall see in the next chapter.

The Lord's Supper

The Romans Catholic mass remained and remains still a eucharistic service, the climax of which is the elevation of the host (sacramental bread) when it becomes for the faithful the body of Christ, sacrificed once again at the hands of the officiating priest for the sins of the participants. The Medieval doctrine of transubstantiation, declaring that at the words of institution the bread became the substance of the body of Christ and the wine the blood of Christ, remained in effect; and the architecture continued to keep participation in the actions of the priest at the altar by the congregation at a minimum. In addition, since one had to go to confession to become worthy of receiving even the sacramental bread, most Catholics communed just once a year, on Easter.

The Sunday morning services of the main Protestant traditions continued also to center on the Table of the Lord, although as noted above, this proved difficult on the American frontier where ordained ministers could not be present regularly to preside at the table. The New England Puritans practiced communion every month, but their progeny, the Congregationalist churches found this difficult as they spread west, out of reach of ordained ministers to preside.

Praise in Music

Oddly enough, as the descendants of the Reformation began to ossify around their doctrinal orthodoxy, the composition and use of music flourished, as did Baroque art and architecture. Some of the greatest names in the history of western music arise in this period as the results of the Renaissance were put to use by artists. Andrea (1510–1586) and Giovanni (c.1558–1613) Gabrieli (uncle and nephew) and the great Claudio Monteverdi (1567–1643) pioneered the oratorio form in Venice in the early seventeenth century, thus opening church music to the styles used in opera and adding a dramatic flavor to music for the church.[8] This was both good and bad news, since it heralded the opportunity for beautiful music at the service of the church while at the same time developing forms too complicated for congregational participation. Whereas the reformers, and to an extent the Roman Catholic Church at the Council of Trent, had pushed for music the whole congregation could sing, now we find increasing use of music of great beauty but equally great difficulty.

It didn't take long for Lutheran musicians to hear what was happening in Venice, as in Germany Michael Praetorius (1571–1621) began to produce liturgical pieces in the style of the Italians. During this same period the organ increased in popularity, even among Calvinists, who generally did not allow accompanied congregational singing. Jan Sweelinck (1562–1621) was an organist in Amsterdam, and his pupil Samuel Scheidt carried his influence to Germany, where later people like Johann Pachelbel (1653–1706), Dietrich Buxtehude (c.1637–1707), and then Johann Sebastian Bach (1685–1750) wrote many worship pieces for the organ. Soon churches in cities and larger towns were employing music directors, many of whom were expected to teach music in the schools.[9]

Bach was known in his day primarily as a great organist and choir director. However, some of his compositions are so complex and hard to perform on instruments of the day that several of his sons were more popular as composers than he was. Yet today he is seen as a great pioneer in writing music that stirs the emotions. Actually this is what got him into trouble with the pietists, who questioned the wisdom of using music to stir the emotions. While seeking deep religious feelings, the pietists wanted such heartwarming experiences to come from the Scriptures, not from worldly music. This seems odd to us today, since Bach himself was quite pietistic, insisting that everything he composed was for the glory of God.

The pietists, on the other hand, developed music that could be sung by the congregation and the words of which directed the thoughts of the singers to the heart of the gospel—the sacrifice of Christ for the sins of the human race. Especially under the leadership of Count Nikolaus von Zinzendorf (1700–1760), they published thousands of hymns, several of which have come down to us translated by John Wesley.[10]

In England the Reformation took a more radical turn for a time, as Oliver Cromwell (1599–1658) carried the Puritans to the seats of power from 1645 to 1660, leading to the abolishment of the monarchy and the House of Lords. During this brief period the Anglican church lost its dominance, and dissenting churches were given freedom of worship. These churches restored the singing of metrical psalms that were "lined out" (the leader sang one line that was then sung by the congregation and so on through the song). With the restoration of the monarchy in 1660 the more artistic music was brought back, especially in the royal chapels and larger churches. This encouraged the careers of composers like Henry Purcell (1659–1695) and later George Frederick Handel (1685–1759), who composed what is without doubt the best known oratorio, *Messiah*, in 1742.

At the same time, a tradition of hymns for congregational singing arose especially among the English dissenters (Baptists and Congregationalists). The pioneer poet of these worship songs was Isaac Watts (1674–1748). Many of his hymns remain in use among nearly all English-speaking Christian groups today. His work and that of the Wesley brothers, John and Charles (1707–1788), along with the many musicians that set their words to fitting tunes, served the church well by giving it songs of good musical quality and theological significance.[11] Many of their hymns can be found in nearly any hymnal extant now, even more than two hundred years after their deaths. We can best appreciate their contribution by recalling that among the British reformed churches up to their time, congregational singing was limited to the biblical Psalms restated in metrical form and set to music. Watts and Charles Wesley continued that tradition, but they added to it songs of their own composing. Such hymns, as we now take for granted and at times treat as old-fashioned, were so revolutionary in the eighteenth century that they caused great controversy.

In 1761 John Wesley, in a newly edited hymnal, set down the following guidelines for hymn-singing:

> That this Part of Divine Worship may be more acceptable to God, as well as the more profitable to yourself and others, be careful to observe the following Directions:
>
> 1. Learn *these tunes* before you learn any others; afterwards learn as many as you please.
> 2. Sing them *exactly* as they are printed here, without altering or mending them at all; and if you have learned to sing them otherwise, unlearn it as soon as you can.
> 3. Sing *all*. See that you join with the congregation as frequently as you can. Let not a slight degree of weakness or weariness hinder you. If it is a cross to you, take it up and you will find a blessing.
> 4. Sung *lustily* and with good courage. Beware of singing as if you were half-dead, or half-asleep; but lift up your voice with strength. Be no more afraid of your voice now, nor more ashamed of its being heard, than when you sung the songs of Satan.

5. Sing *modestly*. Do not bawl so as to be heard above or distinct from the rest of the congregation, that you may not destroy the harmony; but strive to unite your voices together, so as to make one clear melodious sound.

6. Sing *in time*: whatever time is sung, be sure to keep with it. Do not run before nor stay behind it; but attend close to the leading voices, and move therewith as exactly as you can. And take care you sing not *too slow*. This drawling way naturally steals on all who are lazy; and it is high time to drive it out from among us, and sing all our tunes just as quick as we did at first.

7. Above all sing *spiritually*. Have an eye to God in every word you sing. Aim at pleasing *him* more than yourself, or any other creature. In order to do this attend strictly to the sense of what you sing and see that your *heart* is not carried away with the sound, but offered to God continually; so shall your singing be such as the Lord will approve of here, and reward when he cometh in the clouds of heaven.[12]

Preaching

Although preaching among the ministers of the European Protestant churches degenerated during the period of Protestant Orthodoxy to a scholastic style of defense of doctrinal statements, among other traditions preaching of the gospel flourished.

Even though the Council of Trent had urged better preaching among parish priests, the Roman Catholic church had trouble training preachers. The Jesuits included preaching in their education for ordination, but the church at large had nothing like our present day seminary education with courses in preaching. On the other hand, general education in Europe after the Renaissance was based on classical rhetoric, so the use of commonplaces was widespread. This means that preachers collected wise sayings, anecdotes, illustrations, examples, and proofs that could be fit into sermons. The best of the Baroque preachers in Europe were those who could skillfully chain together such pieces to prove a point.[13] The sermons that have come down to us from this era in Europe are not homilies during mass, but are sermons preached at other special occasions, especially in the royal court or at public gatherings to commemorate battles or the lives of public figures. Thus it is difficult to judge how sermons affected the common people assembled for services of worship.

The seventeenth century opened in Great Britain with James I on the throne and Lancelot Andrewes (1555–1626) being transferred from his position as canon at St. Paul's to dean of Westminster Abbey. Andrewes opened an age of fine preaching in the English language. He and his contemporary and fellow metaphysical preacher, John Donne (1572–1631), polished the art of preaching to a high shine. Donne was appointed Dean of St. Paul's in 1621, and for five years the two of them set high standards for preaching in Britain. Their sermons began with the reading and exposition of a biblical text and moved to an application in life. The exposition often focused on a single word or two, the meaning of which shed light on the whole passage.

Puritanism, on the other hand, began with doctrinal contention that at first dominated its preaching. The brief Puritan ascendancy under Cromwell ended with the restoration of the British monarchy, and Puritanism in Britain was tamed. In the New England colonies of Massachusetts and Connecticut, however, the Puritan preachers were in control of the life of the local communities. Congregations were now seen as assemblies of the elect and not, as in the old country, all the inhabitants of a geographical area. Preachers were expected to proclaim the gospel by which the Holy Spirit called sinners to repentance, thus demonstrating their election.

In the American colonies, the Puritans were led by some fine preachers. John Cotton (1584–1652) was recognized as a good preacher even before he sailed from England. His twenty-year ministry in Boston, Lincolnshire, England, was so effective that he was forced by the Anglican authorities first into hiding and then to America, where former parishioners had already named their town in Massachusetts after their former city. So from 1633 to his death in 1652, he ministered as teacher of First Church in Boston, Massachusetts. Many of his sermons are still available and show a fine hand at exegeting the text and applying it to correct living among his parishioners.

The best known preacher in the second generation of New England ministers is Increase Mather (1639–1723). Educated at Harvard and Trinity College in Dublin, he honed his preaching skills in England during the Cromwell years and then returned to Massachusetts, where he was called to Second Church in Boston, later known as Old North Church. There he ministered for over fifty years. His sermons are models of disciplinary preaching, attacking vices like drunkenness, playing cards, and promiscuous dancing at great length and with something approaching violence. His preaching obviously tried to keep his people on the straight and narrow as Puritanism understood it.

Undoubtedly the best known preacher of American Puritanism is Jonathan Edwards (1703–1758). Widely judged one of the finest intellects born in America, Edwards is still read as a philosopher, a theologian, and as a reporter on life in colonial New England. It seems a shame that Edwards is generally best known for his sermon "Sinners in the Hands of an Angry God." It has become the example of "hell-fire and damnation" preaching. It is admittedly a fiery sermon, and it was a primary impetus in the beginning of the Great Awakening of the eighteenth century; but it does not represent the balanced preaching of this great man. We also have from him a series of sermons on love based on 1 Corinthians 13 and many sermons that tell of the delights and joys of being in the hands of a loving God.[14] Edwards was a pietistic defender of the orthodox Protestant (Calvinistic) faith, who was aware of all the currents of philosophy and science of his day—a great intellectual who valued most highly the deep spiritual life he saw in his wife and who recorded spiritual experiences carefully for the instruction of coming generations.[15] He understood that conversion is the work of God's Spirit and that preaching is the means God uses to make individuals aware that they are among the elect. Thus his sermons follow the Puritan model, beginning with exegesis of the text, continuing to elucidation of the theological issues in the text, and ending with application of those issues in the devotional lives and behavior of his hearers.

In Protestant Europe the outstanding preachers of the post-Reformation era are numbered among the pietists. Johann Arndt (1555–1621), in Germany, pled for heartfelt religious experience. When Jakob Spener (see above) was asked to write a preface to a book of Arndt's sermons he produced *Pia Desideria*, that was soon published on its own to become the manifesto of the German movement of Pietism. The movement was aided in its spread by the preaching and organizational abilities of Hermann Franke (1663–1727) and Melchior Hoffmann, and in the next generation by Count Zinzendorf (see above). One of the outstanding mission sermons of the post-Reformation era was preached by Zinzendorf in London on September 4, 1746, a sermon titled "Concerning the Proper Purpose of the Preaching of the Gospel."[16] It is not clear just where or to what audience it was presented, but judging from the content and date it must have been preached in London to fellow believers in some sort of religious gathering.

The prevailing attitude toward the spread of the gospel among most Protestant Christians in the early eighteenth century was that God would see to the conversion of whatever people God wanted in the kingdom, and that God did not need the help of human beings in this enterprise. The church might pray for the salvation of the "heathen," but that would be the extent of their involvement.

Zinzendorf disagreed. This sermon includes a frontal attack on the prevailing attitude, which effectively curtailed any desire to preach to unbelievers. He clearly claims that the "proper purpose of preaching" is to invite people to the wedding feast of the heavenly Bridegroom. With careful exposition of the text and effective appeals to believers to get out the invitation to the bridal feast of the Savior, Zinzendorf encouraged his brethren to carry the gospel wherever they could go. The modern mission movement would wait until 1792 for William Carey's sermon, "Attempt Great Things for God; Expect Great Things from God," that is credited with launching the mission movement; but Carey was standing on Zinzendorf's shoulders as he preached.

As noted above, John Wesley was deeply influenced by the German Pietists. Their influence appears to have driven him not only to preach in order to encourage in his hearers a closer walk with God, but also to be ready to preach anywhere to anybody in any circumstance. This was a radical transformation for a minister of the Church of England. Wesley's concern for the souls of general humanity led him to preach in small village chapels, in large city edifices, and in open fields in the coal mining and farming regions of England. Wesley not only preached to convert people, he also organized them into societies (small groups) for Bible study, prayer, and accountability. Thus the Methodist movement grew in England and its colonies to be a salutary force in church and society.

The finest preaching of the Methodist movement was done by the Calvinist Methodist, George Whitefield (1714–1770). He was a born orator with a God-given ability to understand his audience and to be heard and understood over vast areas. He traveled widely, crossing the Atlantic many times to preach in various parts of the American colonies. Whitefield found ready audiences in open fields and outside busy city buildings. It was he who convinced Wesley to try open-air preaching when he found church pulpits closed to him. Whitefield was neither the theologian nor the administrator that Wesley was, but he drew crowds of as many as 30,000 people to hear him preach. It is estimated that he preached to more people than anybody else before the age of modern communication technology.

Summary

With the exception of the Society of Friends, this post-Reformation period produced no new patterns of corporate worship. However, we have dedicated more space than usual in this chapter to preaching because, as will be seen, preaching in the next generations will change the form and nature of Christian worship, especially in the United States, and because of the dominance of American missions, the impact will be felt around the world.

For Further Reading

Edwards, O.C., Jr. *A History of Preaching.* Vol. 1. Nashville: Abingdon Press, 2004.

Old, Hughes Oliphant. *The Reading and Preaching of the Scriptures in the Worship of the Christian Church, Volume 5, Moderatism, Pietism, and Awakening.* Grand Rapids: Eerdmans, 2004.

Schmidt, Leigh Eric. *Holy Fairs: Scotland and the Making of American Revivalism.* Grand Rapids: Eerdmans, 2001.

Wilson-Dickson, Andrew. *The Story of Christian Music: From Gregorian Chant to Black Gospel.* Minneapolis: Fortress Press, 1996.

⊰ —— ⊱

[1]Ernest Short, *The House of God: A History of Religious Architecture* (London: Eyre & Spottiswoode, 1955) 276-282. There are many photos of baroque-style church buildings available through an internet search.

[2]Leigh Eric Schmidt, *Holy Fairs: Scotland and the Making of American Revivalism* (Grand Rapids: Eerdmans, 2001) 11-68.

[3]Hughes Oliphant Old, *The Reading and Preaching of the Scriptures in the Worship of the Christian Church, vol. 5, Moderatism, Pietism, and Awakening* (Grand Rapids: Eerdmans, 2004) 51-52.

[4]www.covenanter.org/Westminster/directoryforpublicworship.htm (accessed May 25, 2005).

[5]Darrell Todd Maurina and Doug Adams, "An American Puritan Model of Worship," and Maurina, "John Cotton's New England Congregational Model of Worship," in *Twenty Centuries of Christian Worship,* ed. by Robert E.

Webber, The Complete Library of Christian Worship, 2:227-230, and Old, *Reading and Preaching,* 5:170-172, where he cites John Cotton, *The True Constitution of a particular visible Church, proved by Scripture* (1642) and *The Way of the Churches of Christ in New England, Measured and Examined by the Golden Reed of the Sanctuary* (1645).

[6]**www.kimopress.com/whittier4.html#First** (accessed May 25, 2005). For more information on the worship of the Quakers, see the *Apology* of Robert Barclay (1648–1690), **http://www.ccel.org/ccel/barclay/quakers.html** (accessed May 5, 2005).

[7]See John R. Tyson, "A Methodist Model of Worship: John Wesley's Sunday Service," in Webber, *Twenty Centuries of Christian Worship,* 2:236-245.

[8]See Andrew Wilson-Dickson, *The Story of Christian Music: From Gregorian Chant to Black Gospel* (Minneapolis: Fortress Press, 1996) 84-86.

[9]Ibid., 87-88.

[10]"Jesus, Thy Blood and Righteousness" was written by Zinzendorf and translated by Wesley. "Jesus, Thy Boundless Love to Me" was written by Paul Gerhardt and translated by Wesley, as was "Give to the Winds Your Fears." "O Sacred Head, Now Wounded" is from Bernard of Clairvaux, translated into German by Gerhardt, set to music by Hassler and later arranged by Bach. All of these are published in *The Worshiping Church: A Hymnal* (Carol Stream, IL: Hope Publishing, 1990), as well as many other hymnals.

[11]Watts and Charles Wesley were especially prolific. Watts wrote some 600 hymns and psalm paraphrases, including "Alas! And Did My Saviour Bleed," "At the Cross," "Joy to the World," O God, Our Help in Ages Past," and "When I Survey the Wondrous Cross." Wesley wrote an astonishing 6500 hymns, including the familiar "Christ the Lord Is Risen Today," "Hark! The Herald Angels Sing," "Love Divine, All Loves Excelling," and "O For a Thousand Tongues to Sing."

[12]Gordon S. Wakefield, *An Outline of Christian Worship* (Edinburgh: T & T Clark, 1998/2000) 137-138.

[13]See the discussion of the preaching of Jean-Pierre Camus in O.C. Edwards, Jr., *A History of Preaching* (Nashville: Abingdon Press, 2004) 1:344, and one of Camus's sermons in 2:277ff.

[14]Old, *Reading and Preaching,* 5:274-284.

[15]Jonathan Edwards, *Distinguishing Marks of a Work of the Spirit of God* (Boston: S. Kneeland, 1741), in Edwards, *The Great Awakening,* in *The Works of Jonathan Edwards,* vol. 4, ed. by C.C. Goen (New Haven and London: Yale University Press, 1972).

[16]Francis M. DuBose, ed., *Classics of Christian Missions* (Nashville: Broadman Press, 1979) 290-300.

CHAPTER NINE

The Nineteenth Century

Context

The year 1800 found Napoleon marching eastward to conquer Europe while the United States was forming itself as a constitutional government. By the end of the century Napoleon was a figure of history and the United States a world power. The intervening years saw the birth of steam transportation on the high seas, the development of steam railroads, the harnessing of electricity, the drilling of oil, the invention of the telegraph, the radio, and the telephone. The United States survived both another war with Britain and its own Civil War, before getting into war with Spain in 1898, the year radium was discovered. The artists of the century included Cezanne, Van Gogh, Monet, Renoir; the writers Schiller, Goethe, Dostoyevsky, Tolstoy, Browning, Dickens, Melville; and composers Wagner, Beethoven, Chopin, Tchaikovsky, Brahms, Strauss, and Verdi. Many ways of understanding the world were changed by the work of Charles Darwin, Søren Kierkegaard, Georg W.F. Hegel, Friedrich W. Nietzsche, and Karl Marx. World leaders included Thomas Jefferson, Queen Victoria, Abraham Lincoln, Simon Bolivar, Gladstone, and Bismarck.

The worship patterns and practices of the churches of the world showed little change during the nineteenth century, at least in their home regions. However, the emergence of a mighty mission emphasis among European Protestant churches and the westward expansion of the churches in North America made for decisive adjustments outside Europe. In fact, by the end of the century a European Lutheran or Presbyterian visiting a congregation in the American Midwest might have looked twice at the church name on the sign. The order and mood of worship would have seemed as foreign as the language.

In Africa and Asia the spread of Christianity appears to have gone hand in hand with the colonialism of the powerful European governments. The names William Carey (India), David Livingstone (Africa), Adoniram Judson (Burma), and Robert Morrison (China) evoke awe even today among mission-minded Christians. With few exceptions,[1] the worship patterns in these mission churches were imposed on the indigenous people from European practices. Orders, music, preaching styles, even architectural patterns were merely local adaptations of what the missionaries were comfortable with back home. This lack of contextualization (or indigenization) was partly intentional—to differentiate clearly Christian practices from those of the animist or spiritist religions the missionaries found in these places—and partly unintentional, in the sense that people just had not yet thought through the concept that the practice of Christianity should be any different than the European experience. The general move toward contextualization and the accompanying indigenization of worship practices would await the twentieth century.

On the other hand, independence from Great Britain encouraged American churches to develop their own patterns of worship. Life in those churches in the nineteenth century varied greatly, with styles depending on both denominational affiliation and geographical location. This was true with regard to leadership, architecture, and purpose, as well as modes of worship. The movement of people from Europe to America and the increasing movement of people from eastern cities and towns to western frontier areas had a profound impact on the way Christians worshiped.

Along the eastern seaboard at the dawn of the nineteenth century, most of the churches established by earlier immigrants from

Europe continued worshiping in their accustomed patterns. Those established by the Puritans continued their worship under the strict control of their clergy and with a definite emphasis on preaching as the central act of worship, as well as congregational and community discipline. The Lutheran and Reformed churches continued their European liturgical traditions with an emphasis on preaching accompanied by a sense of the importance of the Lord's Supper. However, the nineteenth century would bring radical changes to some denominational patterns and add stress to those for whom change was more difficult. We shall proceed by surveying each of the primary Christian traditions with regard to corporate worship.

Roman Catholic

The few Roman Catholics in the American colonies had little opportunity for change in the Latin mass, even under frontier circumstances. Their liturgical canons and the training of their priests stipulated that the Sunday mass be celebrated as it had been for centuries. The order had been solidified during the Counter-Reformation and stood fast. The liturgy was firmly in the hands of priests, who presided over the detailed prayers of preparation of the bread and wine for the Eucharist. They were trained to work with great reverence the miracle of transubstantiation, when they believed the bread and wine become the actual body and blood of Christ, sacrificed for the sins of the people. The participation of the congregation was limited to set responses to readings and prayers and the reverent reception of the host. Lay people were permitted to commune only with the bread, the clergy alone deemed worthy to receive the blood of Christ. Since the prayers of the mass were in Latin, there was very little rational reception among the congregation. Homilies were generally brief and mostly focused on moral living or correct doctrine. With the continuation of the seven sacraments of the medieval church, the priest was involved in every one of life's passages, but with such dependence on the priest, the Roman Catholic Church was not able to thrive very well under frontier conditions, where priests were scarce. Therefore, during the nineteenth century Protestant churches outnumbered the Catholics in America, except among the Catholic immigrants coming from Europe into eastern cities.

Lutheran

Martin Luther (1483–1546) had been rather conservative in his reformation of the main service of worship. As we saw in Chapter Six, his *Deutsche Messe* of 1526 was little more than a translation of the Roman mass into the vernacular of Luther's Lower Saxony. He attempted to maintain a balance between preaching and the Lord's Supper, but his followers found it easier to celebrate communion only periodically and to center the normal Sunday service on the sermon. A complicating factor for Lutherans in America was the surge of immigration from Germany in the mid-nineteenth century. These people brought their Lutheran orthodox styles of relating to God into the much less formal American context, which caused some dissension between the newer Americans and those who had been here earlier from Lutheran lands. Thus the nineteenth century saw some variety in the details of Lutheran worship forms, but also basic uniformity.

Reformed

The Reformed family of churches presents a much more varied picture. The tradition of disparate modes of worship among the descendants of the Protestant Reformation goes back at least to the Marburg Colloquy of 1529. Since the Reformed churches first arose in several European centers under several leaders, we should not be surprised to find a variety of worship styles and understandings.

Calvin, for instance, differed from Zwingli on the question of music. He had the biblical psalms translated into French and put to good music to be used in the Sunday services in Geneva and elsewhere, whereas Zwingli did away with music altogether. Singing only psalms was the norm for these churches on into the nineteenth century, and some of them continue in use today. The sermon was very important to both Calvin and Zwingli. Because of their failure to establish weekly communion, the Sunday services turned out to be dominantly rational and pedantic.

John Knox (1505–1572) carried Calvin's reformation to Scotland, and most of the Calvinist communities in America came from the Scots and Irish side of the family. The Westminster *Directory for the Public Worship of God* . . . (1645) became the normative document for reformed worship in the English language. Based on this, *The Directory for the Worship of God* was published in America in 1788 and set the worship scene for American reformed churches well into the 20th century. However, the nineteenth century saw much controversy over the revivalist tendencies advocated by Charles G. Finney (1792–1875), a Presbyterian evangelist. There were attempts to return to Calvin's Geneva worship patterns and teachings, but the revivalist momentum was strong, and hymns and gospel songs, as well as preaching for conversions, became the norm for many, if not most, reformed churches in America. The use of choral groups in revivals also migrated into congregational worship during the nineteenth century, until the presence of choirs on or near the chancel area became commonplace among Presbyterians. Spurred by the rational emphases of the Enlightenment, these changes tended to further weaken any emphasis on the sacraments and to increase the emphasis on the word, which resulted in a highly intellectualized church.

Anglican/Episcopalian

The Church of England had been a latecomer to the Protestant Reformation, but from the time of the publication of Thomas Cranmer's (1489–1556) *Book of Common Prayer* in 1549, its periodical revisions have continued to be the defining statements of Anglican worship down to the present. Since the Church of England was originally the established church in several of the American colonies, the results of the American revolution brought into question its place in American life. However, the publication in 1789 of an American revision of the *BCP* indicated its ongoing place in American life. This version fine-tuned the 1662 revision a bit and included a collection of hymns.

During the nineteenth century Anglicans worldwide instituted a turn back to more formal worship and weekly celebration of the Lord's Supper. By the end of the century the pattern was to have at least one of the Sunday morning services each week a eucharistic service and to be sure that the chief service be eucharistic on the first Sunday of each month. Early in the history of Anglicanism sacramental theology tended to veer far from the Catholic concept of the real presence of Christ in the elements of communion. In fact early Anglicans were less sacramental in that sense than either the Puritans or the Presbyterians. However, the nineteenth century saw a return of Anglicans to an emphasis on the real presence and on baptism as accomplishing regeneration. This move was accompanied by increasing emphasis on the Christian year and the use of seasonal hymns. As was true in England and elsewhere, the Episcopal Church in America attempted to strike a balance between the high liturgy surrounding the Eucharist and the importance of fine preaching, as exemplified in the ministries of Phillips Brooks (1835–1893) in Philadelphia and Boston.

Congregationalist

The Puritans who settled early in New England had separated from the Church of England in 1662. They had been influenced by the doctrines of Calvin, but, contrary to Calvin himself, they took the New Testament alone as normative instruction in worship. However, since they had trouble deciding just which New Testament texts were meant to be applied in worship, the ultimate decisions were left up to the local congregations. This congregational autonomy in matters of worship modes was firmly established, as the Congregationalists became the dominant voices of the separatist movement. Rather than liturgical anarchy, this produced a surprisingly high degree of unanimity in worship practices. The Puritans and their even stricter Separatist relatives (called Pilgrims in America) strove for congregations that lived lives of high morals so as to be worthy of receiving the Lord's Supper.

The Separatists, as their name implies, were happy to leave the fold of the Anglican Church. The Puritans who immigrated to the colonies insisted that they were not leaving the Church, but its corruptions. In fact, they established their church in New England much as the Anglicans did in Virginia. Eventually the Puritans found a home in the folds of the Congregationalists, Baptists, and Presbyterians.

Two movements caused division among these worshiping bodies in the late eighteenth and on through the nineteenth centuries. The Great Awakening (1725–1760) and its second incarnation (after 1800) reawakened the need for personal conversion for Christians, which resulted in both a change in the nature of preaching and a renewed insistence on the moral worthiness of those receiving the Lord's Supper. On the other hand, the Enlightenment and the concurrent movement of Transcendentalism led some Congregationalists away from anything sacramental, and from strict doctrinal orthodoxy, some becoming Unitarians.[2]

So we see among Congregationalists a wide spectrum of modes of congregational life and worship that continued throughout the nineteenth century, especially in America. Toward the end of the nineteenth century leaders like Washington Gladden (1836–1918), P.T. Forsyth (1848–1921), and John Oxenham (1852–1941) were able to strike a balance between evangelism and social action, as well as between sacramentalism and preaching.

Baptist

Baptist churches grew out of the British Congregationalist/ Separatist movement when several ministers decided that infant baptism had no scriptural warrant. They began to baptize only those who related and demonstrated evidence of conversion. The name Roger Williams (c. 1603–1683) is usually mentioned as the patriarch of Baptists in America. Williams was hounded out of the Massachusetts Bay colony and founded Rhode Island as a place of religious tolerance, where he and his followers could worship in peace. However, Baptists grew very slowly in the early years. Their growth was largely from immigration and birth, since most of them were strict Calvinists who depended on the Holy Spirit to point out God's elect and who therefore resisted human attempts at conversion.

During the nineteenth century the Baptists began turning away from their earlier dependence on the direct work of the Holy Spirit toward the normative role of the Bible in both evangelistic and worship practices. At the same time, their freedom from codified liturgical forms gave them helpful flexibility in worship forms for the American frontier. They became quite open to the new approach of Charles G. Finney and others who were preaching for personal decisions for Christ. So by the middle of the century they were a fast-growing group, especially in frontier areas. The church subsisted under the leadership of men who made their living as farmers or merchants. Their patterns of worship came to mirror the revival services from which many new members were coming. Lively singing of gospel songs and hymns on the themes of conversion, extemporaneous prayers, and sermons heavy with doctrine and emotional appeals characterized their services.

Quaker

The Quakers (Society of Friends) arose in the British ferment of the Puritan-Anglican struggle. They and other relatives of the more mystical wing of the radical reformation kept their distance from sacramental and other physical aids to worship, holding to the importance of the direction of the Spirit within each member for all that happens in corporate worship. Their severe persecution in England and in New England prompted their best-known advocate,

William Penn, to establish a colony (Pennsylvania), where they and others could live in peace and security.

From the standpoint of an outsider, Quakers are most easily identified by what they do not do in worship. They reject clergy leadership, service books, physical sacraments, preaching, choirs, musical instruments, and most ceremonial activities. However, an insider would point out that they cultivate a deep life of prayer and that they assemble regularly in expectation of the movement of the Holy Spirit within and among them, described as the Inner Light. For them, this Inner Light is equally accessible to all, and the purpose of worship is to wait upon God and follow God's leading.

The revivalist movement on the American frontier was adopted by some Quaker congregations so that during the nineteenth century those thus affected developed worship forms quite evangelical, with congregational singing, preaching, and altar calls characterizing an alternate form for those western Quakers. However, in England and the eastern United States the old style Quaker worship has remained surprisingly stable.

Methodist

As we saw in chapter seven, the one radical change that was born in the eighteenth century was the Wesleyan movement, which combined public preaching with new music and hymn words in such a way as to lead people to an emotional response in worship. John Wesley (1703–1791) and his brother Charles (1707–1788) were both staunch Anglican ministers from Puritan stock. Their movement and its older cousins in German pietism (especially the Moravians) reacted against the cold formalism of orthodoxy and the radical rationalism of the Enlightenment to promote heartwarming religion. They led people to enthusiastic participation in worship through a renewed emphasis on Eucharist and full-voiced singing of hymns, many of them written by Charles himself, who produced over six thousand hymn texts.

The Wesleys simplified the Anglican service to encourage

weekly communion, and they also turned the attention of their followers to the salvation and improvement of life of the workers in the booming industrial complex of Great Britain and America. The Methodist movement took root quickly in American soil and soon developed its own American style, neglecting the more formal aspects of the English Methodists and fitting into the prevailing informality of the American frontier. Francis Asbury (1745–1816), the leader of American Methodism, applied to the worship of American Methodism Wesley's pragmatism but not his love of the Anglican order. Following the American Revolution and Wesley's death, a new *Discipline* was published in America that effectively did away with the formal liturgies of England and promoted extemporaneous prayers, systematic reading of Scripture, preaching, and periodical (not weekly) communion.

The nineteenth century was a time of change and development of worship forms among American Methodists, especially those west of the Appalachian range. The influence of the camp meeting revivals was keenly felt in local communities. Preaching for a verdict became the norm, so as to lead people to a decisive conversion experience. The individualism of the frontier made its appearance in gospel songs such as those written by the blind poet Fanny Crosby (1820–1915), many of whose two thousand or more songs fit the temper of the day, like "Pass Me Not, O Gentle Savior," and "Blessed Assurance, Jesus is Mine." Wesley's concern for weekly communion disappeared, especially where it was impossible to have clergy present each week. The development of the Sunday School also fit the Methodist mold quite well, since lay people could lead it. Toward the end of the century some movement back to a more seriously eucharistic service was visible, but the majority of Methodists communed no more often than monthly.

African-American Trends

For many years, Christians of African descent, both slave and free, worshiped with their Caucasian masters and neighbors and reserved their African peculiarities for informal gatherings in places they often called "Praise Houses." Following the Civil War they began to establish their own congregations, developing their distinctive worship practices. Most did this in relation to either Methodist or Baptist fellowships, where they felt free to express their spontaneity. The African traditions of call and response invited great congregational participation both vocally and with free movement of the body. Another African tradition, that of the *griot*, or story teller, gave their preachers a model for the sermon that combines a rephrasing of the biblical story with its immediate application to the situation of the hearers.

The African-American funeral is an interesting example of the distinctives of this worship, especially prominent in New Orleans. A solemn procession from the home of the deceased begins the ritual, as friends and relatives accompany the body to the church building. The singing and preaching are aimed at eventual celebration of the deceased's entrance into heaven. The music used in the trip to the grave is slow and somber, but that heard on the return trip is upbeat and lively. Movement, music, and preaching, with vocal congregational response are the expected characteristics of this worship pattern now as in earlier years.

Results of the American Frontier

As the nineteenth century progressed, the revivalism of both Calvinistic and Arminian traditions, as exemplified in the ministry of Charles G. Finney, became the norm of worship style in most evangelical churches in the West, and also in many eastern congregations. The order placed the sermon at the climax of the service, with hymns and gospel songs (both congregational and "special") chosen to prepare people to hear the word preached and to lead people to a decision. Except for singing, the direct participation of the congregation faded as the role of the preacher became more prominent. The frequency of communion had been reduced in many instances already because of the scarcity of ordained clergy, and this new revivalist approach to worship made the Lord's Supper seem even less important.

Architecturally, this development encouraged churches to use a central pulpit and to reduce the size of the communion table, placing it either in front of and below the pulpit or off to the side. Choirs and instruments were now placed at the front, where they could become part of the proclamation process instead of at the rear or on the side, where they appeared to be part of the congregation. Acoustics and sight lines were now geared to the congregation's hearing and seeing the leaders, instead of their participating in worship.

The churches that most successfully resisted the move to informality and deemphasis on the sacraments were the Roman Catholic, the Anglican (Episcopalian), and the Lutheran churches. They all had strong traditions of liturgical direction in their histories, and their leaders were taught to follow the traditions. The Quakers, for the most part, were not swept away by the revivalist movement, since their tradition was one of quiet centering on the Spirit and waiting for the Spirit's moving before anything happened in worship. Thus the exceptions to the revivalist style were those with set liturgical canons and those who rejected all human planning and leadership.

However, the churches growing on the American frontiers during the nineteenth century were those Reformed, Methodist, and Free Churches (mostly Baptist and Restorationist) who evangelized openly, produced a ministry either living in the small communities or caring for a circuit of congregations, and developed a congregational polity and worship style congruent with the developing Jacksonian democracy of the time. Preaching in these churches was normally aimed at conversion. Since many frontier families had little or no religious affiliation at the time, such an emphasis was appropriate. The expected signs of conversion were mostly emotional. Among the Methodists such responses were seen as evidence that the individual was truly repentant and thus converted. Among the

Calvinistic Baptists and Presbyterians such responses were seen as signs of the work of the Holy Spirit to indicate that the individual was among the elect. In either case, people who did not have such an experience were often left in despair.

Out of this mix arose a nineteenth-century reformation movement led by Barton W. Stone (1772–1844) and Alexander Campbell (1786–1866), who determined to find their Christian life and worship modeled in the New Testament itself. Eight years before Alexander Campbell arrived in America from Ireland (by way of Scotland), Stone was involved in what has come to be called The Cane Ridge Meeting. What sort of meeting it was has been the subject of debate, but the earliest records of it refer to it as a sacramental meeting. These "Holy Fairs," as we saw in chapter eight, were not uncommon in Scotland, where the Lord's Supper was celebrated only occasionally and often in open-air meetings to accommodate the crowds. Stone had experienced at least one such meeting in southern Kentucky, and so he organized one on the grounds of the Presbyterian church he served in Cane Ridge, northeast of Lexington. He had convinced a number of other ministers, from several denominations, to cooperate in the venture, and when they met in August 1801, they were overwhelmed by the response. Participants reported that at least 12,000 people took part over the six days—people of many traditions and some of no Christian background at all. Preparation for the Lord's Supper lasted several days, during which people heard preaching aimed at leading them to repentance. They were encouraged to pray for forgiveness and to fast in preparation for communion. The phenomena experienced by hundreds of these participants seem very strange to us. They included fainting, howling, barking, and dancing—and perhaps the strangest of all, a beautifully sweet odor that surrounded many of them. There were, of course, skeptics, but for the most part the "exercises" were understood as powerful and miraculous works of the Holy Spirit.[3]

In some contrast to the enthusiasm of the Cane Ridge sacramental meeting, Alexander Campbell's movement in Western

Pennsylvania and down the Ohio River Valley distanced itself from what its leaders saw as the excesses of the revivalistic approach to both conversion and Christian worship. Stone himself appears to have seen such Holy Spirit phenomena not as ongoing experiences for the church, but as urges toward the unity of Christians at the Lord's table.[4] Rejecting the scandalous divisions of the Protestantism of the time and the creeds they saw as encouraging such divisions, they rediscovered the centrality of the Lord's Supper in weekly corporate worship and encouraged its practice under the leadership of local elders instead of ordained clergy alone. They neither sought nor found a specific liturgical order in the New Testament, but maintained freedom for each local congregation to proceed with prayers, praises, The Lord's Supper, and the presentation of the word in an appropriate, orderly fashion. Campbell highlighted two characteristics of corporate worship: the centrality of the Lord's Supper and the inappropriateness of a sermon.[5] This latter stemmed from his strict distinction between preaching (*kerygma*) and teaching (*didache*), the former being primarily for evangelism and therefore not appropriate for Christian worship, and the latter being appropriate for worship.

Thus the order of worship was left up to each local congregation, although Campbell did publish his approbation of one congregation's order: call to worship, a hymn, a gospel reading, a prayer, an epistle reading, a communion hymn, a statement about the Lord's Supper, a prayer for the bread, breaking and distribution of the bread, a prayer for the cup, distribution of the cup, a prayer, the offering, various members speaking to edify the assembled Christians, several songs, and a benediction.[6] This rather straightforward order, with some minor variations, appears to have been the general custom among those early reformed congregations.[7] This simple order reflects as much the simplicity necessitated by frontier living as the way the leaders understood the worship patterns in the New Testament. In fact, the simplicity dictated by the American frontier culture made it difficult, if not impossible, for these folks to recognize the set prayers and more formal liturgies we pointed to in chapter two in the New Testament documents.[8]

Another peculiarity of the Stone-Campbell Movement has been the practice of having local elders preside at the Lord's Table. On the frontier most denominations found it difficult to offer the sacrament very often because of the impossibility of having an ordained minister present for meetings of the church. Alexander Campbell's early negative reaction to the actions and attitudes of the clergy led him to see himself as a teaching elder and to encourage congregations to choose and ordain elders to do the work of shepherding, teaching, and leading worship. This made it possible for congregations to offer the Lord's Supper every Sunday, whether or not there was a preacher present. They saw this fulfilling the description in Acts 20:7, where we find, "On the first day of the week, when we met to break bread, Paul was holding a discussion with them. . ." (NRSV). They took this to indicate that the primary purpose of the Christian assembly was (and is) the Lord's Supper, with words from a visiting preacher as important, but secondary.

Stone's idea of church governance remained clergy-oriented (according to the Presbyterian model) until late in his life; but Campbell's attacks on paid clergy as hirelings out to protect their incomes determined the approach of the movement following the uniting of the two movements in 1831. This anticlergy attitude means not so much that the congregation is lay led, but rather that all Christians are called to minister. Elders in local congregations were generally ordained to that position. However, as paid and educated ministerial leaders appeared, the question of the purpose of ordination became an issue debated long and intensely among the churches. It remains a question for many today.[9]

The practice of baptism was also influenced by this priesthood of all believers principle. Very early in the movement's history the early church's practice of immersion for the remission of sins of believers was adopted and has remained the general practice ever since. The early leaders saw the efficacy of baptism as depending not on the status of the person who did the baptizing, but on the faith of the person being baptized. This means that any believer can do the baptizing, and it thus does not depend on the actions of an ordained minister.

Following the Civil War, with the rise of a paid and educated ministry, the sermon began to move into a place of dominance, along with the invitation time. A primary influence in this change was the important role being played on the frontier by traveling evangelists, who organized their services to culminate in a sermon calling for public acknowledgment of conversion during the singing of a song designated as an invitation or decision hymn. "By 1910 . . . the sermon had replaced communion as the high point of worship."[10] In fact, one student of the subject has stated, "worship is largely seen as a means to an end, and that end is evangelism."[11]

Preaching in the early years of this movement was oriented more to the mind than to the emotions. Faith was seen neither as an emotional response to the preaching nor as a miracle of grace, but rather as a natural human rational response to the presentation of the facts of the gospel as testified to by the biblical text and the history of the Church. Such evangelistic preaching was generally separated from the worship of baptized believers. Therefore worship was seen not so much as response to the moving of God's Spirit but as the congregation's obedient action to please God and to learn from God. What others called *sacraments*, the Campbellites and Stoneites called *ordinances*, thus emphasizing the obedience of the participants over the efficacy of the actions.

Summary

As expected, we see a quite varied worship scene in nineteenth century America—a spectrum stretching from the outwardly unformatted Quaker meetings to the ancient forms of Roman Catholicism. We also see the peculiarly American patterns growing out of frontier life and the revivals that spread over those western reaches. There appears to be an American longing for something different—an experience of God that touches mind, body, and emotions—a longing only partially filled by any single tradition. The search continued through the 20th century and continues today.

For Further Reading

Costen, Melva Wilson. *African American Christian Worship.* N a s hville: Abingdon Press, 1993.

Foster, Douglas, Paul M. Blowers, Anthony Dunnavant, and D. Newell Williams, eds. *The Encyclopedia of the Stone-Campbell Movement.* Grand Rapids: Eerdmans, 2004.

Hieronymus, Lynn. *What the Bible Says about Worship.* Joplin, MO: College Press, 1984.

Maring, Norman H. *American Baptists: Whence and Whither.* Valley Forge, PA: Judson Press, 1968.

Schmidt, Leigh Eric. *Holy Fairs: Scotland and the Making of American Revivalism.* Grand Rapids: Eerdmans, 2001.

Webber, Robert E., ed. *Complete Library of Christian Worship.* Volume 2. Nashville: Star Song Publishing, 1994.

White, James F. *A Brief History of Christian Worship.* Nashville: Abingdon Press, 1993.

_____. *Christian Worship in Transition.* Nashville: Abingdon Press, 1976.

_____. *Protestant Worship in Transition.* Louisville, KY: Westminster/John Knox Press, 1989.

⸺ ——— ⸺

[1]See the story of the remarkable Johannes Van der Kemp (1747–1811) in Frederick W. Norris, *Christianity: A Short Global History* (Oxford: One World Publications, 2002) 210-211.

[2]Ralph Waldo Emerson (1803–1882), a Unitarian minister, refused in 1832 to celebrate the Lord's Supper.

[3]Leigh Eric Schmidt, *Holy Fairs: Scotland and the Making of American Revivalism* (Grand Rapids: Eerdmans, 2001).

[4]Paul M. Blowers and Bruce E. Shields, "Worship, Nineteenth Century," in *The Encyclopedia of the Stone-Campbell Movement,* ed. by Foster, Blowers, Dunnavant, and Williams (Grand Rapids: Eerdmans, 2004) 786-788.

[5]Lynn Hieronymus, *What the Bible Says about Worship* (Joplin, MO: College Press, 1984) 4.

[6]Alexander Campbell, *Christianity Restored* (Bethany, VA: M'Vay and Ewing, 1835, later editions titled *The Christian System*) 340-342.

[7]Some of this material was published earlier as part of an article in *The Encyclopedia of the Stone-Campbell Movement*, 791-792.

[8]Hieronymus, *Worship*, 7.

[9]See the helpful article on "Ministry" in *The Encyclopedia of the Stone-Campbell Movement*, 521-533.

[10]Hieronymus, *Worship*, 11.

[11]Ken Read, "Christian Churches and Churches of Christ," in *The Complete Library of Christian Worship*, ed. by Robert E. Webber (Nashville: Star Song Publishing, 1994) 7:20.

CHAPTER TEN

The Twentieth Century

Context

The twentieth century appears in retrospect to have been a century of wars and upheaval. It was ushered in by a war between the United States and Spain and was greeted only a few years later by what came to be called World War I. That was followed by a worldwide monetary crisis and a great depression. Then came World War II that turned Europe once again into a battleground, this time involving also nations of the orient. The horrors of the Nazi attempt to eradicate the Jews in Europe shocked the civilized world. At the mid-point of the century an armed conflict in Korea and a cold war between the nations of the West and those under the dominion of the Soviet Empire captured attention. All the while, people were living under the fear of a nuclear attack, having seen the devastation of the two nuclear bombs that had brought Japan to the surrender table in 1945. The second half of the century was punctuated by smaller wars in places like Viet Nam, the Middle East, Africa, and the former Yugoslavia, along with armed rebellions in Northern Ireland, Africa, and South America.

However, it wasn't all bombs and bullets. The twentieth century also saw great developments in medical care, food production, and industrial technology. Transportation and communication gained speed, and with that gain came increasing international business. Following World War II the war-weary western European countries moved inexorably in the direction of cooperation, first economically and then politically. With the downfall of the Soviet Union, many of the newly independent nations of eastern Europe began opening to the western nations until the end of the century, when it looked as though Europe would be working together so as to become a world power, both economically and politically. During that same period, the United States went through a tumultuous period of racial tension and civil rights demonstrations, while at the same time being stymied by a war in Viet Nam from which we ultimately had to withdraw. Satellite television that brings events from around the globe into every living room and computers that make possible instantaneous and inexpensive communication everywhere on earth encourage democratic action that brings political change in surprising places. The century reached from the horse and buggy to space travel and from Morse code to e-mail. The changes in worship were no less profound.

Space

Church architecture followed the patterns of architecture in general during the twentieth century, which means that churches built very sparse, modern structures, as well as more traditional Gothic or colonial style buildings. One can find in the United States the Crystal Cathedral in southern California[1] as well as the so-called National Cathedral in Washington, D.C.[2] We find this same eclectic trend in Europe, while in other parts of the world churches began to use local materials and building styles instead of importing European or American designs that appear so foreign.

Time

Along with the liturgical renewal among many churches that we shall see below, came an interest in the Christian year that many traditions had earlier either neglected or rejected as "too Catholic." As the Roman Catholic church stepped back from its confusing array of saints days, many Protestant churches began to emphasize more special days of the calendar than just Christmas and Easter and the seasons around them. All Saints Day began to be recognized, as well as Pentecost. With the growing use of the lectionary, Advent and Lent as well as special services during holy week increased in popularity. There was also an increased appreciation among ministers of the daily office and other approaches to spiritual formation that came down from ancient times.

Orders

Since music and liturgical renewal have played such a vital role in the development of worship patterns through the twentieth century, this section of the chapter will be much fuller than the others. Two movements that began early in the century influenced Christian corporate worship around the world. They are the Pentecostal/ Charismatic movement and the liturgical renewal movement. We shall look at them in that order.

Pentecostal/Charismatic Movements

The Pentecostal movement has its roots in the Holiness trends begun by the German Pietists and in the English speaking areas by John Wesley and his followers. The insistence that a conversion experience is necessarily followed by a second experience of grace for sanctification characterizes the Holiness movement. The emphasis on enthusiasm or emotion found a receptive audience among the people of the American frontier, and the eucharistic occasions followed by revivals and camp meetings that we described in chapter nine gave the movement a method. Over a period of years several of these groups left the historic denominations to form a new cluster of church connections, including the Church of the Nazarene, the Free Methodist Church, and the Wesleyan Church. The Salvation Army can also be associated with this movement, being the one best known for its work outside the regular church walls. In many cases the services of worship were free-flowing, boisterous assemblies where all in attendance were invited (even expected) to participate actively with singing, testimonies, shouts of praise, and prayer times when many people prayed aloud at the same time. Some of the more radical preachers and congregations handled snakes and drank poison as testimony of their faith in the God who promised believers safety (Mark 16:18).

In the first few years of the twentieth century Pentecostalism gained a strong foothold in the United States, as at Bethel Bible School in Topeka, Kansas, and in a great revival meeting on Azusa Street in Los Angeles people began experiencing the gift of speaking and praying in unknown tongues. In 1901, at Bethel, the evangelist and teacher Charles Parham urged his students to pray for the Holy Spirit with miraculous power, and student, Agnes Ozman, began speaking in tongues. Then in 1906 William Seymour, a former student of Parham's, opened a revival at Azusa Street that lasted until 1913, where many people experienced miraculous gifts. Proclaiming this experience to be the direct work of the Holy Spirit, people carried the message and the experience far and wide.

Music played a major role in both the worship and the evangelism of the Pentecostals. They sang great old hymns of the church, traditional southern gospel songs, and newer gospel songs. "Through songs, people expressed emotions, declared doctrines, glorified God, exhorted one another, entreated sinners, responded to testimonies, invoked miracles, and yearned for God's tangible presence."[3] They also enjoyed the phenomenon of singing in the Spirit, in which a group of worshipers sang together in moving, uncomposed harmonies, sometimes in tongues, sometimes in the vernacular, and sometimes, in a hum or nonlinguistic sound.[4] In the 1920s Aimee Semple McPherson built a Pentecostal congregation in Los Angeles that drew upwards of 5,000 people to her services. She used the music of choirs and orchestras, as well as full-voiced congregational singing to reach the masses. She composed her own music at times and used it to good effect to prepare for and follow up on her preaching. This led in 1927 to the founding of the International Church of the Foursquare Gospel. By mid-century larger Pentecostal churches were hiring professional musicians to help in the planning and leading of services. The use of music then became regularized, since with congregations in the thousands it became impossible to encourage spontaneous singing to break out whenever the Spirit moved.

These church musicians became adept at setting Scripture to music and at developing praise choruses that could be sung repeat-edly by congregations for specific emotional effects. As these songs began replacing the older style hymns, the churches lost the theolog-ical content and exhortations to ministry and missions that character-ized the songs of the Wesleys, Watts, and Fannie Crosby. To some extent they also lost interest in the historical creeds and sacraments, emphasizing the feelings over the actions and beliefs of the wor-shipers. Thus what was gained in simplicity and attraction caused a loss in doctrine and connection with the history of worship.

In 1959 the effects of Pentecostalism began to be felt within mainline denominations. It first broke into the Episcopal Church, and then into nearly every Protestant denomination, finally showing itself among Roman Catholics at Duquesne University in Pittsburgh and simultaneously in Bogotá, Columbia, in 1967. This broadening spread of Pentecostal gifts became known as the Charismatic Movement.

A typical charismatic prayer service (usually not a Sunday morning service) is quite spontaneous. Participants often sit in a cir-cle. An opening hymn or chorus is followed by a Scripture reading and silent meditation and prayer. The silence is broken in a few minutes when somebody prays aloud, perhaps responding to the text that was read. More silence is broken from time to time with more audible prayers. A guitar begins a praise chorus in which the others join. A few people give testimonies of God's power helping in life situations. Someone asks for prayers for a difficult situation. He/she sits or kneels in the middle of the circle while others gather around, laying on hands and praying. One or two pray in tongues. They go back to their places, and somebody reads a Psalm, followed by silence. There might be a refreshment break and then a resump-

tion of the service. More prayers ensue followed by the group praying the Lord's Prayer. Somebody speaks a prophecy. Somebody else
begins singing in tongues, and soon the whole group is involved in
what became known as the "heavenly choir." The group recites a
Psalm and the meeting closes. In contrast to larger Pentecostal
assemblies, this Charismatic service is subdued, but still charged
with the awareness of God's presence.[5]

This larger Charismatic Movement resulted in disruption and
many congregational splits over the next decades as Charismatic
groups formed within traditional congregations. In most cases communication broke down as the more radical on both the traditional
and the Charismatic sides decided that the other side was not
Christian or not fully Christian. I am aware of one case where an
elder stated publicly that speaking in tongues was the work of the
devil, only later to request that the Charismatic group in his congregation pray for his healing of cancer, which they did.

Most obvious of the results for worship of the Pentecostal/
Charismatic movements is their music, which combined with that of
the Jesus Movement in a way that touched many young adults of
the late sixties, seventies, and eighties. The Pentecostal/Charismatic
musicians also encouraged the development of an industry to print
and distribute their music, which led to recordings, concerts, and
concert tours of soloists and musical groups. This tendency grew to
the point of becoming a major factor in the entertainment business,
with Christian bands rivaling secular rock bands for popularity and
name recognition.

The resounding success of this music in drawing people to the
Christian faith during the sixties and seventies continued through
the end of the century. The music was also quickly incorporated
into the services of congregations looking to attract younger people.
The Willow Creek congregation was just the earliest of many that
developed "seeker services" in which contemporary music and a
very informal approach to worship were applied. In fact, it might be
argued that the seeker services were not worship at all, but rather

evangelistic services. Willow Creek and others developed services during the week for Christian worship, including the Lord's Supper, which was absent on Sunday mornings. Many of these churches grew very quickly, and a church growth movement appeared, along with a great interest in planting new churches that would not look or sound like the "traditional" congregations.

Since Pentecostals, Charismatics, and the Evangelicals who have adopted (and adapted) their approach to worship do not use set worship orders or prayers, we cannot point to documents of services with any confidence that we would be seeing how these churches worship. We can, however, point to music as a defining characteristic of worship, as we saw above. In many instances congregational singing, led by a praise band, lasts thirty to forty-five minutes, interspersed with prayers by the leaders and brief, inspirational introductions to songs. Interestingly, music/worship ministers have developed a kind of ritual order, patterned after the Jerusalem temple or the tabernacle. The idea is that the worshipers begin outside the temple, proceed into the outer courts and progress inward, ever closer to the presence of God in the Holy of Holies. The journey begins with choruses of personal experience, songs of praise, phrased mostly in the first person singular or plural. Entering the gates is accomplished with songs that lead from praise to worship, songs of thanksgiving. This makes the worshipers conscious of both themselves and their God. Third comes a step into the Holy of Holies, where worshipers are conscious of God alone. Now the dominant pronoun is second person singular, as people express their worship directly to God. Not only does the verbal expression change in this order, but the mood changes from jubilant, hand-clapping praise to reverent, raised-hands worship, often with tears.[6] This song service usually leads to times of teaching/preaching, intercessory prayer, and ministry, to which the congregation is commissioned and dismissed.

Since the domination of the clock has not been a factor among these congregations, a forty-minute sermon is not unusual. In some instances the Lord's Supper is offered during the service, but quite often it is served in an anteroom following the closing prayer. The larger churches have developed drama ministries so that Bible stories acted out or illustrative contemporary skits play a role in eliciting an emotion or making a point. This has been paralleled by the development of dance troupes who do choreographed movement to songs or Scripture readings. As such presentations became increasingly professional, the services themselves became more and more centered on the platform, thus making the congregation more of an audience than a community of participants. This is why in chapter six we pointed out that some of the tendencies of medieval Catholicism returned among twentieth-century Evangelicals. For the seeker who feels more comfortable as an anonymous face in a crowd and who is accustomed to attending concerts or films, this is a welcoming environment. Thus these churches experienced phenomenal growth among the baby-boomer generation.

African American worship, while in many ways related to the Holiness or Pentecostal movement, has had its own style and characteristics. There is no single worship pattern, but there are some dominant characteristics. Whereas the African Methodist Episcopal Zion Church has continued the staid worship order established by Francis Asbury in the early years of American Methodism,[7] most predominantly black churches prefer a more spontaneous and participatory style. The sermon is usually the climax of the service, with people encouraging the preacher with their "amen," "praise the Lord," and "Help him, Jesus" utterances. There is little one would recognize as set liturgy, but there is a definite emotional shape to these services—a sequence of calm, rational thought and exuberant emotion, ending in a grand celebration.[8]

African American worship is at least tangentially related to the Pentecostal/Charismatic approach; although it has roots that extend all the way back to Africa and which developed in the "middle passage" in the Caribbean islands and during the years of slavery and segregation in the United States.[9] Instead of rejecting the religion of their masters, these slaves by and large adopted it, adapting it to their remembered traditions and their oppressive situation. Costen outlines a general order of worship in many African American churches thus:

> God's Divine Initiative (Call)
> Fellowship (Gathering)
> Adoration and Praise to God (Personal Testimonies)
> Penitence (Prayer)
> Hearing and Receiving the Word (Illumination)
> Renewal, Self-offering, and Dedication
> Service in the World (Mission)[10]

This open outline affords worshipers opportunities for the direct participation that is characteristic of their worship. By far the best known element of African American worship is the music. Many people hold that the blues and jazz, America's gifts to the musical arts, come straight out of this church music. The spirituals that arose as oral folk music closely related to African chants are known and appreciated in much of the world even today. The slaves learned the metric hymns used by their masters, but they sang them in their own oral style, a leader singing out a line and the congregation repeating it after him or her. In this way they developed their own rhythms for "Dr. Watts." Out of this mixture was born the Black Gospel style—a designation given it by Thomas A. Dorsey, a fine musician and composer best known for his "Precious Lord, Take My Hand," written in response to the death of his wife and newborn son in 1932.[11] Dorsey's contributions to Christian music have been updated and continued by Andraé Crouch[12] and others who have brought Black Gospel into the Modern and Postmodern eras with new rhythms and harmonic structures. Three part harmony (melody, alto, and tenor) and a lead singer improvising often above the melody give this music its special sound and emotional impact.

The typical preaching of African American churches has been studied much more broadly than has worship in general. Part of the impact of Martin Luther King, Jr., was an interest in the power of black preaching. These sermons do more than convey information. "The word from the Lord is heard with the ears of one's total being, and it is experienced in the poetic flow of the preacher."[13] The crescendo and decrescendo of emotion accompanied by the verbal encouragement of the congregation make the sermon a participatory art form, a holistic experience.[14]

Times of prayer are also times of full participation when, in contrast to most Euro-American churches, people add to the prayers of the pastor with "Yes, Lord," "Thank you, Jesus," "Amen," and other phrases. Thus, music, preaching, and prayers of many sorts combine to give the African American worshipers the divine power that society so often denies them.

Liturgical Renewal Movements

Eastern Orthodox

On the other hand, the movement of liturgical renewal was developing at the same time as the Pentecostal/Charismatic Movements. As we saw in Chapter Five, the Eastern Orthodox liturgy was set in the fourteenth century and was passed from generation to generation with little change. It is credited to St. John Chrysostom who, with his fourth-century colleague Theodore of Mopsuestia, developed both the service of worship and the theological rationale for it. Even though other eastern churches (East and West Syrian, Armenian, and Alexandrian liturgical families) have their own liturgies, the Byzantine churches (Greek and Russian primarily) are most commonly known in the West. Therefore we offer this Byzantine order for comparison with the Roman Catholic order to follow:[15]

> ➤ Introductory and Entrance Rites
>> ➤ Liturgy of Preparation (*Proskomidia*)—in Prothesis:
>> ➤ The Great Litany (*Synapte*)
>> ➤ The 3 Antiphons
> ➤ Reading of Scripture and Supplications
>> ➤ The Little Entrance (Procession of the Book of the Gospels) with Trisagion Hymn

> The Epistle Reading
> > The Gospel Reading preceded by Threefold Alleluia
> > Homily
> > Litany and Dismissal of the Catechumens
> > Prayer of the Faithful
> The Procession to the Altar
> > The Great Entrance with Cherubic Hymn
> > Litany of Fervent Supplication and Prayer of Prep-
> > aration (*Ektene* and *Proskomide*)
> > Kiss of Peace
> > Nicene-Constantinopolitan Creed
> The Eucharistic Prayer and Communion
> > Eucharistic Prayer (*Anaphora*)
> > The Lord's Prayer
> > Communion Invitation, Communion, Communion
> > Hymn
> Concluding Rites
> > Post-Communion Hymn(s) and Prayer of Thanks-
> > giving
> > Various liturgical additions (Homily, Memorial Ser-
> > vice for the departed, etc.)
> > Dismissal Rites: Blessing, Distribution of Antidoron

This Orthodox order can be confusing to those who are not accustomed to it, since the priest is often hidden behind the iconos-tasis (icon screen), which should not be understood as a barrier but rather a bridge between the earthly worshipers and the heavenly worshipers. Prayers and hymns are spoken and sung by the people, led by a deacon (a clergy order) while the priest and his concele-brants prepare the loaf and cup in intricate ways, as well as prepar-ing themselves and praying for the congregation. The service focus-es on the resurrected and reigning Christ and his presence among his people; and the architecture, vestments, music, incense, and bib-lical statements of praise are designed to make the experience of worship as transcendent of this world as possible.

Roman Catholic

Meanwhile, the twentieth century was a time of restudy and reform of the Roman mass. As early as 1903 Pope Pius X began to encourage the study of the ancient liturgical forms of the church. Pius XII furthered the movement, as did an international pastoral conference in Assisi in 1956. This set the stage for a long look at the worship of the Roman Catholic Church, which came to fruition at the Second Vatican Council in early 1962. A serious attempt was made by the bishops and their advisors during the years of preparation for the council to look carefully at the worship patterns seen in the Bible and in the earliest documents of church history and to consider how these might be applied to the contemporary church.

Keeping in mind the developments of the mass during the middle ages that we described in Chapter Six and the hard-edged ritual strictures of the Counter-Reformation by the Council of Trent that we saw in chapter seven, one can appreciate the distance traveled by the Catholic hierarchy at Vatican II. However, the adoption of the new guidelines was neither easy nor unanimous. In fact as late as the early twenty-first century there are still priests and parishes resisting the changes.

The heart of the *Constitution on the Sacred Liturgy*[16] of the Second Vatican Council is in Article Ten, which states the centrality of the church's worship:

> . . . the liturgy is the summit toward which the activity of the Church is directed: at the same time it is the fountain from which all her power flows.[17] For the goal of apostolic works is that all who are made sons of God by faith and baptism should come together to praise God in the midst of His Church, to take part in her sacrifice, and to eat the Lord's supper.
>
> The liturgy in its turn inspires the faithful to become "of one heart in love"[18] when they have tasted to their full of the paschal mysteries; it prays that "they may grasp by deed what they hold by creed."[19] The renewal in the Eucharist of the covenant between the Lord and man [*sic*] draws the faithful into the compelling love of Christ and sets them afire. From the liturgy, therefore, and

especially from the Eucharist, as from a fountain, grace is chan-
neled into us; and the sanctification of men in Christ and the glo-
rification of God, to which all other activities of the Church are
directed as toward their goal, are most powerfully achieved.[20]

We can see in this emphasis why the liturgy had been worked
on for so long before the Vatican Council met and why this *Constitution on the Sacred Liturgy* was adopted first and applied so rigorously. We can also see that certain aspects of the Catholic understanding of liturgy were not to be revised. The clearest example of
this is the reference to sacrifice and the strong sacramental language in terms of the channeling of grace through liturgical actions.
At the same time, it becomes obvious that the understanding and
participation of the whole church (laity as well as clergy) will be
important. In fact, the very next three articles deal with the preparation of participants so the faithful can "take part knowingly,
actively, and fruitfully."[21] In addition, Section II, comprised of
Articles 14 through 20 commend and outline the instruction of the
faithful in appropriate preparation and active participation in the
liturgy.

The general norms of reform state that there are unchange-
able liturgical acts, but there are also elements that may and should
be changed from time to time. The Bible is seen as the ultimate and
decisive norm:

> Sacred Scripture is of paramount importance in the celebration of
> the liturgy. For it is from Scripture that lessons are read and
> explained in the homily, and psalms are sung; the prayers, collects,
> and liturgical songs are scriptural in their inspiration, and it is
> from Scripture that actions and signs derive their meaning. Thus
> if the restoration, progress, and adaptation of the sacred liturgy
> are to be achieved, it is necessary to promote that warm and liv-
> ing love for Scripture to which the venerable tradition of both
> Eastern and Western rites gives testimony.[22]

Under norms based upon the educative and pastoral nature of
the liturgy, the *Constitution* opens the door, in Article 36, for much

broader use of local vernaculars in worship, and thus limited use of Latin.[23] This was one of the first changes traditional Catholics noticed, and it caused much debate because of the concern that it tended toward local distinctions and threatened the global unity of the Catholic (universal) Church. Homilies and Scripture readings had long been in the vernacular, but now the prayers of the priest at the altar were to be understandable, too. The extent and pace of this change were left to the discretion of local bishops in consulta-tion with other bishops and ultimately with the Vatican.

One of the more radical reforms is outlined in Articles 37–40, where bishops (again with proper consultation) are encouraged to study local traditions and art forms with a view to incorporating them into the liturgy. This is especially important to churches on non-Western mission fields, where western customs seem too strange to be attractive.

To facilitate reform on the local level bishops were instructed to establish diocesan commissions on the liturgy and to see to it that liturgics becomes a primary part of priestly formation from semi-nary through continuing education. Then in the articles on the reform of the Eucharist the use of more Scripture and an emphasis on preaching (Articles 51 and 52) should be included in the mass.

Bishops were also given permission to offer both the bread (host) and the wine to clergy and laity alike in the Eucharist, but in certain special services only. This was again an important opening, and Article 55, which deals with both elements, refers back to the decrees of the Council of Trent that also permitted communion in both "kinds" in several specified occasion masses. The new state-ment, however, is worded so as to teach that this is the original practice with the implication that it should be the present practice at every occasion, even though it continues to be limited. The revi-sions that came out of the guidelines set forth in the *Constitution* included moving the main altar away from the wall, where for cen-turies the prayers of the priest were said or sung with his back to the congregation. Now the priest and those assisting him were expected to stand behind the altar facing the congregation, thus signifying that the altar is essentially a table around which the whole church gathers with its Lord.

These changes in the Eucharist are followed by Articles 59 to 82, listing similar revisions in the other sacraments and the sacramentals (rituals for various occasions of life, including funeral services). Once again we find here the insistence that the understanding of all participants is vital, so instruction, as well as the wording of the ritual itself should be in the language of the people, and the people should be instructed in the meaning, where that is not obvious. To accomplish all this, instruction is given to revise and enrich all these ceremonies so as to focus on their meaning and significance. No longer is the medieval dictum that a sacrament is efficacious in itself (*ex opere operato*) enough; now it is clear that the understanding and therefore the participation of all who are involved is vital.

Articles 83 to 101 deal with the Divine Office, the prayers, Psalms, and other readings to be used as personal and choral devotions at specified times of each day. Again we find permission to use the vernacular if that is more effective. There are other revisions called for to make the Office better suited to the otherwise busy days of parish priests and nuns, while keeping monks and others on a tight devotional schedule.[24] The morning and evening times (Lauds and Vespers) are underscored as most important, with a simplified prayer at bedtime (Compline). Matins, which was originally the end of an all-night vigil and which was later applied to the prayers in the middle of the night, was changed to be used any time during the day, while Prime, Terce, Sext, and None (first, third, sixth, and ninth hours prayers) were allowed to disappear as required actions.

The liturgical year is dealt with in Articles 102 to 111. The primary festival is that of the resurrection of Jesus, which is celebrated each Sunday but emphasized especially on Easter. The statement of purpose of the cycle of the year here is worth quoting in full:

Recalling thus the mysteries of redemption, the Church opens to the faithful the riches of her Lord's powers and merits, so that these are in some way made present at all times and the faithful are enabled to lay hold of them and become filled with saving grace.[25]

Even though the importance of days to honor the virgin Mary and the saints and martyrs is upheld, Article 108 makes it clear that the cycle of events in the life, death, and resurrection of Christ are most important. Therefore, Lent and Holy Week are specifically dealt with as important preparations for baptism and for the celebration of salvation, while saints days are relegated to a minor place.

Sacred music is encouraged in Articles 112 to 121, where music of all kinds is permitted, as long as it is appropriate to the setting and purpose. Gregorian chant is still accorded pride of place, and the pipe organ is noted as the traditional instrument, but composers are encouraged to compose music fitting to their cultures, and priests (especially missionaries) are instructed to learn as much as possible about music in their cultures so as to be able to make intelligent decisions about its use in the liturgy. In much the same way, the final five articles deal with the fine arts used as part of sacred space for the edification of the faithful.[26]

The resulting Eucharistic Mass of the Roman Catholic Church follows this pattern:

> Entrance
>> Entrance Procession with congregational song
>> Greeting with congregational response
>> Rite of Blessing and Sprinkling Holy Water (to remind worshipers of their baptism)
>> Gloria
>> Opening Prayer
> Liturgy of the Word
>> First Reading with response: "The Word of the Lord. **Thanks be to God.**"
>> Responsorial Psalm
>> Second Reading with response above
>> Alleluia
>> Gospel Reading with response: "The Gospel of the Lord. **Praise to you, Lord Jesus Christ.**"

> ➤ Homily
> ➤ Profession of Faith (Apostles' Creed or Nicene Creed)
> ➤ General Intercessions, each prayer ends with ". . . let us pray to the Lord. **Lord, hear our prayer.**"

➤ Liturgy of the Eucharist
>   ➤ Presentation of the Gifts/Preparation of the Altar
>   ➤ Prayer over the gifts
>   ➤ Eucharistic Prayer
>   ➤ Memorial acclamation: "Let us proclaim the mystery of faith. **Christ has died, Christ is risen, Christ will come again.**"
>   ➤ Doxology and the Great Amen
>   ➤ The Lord's Prayer
>   ➤ The Sign of Peace
>   ➤ The Breaking of the Bread
>   ➤ Communion with a song as people go forward and receive the bread
>   ➤ Silence or song of praise
>   ➤ Prayer after Communion
>   ➤ Greeting and Dismissal

Mainline Protestants

An interesting detail of the Second Vatican Council and our purpose in reviewing so much of its work here was the presence of observers from other churches and traditions. This refreshing openness encouraged the mainline Protestant denominations to look at their own worship traditions in the light of the research into Christian origins done by Catholic scholars; and it came at a time when the Charismatic Movement was bringing traditional Protestant worship orders into question. Even though none of them merely adopted the Roman Missal as a guide, the Presbyterians, Lutherans, and Methodists, as well as other groups, began to use ancient prayers, confessions of sin, creeds, and responses in their worship assemblies. Whereas the former two centuries had seen increasing diversities among Christian denominational families, the late twentieth century saw increasing convergence. This trend showed itself not only in Sunday morning worship, but also in the use of the church calendar and lectionary, the Lord's Supper, baptism, ordination, marriage, and funeral ceremonies. Indeed, guides for daily prayer and devotional reading began to be marketed across denominational lines, and this, together with the additional opportunities for lay participation in worship assemblies, got increasing numbers of church members directly involved in worship instead of being passive recipients of music, prayers, and sermons.

One especially encouraging turn among Protestants was the regular use of multiple Scripture readings in services of worship. The lectionaries edited by ecumenical committees (with Roman Catholic observers), using modern translations of the Bible and combining the choosing of smaller texts (pericopes) with the *lectio continua* approach of the Reformation, encouraged the use of three or four (Old Testament, Psalm, Epistle, and Gospel) readings in each service, read in many cases by different men and women from the congregation. In this way, millions of churchgoers were hearing the same texts at their weekend services as were their neighbors in other churches. Preachers were preaching on one or another of those texts (most often the Gospel text), which encouraged them to discuss sermon preparation with their colleagues in other denominations.

The ecumenical movement of the twentieth century encouraged congregations of various denominations to worship together and to develop services that would facilitate such interdenominational worship. In 1950 the Anglicans, Methodists, Presbyterians, and Congregationalists of southern India united into the Church of South India and began to worship with an ecumenical liturgy, as follows:

➤ The Preparation
  ➤ Ministers enter, carrying the Bible to the lectern
  ➤ Presbyter leads an opening prayer with a praise response from the congregation
  ➤ Confession of Sin
  ➤ Assurance of Pardon

> The Ministry of the Word of God
> > "The Lord be with you; **And with your spirit.**"
> > Prayer
> > Hymn
> > Old Testament Lesson. People respond: **"Thanks be to Thee, O God."**
> > Epistle Lesson. People respond: **"Thanks be to Thee, O God."**
> > Gospel Lesson. People respond: **"Praise be to Thee, O Christ."**
> > Sermon
> > Nicene Creed
> > Bidding Prayers. People respond to each petition: "**Hear us, we beseech thee, O Lord**" or "Lord, have mercy."
> > First Benediction
> The Breaking of the Bread
> > Passing the Peace
> > Offering of Alms and bringing the communion elements to the table
> > "**Be present, be present, O Jesus, thou good High Priest, as thou wast in the midst of thy disciples, and make thyself known to us in the breaking of the bread, who livest and reignest with the Father and the Holy Spirit, one God, world without end. Amen.**" [kneeling]
> > Sursum Corda and Eucharistic Prayer, followed by the Lord's prayer and: "**We do not presume to come to this thy Table, O merciful Lord, trusting in our own righteousness, but in thy manifold and great mercies. We are not worthy so much as to gather up the crumbs under thy Table. But thou art the same Lord, whose property is always to have mercy: Grant us therefore, gracious Lord, so to eat the Flesh of thy dear Son Jesus Christ, and to drink his Blood, that our sinful bodies and souls may be made clean by his most precious Body and Blood, and that we may evermore dwell in him, and he in us. Amen.**"

> ➤ Bread is broken, wine is poured out, and the people receive both, while singing an appropriate song.
> ➤ Prayer of Thanksgiving
> ➤ Final benediction.[27]

In 1982 the World Council of Churches published a Faith and Order Paper (Number 111) titled *Baptism, Eucharist and Ministry.* This booklet calls the various denominations to study the roots and meanings of these three divisive issues to determine what is essential and how adherents of the varied traditions can recognize and honor the baptism, communion, and ordination of other traditions. This was followed in 1990 by the publication of a report on progress.[28] This report indicates that more progress has been made on the sacraments than on mutual recognition of ministry and that more study is needed on the roles and offices of bishop, presbyter, and deacon.

The best known liturgy to come out of these ecumenical discussions is the Lima Liturgy, used first at the World Council of Churches meeting that approved *Baptism, Eucharist and Ministry* in Lima, Peru, in 1982. It follows this order:

> ➤ Liturgy of Entrance
>   ➤ Entrance Psalm
>   ➤ Greeting
>   ➤ Confession of sin
>   ➤ Absolution
>   ➤ Kyrie Litany
>   ➤ Gloria
> ➤ Liturgy of the Word
>   ➤ Collect
>   ➤ First Lesson
>   ➤ Psalm of Meditation
>   ➤ Epistle
>   ➤ Alleluia
>   ➤ Gospel
>   ➤ Homily

➢ Silence
➢ Creed
➢ Intercession
➢ Liturgy of the Eucharist
   ➢ Preparation
   ➢ Dialogue (sursum corda)
   ➢ Preface
   ➢ Sanctus
   ➢ Epiclesis I
   ➢ Institution
   ➢ Anamnesis
   ➢ Epiclesis II
   ➢ Commemoration
   ➢ Conclusion
   ➢ The Lord's Prayer
   ➢ The Peace
   ➢ The Breaking of the Bread
   ➢ Lamb of God
   ➢ Communion
   ➢ Thanksgiving Prayer
   ➢ Final Hymn
   ➢ Word of Mission
   ➢ Blessing[29]

As we approach the fiftieth anniversary of Vatican II, we see increasing effects of its work on worship, as ever more congregations look again at ancient forms and adapt them to contemporary situations and styles, thus coming ever closer to unity in Christian corporate worship forms.

Initiation

Very little changed during the twentieth century in reference to practices of Christian initiation (baptism and confirmation), with the exception of the development by the Roman Catholic Church of a ritual for adult initiation. This is a year-long process of learning and spiritual formation in preparation for baptism and communion (usually on Easter).[30] As we have seen in earlier chapters, the history of initiation in the Catholic Church had shifted from adult baptism to infant baptism so that the rituals assumed that the candidates were babies. After Vatican II the need was seen of preparing rituals (again) for those who could answer for themselves.

The Lord's Supper

As we noted in Chapter Seven, The Reformation period produced many different understandings and practices of the Lord's Supper. The spectrum runs from the extreme sacramentalism of the Orthodox and Catholics to the extreme nonsacramentalism of the Quakers.[31] We offer here just an overview of this spectrum.

➤ Roman Catholics and Eastern Orthodox churches hold to the doctrine of transubstantiation, believing that the bread and wine become the body and blood of Christ sacrificed again at the hands of the priest as he utters the words of institution. The difference between the two is just that Catholic theologians and liturgists attempt to explain the change in terms of Platonic philosophy and the Orthodox merely claim that it is a mystery.

➤ Lutherans generally hold to the real presence of Christ in the bread and wine, but deny that the actions of the presiding minister effect a sacrifice. There have been many attempts to explain the presence (cf. Luther's "consubstantiation"), but none of these have become essential doctrines.

➤ Calvinistic approaches to the Supper, which include a broad range of churches, including Reformed, Presbyterian, Anglican, and Methodist, hold to a spiritual presence of Christ in the rite of the Lord's Supper, but not especially in the elements themselves.

➤ Churches following the pattern of Zwingli include most Baptists, Mennonites and Amish, Restoration Movement congregations, Evangelical Free Church, and most Pentecostals and Adventists. They understand the bread and wine to be symbols of Christ's body and blood and nothing more. However, the practice of these churches differs widely, from the insistence of the Restoration Movement that the Lord's Supper is the central act of worship and should be observed every week to the Quaker teaching that Christ never meant the Supper to continue past the first generation of Christians.

Interestingly, among many of these denominations, movements started during the later years of the century to return the Lord's Supper to its place at the center of weekly worship, and many congregations have increased the frequency of communion, often making it available every week. If not the theology of communion, certainly the frequency is becoming more common.

Praise

As we saw above, there was an emergence of praise music among Pentecostals, Charismatics, and then evangelicals in general in the twentieth century. By the end of the century such music was in use even in rather formal liturgies among the mainline denominations. The influence of the Christian music industry and the concerts and recordings of this music was being felt worldwide and across the denominational board, as congregations attempted to attract and retain young people.

Preaching

The importance of the sermon was brought into question during the 1960s, when many Christians became convinced that social and political activism and not worship and preaching was the primary mission of the church. However, beginning in the 1970s preaching made a comeback, led by Fred Craddock and others who were experimenting with new forms for the spoken word. Since the publication in 1971 of Craddock's *As One without Authority*,[32] the books and articles about preaching have comprised a veritable flood. Therefore, among the heirs of the Protestant Reformation preaching continues to be an important element of Sunday worship, with renewed interest stemming from the use of narrative and inductive or indirect structures of thought. Even more surprising has been the growing concern for preaching among Roman Catholics. There continues to be frustration among parish priests about the tight time schedules of multiple masses which make it difficult to develop homilies systematically; yet they are being urged to spend more time in sermon preparation and to make the homily a more important and interesting element of the liturgy.

Conclusion

The close of the twentieth century saw what appeared to be a widening gap between Evangelical and Fundamentalist Protestants on the one hand and Mainline Protestants, Eastern Orthodox, and Roman Catholics on the other, especially in terms of worship style and orders. The former preferred a casual, free-flowing, seemingly spontaneous service with a preponderance of music, mostly sentimental choruses (the words of which are projected on a screen); while the latter worshiped with the aid of books of worship, using set prayers, clerical vestments, and litanies often dating back 1500 years or more. The former was more horizontal, focusing on the experience of the worshiper; the latter more vertical, focusing on the transcendence of God. However, as we shall see in Chapter Eleven, this divergence appears not to have been permanent. The most encouraging aspect of all this for Christian unity was the sincere desire on all sides to use Scripture as the primary norm for developing services of worship. There was and continues to be great disagreement about which texts are to be seen as normative and about just how to read and apply those texts, but in all traditions Scripture now outweighs denominational tradition as the primary authority in making decisions about worship.

For Further Reading

Abbott, Walter M., S.J., General Editor. *The Documents of Vatican II: With Notes and Comments by Catholic, Protestant, and Orthodox Authorities.* New York: Guild Press, 1966.

Baptism, Eucharist and Ministry, Faith and Order Paper No. 111. Geneva: World Council of Churches, 1982.

Bartels, Ernest. *Take Eat, Take Drink: The Lord's Supper through the Centuries.* St. Louis: Concordia, 2004.

Best, Thomas F., and Dagmar Heller, eds. *Eucharistic Worship in Ecumenical Contexts: The Lima Liturgy—and Beyond.* Geneva: WCC Publications, 1998.

Burgess, Stanley M., ed. *The New International Dictionary of Pentecostal and Charismatic Movements.* Grand Rapids: Zondervan, 2002.

Costen, Melva Wilson. *African-American Christian Worship.* Nashville: Abingdon, 1993.

For the Lima Liturgy see: http://www.wcc-coe.org/wcc/what/faith/lima-e.html.

For the Liturgy of the Church of South India see:
http://justus.anglican.org/resources/bcp/India/SIndia_euchr_intro.htm.
or: http://michigan.csichurch.com/Services.html.

For the Liturgy of the Eastern Orthodox Churches see:
http://www.ocf.org/OrthodoxPage/liturgy/liturgy.html.

❧ —— ☙

[1] See http://www.crystalcathedral.org/ (accessed July 12, 2005).
[2] See http://www.cathedral.org/cathedral/ (accessed July 12, 2005).
[3] Edith Blumhofer, in *Twenty Centuries of Christian Worship,* The Complete Library of Christian Worship, ed. by Robert E. Webber (Nashville: Star Song, 1994) 2:106.
[4] This appears to be similar or identical to the "singing exercise" of the Cane Ridge meeting, as described by Barton Stone. Blumhofer, *Twenty Centuries,* 107.

[5]Richard M. Riss, in *Twenty Centuries*, 2:121-125.

[6]Webber, *Twenty Centuries*, 2:132-133.

[7]Andrew Foster, "The African Methodist Episcopal Zion Churches." in *The Renewal of Sunday Worship*, The Complete Library of Christian Worship, ed. by Robert E. Webber (Peabody, MA: Hendrickson, 1993) 3:8-9.

[8]See Henry H. Mitchell, *Celebrations and Experience in Preaching* (Nashville: Abingdon Press, 1990).

[9]A good overview of this history is available in Melva Wilson Costen, *African American Christian Worship* (Nashville: Abingdon, 1993).

[10]Ibid., 92.

[11]Richard J. Stanislaw and Donald P. Hustad, *Companion to The Worshiping Church* (Carol Stream, IL: Hope Publishing, 1993) 142-143.

[12]See his "Bless His Holy Name," "My Tribute," "Soon and Very Soon," and "Through It All."

[13]Costen, *African American*, 105.

[14]Henry Mitchell, *Black Preaching: The Recovery of a Powerful Art* (Nashville: Abingdon, 1990).

[15]The details and explanations of the Orthodox service can be found in Chapter Five and at http://www.ocf.org/OrthodoxPage/liturgy/liturgy.html (accessed July 11, 2005).

[16]Walter M. Abbott, S.J., gen. ed., *The Documents of Vatican II: With Notes and Comments by Catholic, Protestant, and Orthodox Authorities* (New York: Guild Press, 1966) 137-182.

[17]This solemn paragraph represents the core of the Church's official teaching on the liturgy. It is thus something central, by no means secondary or peripheral. [This and the following two footnotes are in the version noted in footnote 16.]

[18]*Postcommunion in the Easter Vigil Mass and the Mass of Easter Sunday.*

[19]*Collect* (prayer) *of the Mass for Tuesday of Easter Week.*

[20]*The Documents of Vatican II*, 142-143.

[21]Ibid., 143.

[22]Ibid., 147.

[23]Ibid., 150-151.

[24]The Daily Office in English is easily accessible at http://www.universalis.com/ (accessed June 30, 2005).

[25]*The Documents of Vatican II*, 168.

[26]An especially clear and accessible outline of the contemporary Roman Catholic mass can be found at http://myweb.lmu.edu/fjust/Mass.htm (accessed June 30, 2005).

[27]This service has been updated, and one can compare the original with the more recent on this website: http://michigan.csichurch.com/Services.html (accessed July 6, 2005).

[28]*Baptism, Eucharist and Ministry 1982–1990*, Faith and Order Paper number 149 (Geneva: WCC Publications, 1990).

[29]See http://www.wcc-coe.org/wcc/what/faith/lima-e.html (accessed July 6, 2005).

[30]Details of the preparation period and rituals can be found at http://www.ecatholic2000.com/rcia/rcia.shtml (accessed July 12, 2005).

[31]A helpful history and outline of present positions are available in Ernest Bartels, *Take Eat, Take Drink: The Lord's Supper through the Centuries* (St. Louis: Concordia, 2004).

[32]Fred Craddock, *As One without Authority* (Nashville: Abingdon, 1971).

CHAPTER ELEVEN

The Present
and
Trends

*T*his final chapter will be a more personal statement from the authors, in contrast to our attempt to be objective in the rest of the book. We both have worship biographies, and they are vastly different, as you will see. In addition, Bruce did quite a bit of traveling during a sabbatical leave in 2004, during which he visited services of worship in Germany, southern and northern India, Thailand, Korea, Hong Kong, and Singapore. He has also solicited video tapes of worship in other parts of the world. His impressions of worship in parts of the world outside North America are just that—impressions and not objective or scientific studies. We were also asked to speculate about worship in the church of 2020 for a conference at Emmanuel School of Religion, and some of those speculations will appear in this chapter. So please keep in mind as you read this that it is made up of personal recollections, impressions, and speculations. Only time will tell whether the latter have any validity.

Bruce's Worship Biography

I was born in 1937 to parents who were very active at First Christian Church in Tarentum, Pennsylvania. My father was an elder who sang in the church choir and in a male quartet, and my mother was the choir director. This was before children's worship or, in our church, even nurseries during the worship service, so when I was two weeks old I was in the adult service with my parents and grandmother, who took care of me when my parents were busy with music or serving the Lord's Supper. Thus I grew up with weekly worship. Actually the order of worship at that congregation has changed little over the years. They have a more up-to-date hymnal now, but the order is simple:

> ➤ Call to Worship (often a few verses of a Psalm)
> ➤ Opening Hymn
> ➤ Opening Prayer
> ➤ Announcements
> ➤ Prayer Hymn
> ➤ Pastoral Prayer
> ➤ Communion Hymn
> ➤ The Lord's Supper
> ➤ Offering
> ➤ Scripture Reading
> ➤ Sermon
> ➤ Invitation Hymn
> ➤ Closing Prayer
> ➤ Closing Chorus

This is a typical order of the mid-twentieth century. As we saw earlier, it is a combination of the centrality of the Lord's Supper of the early Stone-Campbell Movement and the emphasis on preaching and conversion of the nineteenth-century revivals. Most of the congregational music was of the gospel-song genre of Fannie Crosby, the Havergals, and others who followed them. I heard (and sang) many solos written or arranged by Homer Rodeheaver, the great song evangelist. I saw him in concert once, and his trombone playing stimulated an interest in me that lasts to this day.

When in 1955 I moved to Tennessee to begin college, I was introduced to southern gospel music, which north of the Mason Dixon line we "sophisticates" had disregarded as "hillbilly music." I was already a fan of swing and jazz and soon learned to appreciate and worship with gospel songs with a southern accent. It wasn't long until Elvis Presley and then the Beatles introduced a new beat to secular music and some young people were trying to introduce rock into church life. In spite of hard resistance from many older church leaders Christian words were soon being sung to a decidedly rocklike rhythm (with the accent on the second beat instead of the first beat of the measure). This was the sixties, when many Christians were demonstrating for civil rights and against the war in Viet Nam, singing protest songs with folk and rock genres. The "Jesus People" developed songs that expressed their personal relationship with Jesus, but which neglected (sometimes even rejected) the assembled church as the body of Christ. Choruses that were easily memorized and sung to four chords on a guitar began to spring up in Christian circles. The Charismatic Movement was noticeable by 1970, and it continued the "Jesus and me" kind of sentimental music in small circles of people who were together but worshiping as individuals.

In 1972 I moved my family to Tübingen, Germany, where I became the missionary pastor of a small congregation in that university city. I found a church there that was using mostly hymns and gospel songs from the German pietistic movement, but there were other Christian groups in the region connected to the Charismatic Movement and to more upbeat music, some of which we were able to incorporate into the worship of the "*Christliche Gemeinde.*" Our return to the United States in 1977 ushered us into worship services that were quite different from those we had experienced earlier, especially with regard to music. Although some churches were resisting the change, most were beginning to use more simple choruses and fewer of the profound lyrics and staid music of Wesley and Watts. The focus appeared to be on individual salvation and relationship with Jesus and less on adoration of an almighty creator God. I watched this trend continue for the next twenty years. In fact, it was my concern about this that led me to volunteer to develop and teach a course in Christian worship first at Lincoln Christian Seminary (Lincoln, Illinois) and then at Emmanuel School of Religion (Johnson City, Tennessee), a course that I continue to teach.

By the nineties many congregations had adjusted their order of worship to begin with a "song set," a ten to fifteen minute (sometimes longer) time of congregational song, often alternating between newer choruses and older hymns and gospel songs. Characteristically, the words of the songs are projected either on a screen or blank wall to encourage the worshipers to hold their heads up while they are singing. Usually the leaders are a praise band with guitars, drums, and keyboard instead of the traditional organ or piano. My reaction to this is mixed, I must admit. I appreciate the enthusiasm with which people, especially younger people, participate in these "contemporary" or "blended" services, while mourning the loss of theological content and challenging (read: interesting) musical forms. At the same time, I am excited about what's next. As we'll discuss later, it appears that the emerging church, which is not so much a generational designation as a cultural one, is seeking roots in the history of worship to merge with up-to-date styles and technology. I am eager to see what is to come next.

David's Worship Biography

This book has been a story about real people throughout the ages rendering what they have believed to be their highest expressions of worshiping God. Like other stories, it would be difficult to extricate the people from the plot, and so in our study we have been introduced to something of a historical "Who's Who." We saw how the following well-known biblical characters changed the shape of worship: Abel, Melchizedek, Abraham, Moses, David, and the Prophets; and, unquestionably, Jesus, the Apostles, and Paul. Then we were introduced (many of us for the first time) to other Christians and their worshiping communities such as Justin, Irenaeus, Tertullian, Cyril, Ambrose, Basil, Gregory, Chrysostom, Maximus, Benedict, Luther, Zwingli, Calvin, Cranmer, Knox, and Campbell. As the list of names approaches our own contemporary historical consciousnesses, we begin to see ourselves as characters within the larger story and find ourselves as participating in the plot.

In Detroit, one Sunday morning, my grandmother and several of her ten children missed the streetcar that would have taken them to the small Pentecostal mission church on Miller Road. This, she insisted, was a "sign from God." And since she knew of a woman who had recently opened a small storefront church on Nevada Avenue, grandmother decided to take her family on a walk to the building that had formerly been a tire repair shop. There, back in 1934, they found themselves numbered among fewer than twenty worshipers. By the mid-1950s, the church (then called Bethesda Missionary Temple) housed Michigan's largest Sunday school, and by the 1970s had approximately three thousand in the membership, thus becoming one of the first megachurches in the Pentecostal tradition.

By the time I had arrived on the planet—smack dab in the middle of the Detroit riots in the summer of 1967—several "innovations" were taking place at the church. The founder's daughter had it in her mind to set up a nine-month catechumenate for seventh graders that would teach them the basic tenets of the faith (or at least our Pentecostal version of it) and prepare them for initiation into the sacramental life of the local church. Not a few zealous detractors decided that the whole idea sounded "too Roman Catholic." They were suspicious of words like catechism and sacrament, even though they had no objection to our method of baptism and our practice of receiving the Lord's Supper monthly on Sundays and weekly on Thursdays. Since, at Bethesda, church government was singularly located in the office of the pastor, the daughter's proposal was accepted by her mother/pastor/founder without the least bureaucratic delay, and Bethesda had its catechism program.

In 1979, the year I was old enough to attend catechism, there were over 160 adults and 90 adolescents registered in three different sections. The catechumenate at Bethesda was surprisingly faithful to the historical model on the whole, but with amusing Pentecostal elements that often played fast and loose with theology. Students learned the biblical history of salvation in Christ, the Ten Commandments, the Lord's Prayer, the Apostles' Creed, and were given a cursory explanation of the Sacraments. The entire class was baptized in a special service apart from the weekly Sunday morning gathering. Confirmation was separated from baptism by approximately three months during which time there was regular prayer for the reception of the charismatic manifestations of the Spirit on those previously baptized. It was a very interesting juxtaposition of the ancient catechumenate with those phenomena of charismatic worship described in 1 Corinthians.

Concurrent with the development of the catechism program at Bethesda was a growth surge in the area of worship music. In this case, it was the founder's youngest son who had ascended to the choir director's podium. Along with many other thriving Pentecostal churches of its day, the music program grew exponentially, boasting a choir of approximately one hundred voices and a 25-member orchestra. Besides the staple 1970s Gospel selections (largely Bill and Gloria Gaither fare), the music department's repertoire also included Bach chorales, Handel's *Messiah*, Mendelssohn's *Elijah*, and several 20th-century sacred works that few Pentecostal choirs would have dared to perform, much less would have performed well.

Worship choruses had been a part of congregational singing ever since the early days of the church in the 1930s, but members of Bethesda were also active contributor-composers to the proliferation of worship choruses that made their way around the world as the practice was reaching its national acclaim in the late 1970s. A vast network of pastors, musicians, and traveling pilgrims of charismatic ilk can be credited to those golden years of chorus-swapping before publishing companies began to make the whole thing an industrial venture and copyright ownership began to be taken seriously in legal suits. Moreover, a remarkable feature of worship-chorus singing found its Midwest epicenter in Detroit: the practice known variously as *free praise, corporate praise,* and *singing in the*

Spirit. Briefly described, this is a congregational "song" that has no set lyrics, melody, or rhythm; only harmony (usually on the single chord that brought the previous worship chorus to its end). The words and melodies are free-composed by the worshiping individuals who usually use stock "clichés," biblical expressions of praise or, in some occasions, glossolalia (ecstatic speech). Charismatics would describe all of it as a beautiful, choral chaos. Non-Charismatics would simply call it strange and odd. Regardless, whatever of this exists in charismatic communities to this day can be traced back to only a handful of North American churches in the 1940s.

I have given this lengthy exposé of my family's church because it is against this background that my interest and involvement in worship and its history makes the most sense. I began playing the piano at three years old, was giving public performances at five, and began accompanying congregational worship services at ten. When people ask me how long I have been "doing what I'm doing" the answer is usually, "Since I was very young." Family, friends, and the musical community in Detroit all helped to introduce me to the worship styles of numerous Christian traditions other than my own. In fact, for much of my elementary school years it seemed as if I were being perpetually taxied somewhere to play the piano or organ in a new worship setting. I attended a Missouri Synod Lutheran School for junior high and thus had a fair amount of exposure to the Lutheran liturgy but found little appreciation for it. (During those years any substantial interest in Lutheranism was eclipsed by the larger distress of having to learn Bach's Three-Part Inventions, or trying to avoid being hazed on the playground at St. Thomas.) In the ninth grade I was introduced to the Episcopal Church at a Service of Lessons and Carols where the combination of Gothic architecture, choral music, and the beauty of the Church Year began to speak deeply to me. During my undergraduate years of studying music theory at the University of Michigan, I served a Baptist congregation as organist and, three years after that, a Presbyterian congregation. This usually meant four services each Sunday while providing musical accompaniment at Catholic Masses a few Saturdays in the month. I had become an ecumenical-musical mutt.

In all of this, especially during undergraduate studies, I had discovered that in order to learn the history of western music it was necessary to learn much of the western liturgy! In fact, my first exposure to the Kyrie, the Gloria, The Creed, and the Lamb of God of the Roman Rite came by singing Palestrina, Victoria, and Josquin des Pres in the University Chamber Singers!

As everyone who knew me expected, I returned to Bethesda after my studies in Ann Arbor, and went to work full-time in the music ministry. We had two thriving choirs: the larger of the two performed a couple of selections every Sunday, often accompanied by a small orchestra. On good days we numbered 80 voices. We used no written music in rehearsals; everything was learned in the African-American Gospel tradition of singing by rote. The selections were high-energy (an intense vocal workout) but always something the congregation could remember long after they went home from church. The second choir also rehearsed weekly, but performed only twice a year and in a concert setting. We formed the concert choir in response to the requests from proficient singers who were interested in the classics of sacred music and understood the necessity of spending several months of rehearsals for only ten or twelve selections. We also realized that the Concert Choir's repertoire (which included Lotti, Haydn, Mozart, Schubert, Verdi, and John Ness Beck) no longer fit the Sunday morning style of our Pentecostal church and would not have helped all of our people to worship.

It wasn't very long, however, until larger questions began to occupy my thoughts as music director: Why were we worshiping the way(s) we were? What about the Brooklyn Tabernacle style was suitable in Brooklyn, New York, but would not have been received by our people in Detroit? What was missing from our relatively young tradition as Pentecostals that could only be supplied by a connection with the Credo of Schubert's *Mass in G,* or an *Agnus Dei* by Hans Leo Hassler? What about all the formality that surrounded the Lord's Supper as we celebrated it, and why only once a month? Why was I disturbed when asked if the choir could perform Frank Sinatra's rendition of "I Did It My Way" to illustrate a sermon about Samson? Why did our local church take arbitrary positions on what constituted a valid "charismatic" worship expression? I did not realize that I was asking questions about liturgy and enculturation, church history, sacramental theology, biblical interpretation, and pastoral ethics. It was time to seek out the answers to those questions, and so I enrolled in the Master of Divinity program at Emmanuel School of Religion (Johnson City, TN). It was a comprehensive program of study; but for as many questions as were answered in those three years, a few hundred more sprang up.

Two years of doctoral coursework at Catholic University of America allowed me to concentrate on the historical development of the liturgy itself and experience the worship at the National Basilica from a baritone's perspective in the 30-voice choir. During my studies, I was invited to board with a religious community in Washington, D.C. In their daily times of worship, work, and fellowship, the Oblates of St. Francis de Sales taught me how the liturgy could be celebrated daily without the need of a professional choir, a three-million-dollar pipe organ, or a 3,000-seat Romanesque basilica. The experience with the Oblates reminded me of another spiritually formative time a few years prior when several of us at Emmanuel gathered each morning as friends to pray together the Daily Office from the Book of Common Prayer. The difference in Washington, however, was that necessary dimension of life lived together in a *community* whose focus was to "live Jesus," celebrating prayer and liturgy as it extended into the missional work of the community.

Johnson City, Tennessee, has now become my home. Here I have found a place among a genuine community of worshipers at Hopwood Memorial Christian Church. The church is serious about how it shapes its worship and about how that worship in turn shapes the community. Hopwood resembles my Pentecostal church when there is such a deep engagement with the worship that it moves the heart of some to weep, to speak out with a word of testimony or confession, or to be energized enough to clap and sway with Gospel-style rhythms. Hopwood reminds me of my more liturgical experiences when worship planning takes on an ecumenical perspective and attention is given to historical and theological integrity. As I see it, those are the two criteria that are the most important for the real worshipers: Spirit and Truth. Of course, we all hope to grow more deeply in both of these areas.

Bruce's Global Observations

During several sabbatical leaves and summers I (Bruce) have been privileged to travel widely, and in those travels I have worshiped with many different people groups and in many different languages. I cannot claim to have covered the earth. In fact, I have yet to set foot on South America; but I have read about and discussed worship in those places with people who know. Thus I have some research to back up my impressions. With that disclaimer, here are my observations.

Space

I have worshiped in a great variety of different buildings—from European cathedral structures to a bamboo hut in a rural village. In a well-appointed sanctuary on a main street in Tokyo I heard a fine pipe organ produce the music of Bach. In a cement-block structure with about two hundred people in a village in southern India I heard spirited singing accompanied only by two drums. In Thailand I worshiped with college students with the help of guitars and a set of drums, but I also worshiped to the sound of traditional Thai instruments and music suitable to them. In Singapore we met in a large room in a building surrounded by apartment buildings, and in Hong Kong we were in a small room used during the week as a Bible college classroom. Different kinds of space make for different kinds of experience, but Christian worship happens even with no enclosure at all, as is the case in many parts of Africa, where people might meet under a tree.

Time

I have noticed that time is experienced differently in cultures outside North America. Even in Europe in many cases believers are in no rush to begin or to end services of worship at a set time. This casual attitude toward time is even more pronounced in Asia, Africa, and Central and South America, where services often last two hours or more and where worshipers are disappointed with a sermon lasting only twenty minutes.

I also have the impression that Christians outside North America have fewer tendencies to confuse political celebrations with Christian holy days. I did attend a Sunday service in Singapore that had a special speaker from the Philippines because it was Philippine Independence Day. However, I heard no mention of that national day in the service itself, and the preacher delivered a stirring testimonial evangelistic sermon, not at all political or nationalistic. In those places where Christianity has been under governmental pressure, there is a natural and obvious concept of separation of church and state. Otherwise, the Christian calendar determines the special emphases of the year and is more or less followed in a variety of ways in many parts of the world.

Orders

Even though the Anglican Evensong service at Westminster Abbey left a deep impression on me, most of my experiences of worship on foreign soil have been in churches connected with the Stone-Campbell Movement. Thus my personal experience of worship orders is rather limited.

One overall impression I took away from my travels is that the order of worship is not very different in the rest of the world from what I am accustomed to at home. There are prayers, songs, sermons, and the Lord's Supper in some sequence or another everywhere I have gone. In most cases the sequence is not much different from the order I outlined above from my home church. This is likely because the churches I visited were planted by missionaries from the West who had been educated in the early decades of the twentieth century. These dedicated men and women naturally replicated what they were familiar with at home for use on the mission field.

Initiation

My impression is that baptism of believers by immersion in water is the prevailing mode of Christian initiation in the various churches of Africa, India, and Southeast Asia. In many instances missionaries even from paedobaptist traditions have taught and practiced immersion of believers as the primary mode of baptism in the early church.

The Lord's Supper

Here is where I found myself concentrating on the many languages I heard and could not understand. Here is the common act of worship that communicates well even to worshipers who cannot understand the spoken language. No matter where a Christian worships, when the bread is broken and the wine poured and served, the visual, the tactile, the olfactory, and the taste senses come into play, even when the words (the auditory sense) sound foreign. Most of us could even say the words with the presider and be close to accurate. I found myself fully engaged in communion services and fully disappointed when the church I was visiting did not have communion that day.

Perhaps a word of encouragement is appropriate here. Whether or not we have strangers or foreigners in our services, it seems to me that we should carefully do the actions of the Lord's

Supper, following closely the New Testament accounts of the last supper—not so much to say the right words as to do the right actions. As Jesus did, to take the bread, bless it, break it, and pass it to the believers; to take the cup, bless it, and share it with the others is a clear mode of communication. Also, for the congregants to receive, eat, and drink is a total communication experience, no matter how deeply we understand the meaning of "This is my body." I say this in light of the practice in many churches of bringing the communion trays from the rear of the nave, in which case the people never see unbroken bread or a large container of "the fruit of the vine." They also do not see the breaking, blessing, and distributing.

Praise

Music is another aspect of worship that I found everywhere I went. Furthermore, for good or ill, most of the music I heard sounded very western—much like what most of our American churches use. The exceptions to this stand out in my memory. In Thailand my host was able to find a church that used traditional Thai instruments and music in the service, although he indicated that this was unusual. Some of the music I heard in India sounded indigenous and some of it western. I was thrilled to hear in Hong Kong that Christians in mainland China are beginning to use freshly minted music, much of which is written and composed by a young rural Chinese woman with little education.[1]

I also saw a dance troupe of young women in a church in Singapore, who did a dance interpretation of a contemporary praise song. This reminded me of hearing about dance in worship among African Christians. I have also seen a Christian dance group from Thailand that uses Thai traditional dance movements in praise of the Lord. American churches could learn from these others that there is more to praise than music. Some of us are awkward in our movements, and some do not sing very well, but all should be able to find ways to praise God.

Preaching

In an earlier trip I did some research on preaching in various cultures.[2] I found, to my chagrin that only rarely are Christians using the variety of oral communication forms in their cultures to herald the good news. I specifically asked preachers how their children learn to be good citizens of their nations and good members of their society. They were able to tell me about different ways such things are taught in different cultures, but in only a few instances did I hear of preachers employing any of these genres of communication. Where I did find such creativity (Thailand and Korea), I found also good growth among the churches. In Japan, where the preaching appears to be a carbon copy of American evangelical preaching from around 1940, I found very little growth.

At Tokyo Union Seminary, I preached a sermon in chapel in which I moved from behind the pulpit and ended in the center aisle with the congregation. I was told that the sermon was strangely moving, but no Japanese preacher could do it that way. Preaching remains important, but where it is ossified into a pattern that does not communicate to people with iPods and cell phones, it is not heard in a way that will produce faith. "Faith comes by hearing," not by preaching.

I wish all congregations could have input from those in other parts of the world, since it is only such cross-cultural experience that raises our consciousness of our own cultural influence. It wasn't until I showed photos of the interior of American churches to believers in Germany and heard their shock that we would display an American flag in the sanctuary that I began thinking about the issue of separation of church and state. We could all profit from such exchanges.

Trends We See for the Future

Historical inquiry is not merely helpful for understanding the way things were. A knowledge of history is helpful for understanding the way things presently are, and how they may yet be. If, after reading this book, you are able to draw a few connections from ancient to modern worship, see a more defined contrast between the two, note how the theological pendulum has swung over trends and epochs, or can compare one modern worship tradition with another, then this book will have served its purpose. But possessing a modicum of knowledge can be a perilous thing for anyone, and speculating about the future is simply a dangerous venture no matter how much data is available. Therefore, the basic method underlying the projections which follow is simply this: worship among the various Christian expressions will continue to follow their present course.

1. Liturgical Churches / Historical Churches: Having yet to fully implement the liturgical renewal of Vatican II, it would appear that the Roman Catholic Church will continue its scholarly work of revisiting the ancient roots of the Roman Rite and reassessing the modern editions of liturgical books. The greatest challenge, however, will be the inculturation of the Roman Rite among various modern languages and people groups. Rome has always been slow to change, has been protective of its tradition, and has been markedly Euro/Italo-centric in its governance. Newer international translations/adaptations of the Roman Rite have been met with less than enthusiastic approval by the Curia and, in some cases, the process of having a specific translation officially approved has taken well over half a century. Nevertheless, in places where the liturgy is being celebrated in a way that is culturally relevant, the Catholic Church has had no problem with adding to the number of its adherents, especially among the youth of the world. In America, the tendency toward the Catholic megachurch with its multiplicity of programs, its attention to preacher-personalities, and its culturally accessible musical accompaniment of the Mass, is already being witnessed and will probably continue as smaller parishes with fewer worship resources dwindle.

The Orthodox Churches continue to be the bastion of nationalism in many places. There are converts to Orthodoxy, even among some noteworthy Protestant Evangelicals, but these are often serious students of history who appreciate the Orthodox Churches for their commitment to historical continuity. The Orthodox liturgy is not expected to change at all in the near or distant future, but this does not mean that Orthodox worshipers will be necessarily unable to see their worship as relevant. In fact, it may be that a renewal, similar to Vatican II in the Catholic Church, may restore a fuller participation of the Orthodox laity in receiving communion, as the printed copies of the Divine Liturgy and the advent of the microphone have recently made the inaudible prayers of the priest capable of being heard and understood in the nave—at least in this hemisphere. More than likely, Orthodoxy will continue, as it always has, to exist as a testament to the power of the Byzantine Empire that has withstood the onslaught of time and cultural change.

The Lutheran church, the Episcopal church, and others whose worship has either always resembled or has been realigned to the pre-Reformation liturgies will continue their onward study of the historical data and will continue (as they indeed have) to make more substantial changes in cultural style and theological content of their worship. Some have experimented (to good results) with blended worship by making use of traditional texts in contemporary settings), and the practice is gaining momentum. Others are refining their heritage of choral and organ music, bell choirs, stained glass, liturgical art and architecture—preserving the beauty of bygone centuries in a living, liturgical way. These churches will also continue to advance towards ecumenism based on the interdenominational sharing of the eucharist. It remains now for these and other Protestant communions to more fully realize the sacramental character of the eucharist as the empowering for mission to the world in the face of a North American cultural preference for nonsacramental, antiliturgical bases for mission.

2. Pentecostals and Charismatics. Pentecostals have made great strides in recent years to reach into the history of the Church both academically and ecclesially. It is telling that a major university of one Pentecostal denomination has been intentional in developing a program in Patristic studies. Only time will tell if formal education will produce Pentecostal worship leaders who are historically informed about the entire worship history of the last two millennia. At the present, it is more likely that Pentecostal worship in North America will continue to be molded by key figures who are able to gain national popularity either through the Christian music industry, or through broadcast media. Given the growth of Pentecostalism around the globe, there remains the potential that the "charismatic expressions" of Pentecostal worship will create erroneous and harmful divisions between Christians of other traditions unless, of course, efforts are made between churches to cooperate in their mission to the world.

Charismatics, especially those who have remained within their own denominational traditions, may find it easier to synthesize historical worship with their experience of the charismatic expressions. For instance, Charismatic Catholics in Steubenville, Ohio, have produced a hybrid worship form in which the Mass is interspersed with unique moments for worshipers to respond to the promptings of the Spirit. Other Charismatics, who have left their previous denominational affiliation to form their own local assemblies, may continue to drift further away from their parent worship forms and may establish their own charismatic worship styles. These new structures may betray a suspicion of anything "old" or historic, and will potentially prejudice worshipers to devalue Christians of other traditions as less than equals.

Again, Pentecostals and Charismatics who choose to remain unaware of the dangers of ecclesial independence run the same risks that await the pragmatic and sentimental churches we have mentioned (above). We see the comprehensive education of worship leaders in the history and theology of Christian worship to be the guardrails by which the best pastoral and ecumenical decisions can be made for worshiping communities.

3. Protestant Evangelicals. Since we assume that the majority of readers of this book identify most closely with the worship patterns of Protestant Evangelicalism, this section will be longer than the immediately preceding sections. As it concerns an in-depth enquiry into the historical roots of Christian worship, Protestant Evangelicals on the average often appear to be the least concerned and the least informed. Pragmatics is most likely to blame for this, since the Evangelical, revivalistic worship style has been quite successful (by secular standards) in the past two centuries especially in North America, and has adapted itself with ease to the work of global evangelism. Nevertheless, Evangelicals appear to be at a crossroads of sorts. It is necessary, now, to oversimplify:

On the one hand, the motivation to be pragmatic, utilitarian, rational, culturally congruent, and independent (when it comes to actual ties with the historical churches) will most likely result in a worship style that is increasingly more contemporary than it is Christian. If this is a harsh prediction, it is merely based on current general trends. For instance, the amount of Scripture that Evangelicals currently hear on any given Sunday is considerably less than their liturgical counterparts. Granted, the sheer force of a small amount of Scripture is a characteristic of Evangelicalism, but even this force has been suppressed under the pretenses of preaching to an "unchurched" audience who might not be able to understand more than a verse or two. Furthermore, since the rise of contemporary worship in the Pentecostal/Charismatic communities, the theological education in Evangelical hymnody that once shaped its worshipers has all but disappeared. The newer musical options might find more popular appeal (considered "successful" when the worship space is full), but the songs—no longer being composed by theologians—tend to reflect even more the contemporary culture's proclivities than even direct citations from the Scriptures.

On the other hand, there is a conserving tendency among many Evangelical churches whereby an appeal is made to tradition. But this tradition is often not the larger tradition that dates back through the centuries to the early Church. Rather, it is a nostalgic tradition that links prayers with the familiar people that prayed them, hymns with childhood memories, and other rituals that have mostly local or denominational significance. This type of Evangelical church will often sing an older hymn for its sentimental value, regardless of its potentially dangerous theological content. Prayers will often be a catena of oral-tradition clichés. Ceremonies may even have non-Christian elements that would not be admissible in "ordinary worship" (one thinks of the staggering number of secular songs that make their way into Evangelical Christian wedding ceremonies). This is a curious phenomenon where churches who claim to have rejected the larger Christian Tradition cling tenaciously to their own small traditions with little or no means of evaluating them against the greater historical backdrop.

The middle way between the two crossroads appears to be equally inadequate. There may be nothing more hazardous than blending nostalgia with cultural sensitivity. The result could be a powerful emotional connection with what the contemporary culture believes is valuable, rather than what the Church has preserved for the greater part of its history prior to the Great Awakening. The best answer for Evangelicals may well be the trend that, at the time of the publication of this book, is being called the *emergent* church.[3]

In the western hemisphere there is an increasingly large group of people who might be called post-Christian. Some of them have had some contact with a church or churches and have been alienated from worship that they see as totally unrelated to their lives as they are. Others are children of baby boomers who left Christianity in the 1960s and who, therefore, have had only very superficial contact with Christians or Christian worship—attending a few weddings and funerals in churches. On the other hand, they are attracted to what is generally called "spirituality." Ever since the Beatles and other pop stars went on spiritual treks to India or elsewhere, there has been a growing yearning among people disenchanted with consumerist societies for something deeper. Those two realities have produced a subculture that wants Christian faith to be true but that wants to experience it differently than did their parents and grandparents.

To minister to these people many churches have developed brand new approaches to worship, and to some extent these experiments have led to brand new, but in many ways very old, understandings of church. Whereas the Woodstock generation flocked to churches that used praise bands singing pop-rock music with Christian lyrics, where the band leads worship like rock stars at concerts, and where worshipers can be anonymous, the children of those boomers are being drawn to quiet, meditative, participatory gatherings in smaller spaces, where they can find community and accountability. In many cases, these gatherings are reaching back into the ancient church to find prayers, litanies, hymns, and confessions that express their feelings about God. They do this while using the computers and projectors they are so at home with. Robert Webber calls this interesting convergence "Ancient-Future Worship."[4]

There are a number of books now available that deal with the "Emerging Church" and its worship, but this movement is developing so quickly and in so many different directions that the best way to keep up with it is on the Internet. One of the exciting aspects of this movement is that its leaders are interested in more than "cool" things to do in worship. In fact, they insist that an understanding of the God-given mission of the church is THE important foundation for the developing of any new way to worship. This worship, in its many different formats, is not for spectators. It is for people who want personal involvement and the authentic experience of God that such involvement makes possible. In fact, the two primary buzzwords of the so-called postmodern generation are *authentic* and *relationship.* Thus, these people see a connection with the history of worship as a way to be authentic since it has passed the test of time; and they see the building of community around those historically tested faith statements and worship forms as fundamental to worship.

Since this new approach to worship is so varied and so quickly developing, it is impossible to be very sure that what one community does one week in worship will look much like what that same community does the next week or what another group does at any time. However, there do appear to be some commonalities. We see them as follows.

Space for them is not much of an issue, since they meet in many different venues. On the other hand, ambience is important. Low lighting, the use of Christian symbols, either displayed directly or projected, flexible seating instead of pews (sometimes around café tables), and often candles or even incense are in use. Art is usually in view, including medieval stained glass window art drawn, painted, or projected. If there is a band, it will likely be at the side or behind most of the worshipers—certainly not up front on a raised platform. The teacher/preacher will probably be on a raised platform that juts into the middle of the congregation (similar to the bema of the ancient synagogue and church buildings).

Time is also not seen as sacrosanct, although the church year is used as a way to emphasize the use of Scripture in the gatherings. The heavy emphasis on worship as a lifestyle tends to downplay special times for worship. Even time limits are rejected, the assemblies often lasting two hours or more. Nor is the day of the week seen as important, although most larger gatherings take place on weekends.

Orders change from week to week. Most include congregational singing, prayers, quiet time for individual meditation, and some sort of lesson or sermon. In many cases, there is time for participants to move to different parts of the room where prayer stations or other opportunities of participation are prepared. People are encouraged to draw, to sculpt with clay, to write letters or poems, and to use other personal ways of connecting with God and God's people. In some cases recorded music is playing softly through the whole worship time. The lesson/sermon is likely to be early in the order, and it often ends with a question that the people are to discuss and deal with in creative ways. A variety of people are recruited to read Scripture or poetry, give testimonies, or in other ways participate in the leadership of the assembly. There are usually statements to be said by the whole congregation: prayers, confessions, litanies, etc. All in all, the orders are designed to involve as many people as possible to express in a variety of ways their praise of God. Worship in these orders is much more than music or information; it is a community of believers expressing their worship of God in their own ways.

Initiation appears to us to be up in the air at the present. One factor in this unsettled understanding of initiation into membership is that in a few cases, the emerging worship assembly has recognized that it is a separate church and has developed its own ways of leading people toward baptism, but more often the emerging church congregation is only an adjunct to an established church and leaves this aspect of worship to the rest of the church. Thus, the initiation rites are done by the mother church after the emerging church congregation has drawn the seekers to faith in Christ. We expect this will change considerably in the next few years as these groups become more responsible for their own membership practices.

The Lord's Supper has become very important for many of these groups, and often in contrast to their denominational traditions, many are making communion available every week, or every time they meet, even in house-church settings. Their motivation appears to be either a connection with a long historical practice or a desire for an intimate, individual experience. For some reason there seems to be a lack of recognition of the supper as a communal act, but this will likely develop soon.

Praise, which to the boomer generation means loud music led by an up-front band, is to these people a quiet enterprise. It can be music, and at times it can be loud; but music is always just a part of it. Praise can be expressed by the assembly as they unite their voices in a psalm, a poem, or an ancient litany. It can also be shown through art or written words, through mercy to the poor or otherwise needy people, through prayer alone, with a friend or small

group, or through postures such as dancing, kneeling, or lying pros-
trate. Again, there is much creativity in designing praise times in
these gatherings.

Preaching is bound to change in this sort of environment.
These postmoderns or post-Christians are not swayed by argument,
nor do they seek plain information. They are moved by narratives
(of which the Bible is full) that show the power of God in the lives
of people. They appreciate being stimulated to do their own thinking, so challenges and questions are important. They also hunger for
an understanding of Jewish and early Christian living and worship,
to give them roots. The latter item is a radical departure from their
parents, many of whom had rejected everything old. ("Don't trust
anybody over thirty.") They see that what has been called "contemporary worship" has become traditional, and they want to explore
the roots of their faith and worship in history (thus nomenclature
like "vintagefaith" and "ancient-modern").

So where is all this heading? Only God knows for sure. But we
find it exciting to see young leaders turning back to the biblical
records and to the ancient church and blending what they find there
with modern technology and awareness to form worship that is not
age-specific, but is culture-sensitive. We recommend that Christians
should not reject what is coming next just because it is foreign to our
experience. Rather we should search the Scriptures to see worship
in homes as well as in temples, worship that is quiet as well as worship that is boisterous, worship led by professionals as well as that
which springs spontaneously from hearts dedicated to the Lord.

Soli Deo Gloria

❧ —— ❦

[1]The music of Xiao Min is available on the Internet site **www.chinasoul.org**
(accessed September 25, 2005).

[2]This was published as "Preaching and Culture," *Homiletic* 22 (Winter
1997) 1-9.

[3]Dan Kimball has published two books that grew out of his ministry in Santa Cruz, California, and his contacts with leaders of other similar church groups, *The Emerging Church: Vintage Christianity for New Generations* (emergentYS, 2003) and *Emerging Worship: Creating Worship Gatherings for New Generations* (Zondervan, 2004), but his website includes links to many other sites and blogs that concentrate on this phenomenon: **www.vintagefaith.com** (accessed September 25, 2005).

[4]Robert Webber, *Planning Blended Worship: The Creative Mixture of Old and New* (Nashville: Abingdon, 1998), and *Worship Old and New: A Biblical, Historical, and Practical Introduction* (Grand Rapids: Zondervan, 1994).